Oracle Developer Forms Techniques

Bulusu Lakshman

A Division of Macmillan USA
201 West 103rd St., Indianapolis, Indiana, 46290 USA

Oracle Developer Forms Techniques
Copyright © 2000 by Sams

International Standard Book Number: 0-672-31846-6

Library of Congress Catalog Card Number: 99-068916

First Printing: February, 2000

02   01   00   4   3   2   1

Printed in the United States of America

Trademarks

Warning and Disclaimer

ASSOCIATE PUBLISHER
Angela Wethington

ACQUISITIONS EDITOR
Steve Anglin

DEVELOPMENT EDITOR
Tiffany Taylor

MANAGING EDITOR
Lisa Wilson

PROJECT EDITOR
Elizabeth Roberts

COPY EDITORS
Kate Talbot
Rhonda Tinch-Mize

INDEXER
Sheila Schroeder

PROOFREADERS
Kathy Bidwell
Juli Cook

TECHNICAL EDITOR
David Thompson

TEAM COORDINATOR
Karen Opal

MEDIA DEVELOPER
Dave Carson

INTERIOR DESIGNER
Anne Jones

COVER DESIGNER
Anne Jones

COPYWRITER
Eric Borgert

EDITORIAL ASSISTANT
Angela Boley

PRODUCTION
Lisa England

Overview

Contents

About the Author

Bulusu Lakshman is a seasoned Oracle Forms developer, having hands-on experience in developing and deploying Oracle Forms applications on the client/server and Web environments. He has lectured at various international and national conferences on Oracle Developer and PL/SQL8 and has contributed to lead technical journals and magazines in the United States and UK.

Bulusu holds an Oracle Masters credential from Oracle Corporation and is an OCP-Certified Application Developer. Prior to this, he received double Bachelors honors degrees, in mathematics and in computer science and engineering, in India.

He is employed by Compunnel Software Group, Inc., a leading technical consulting firm in New Jersey, and can be reached at blakshman@compunnel.com.

A partial bibliography of his writings is as follows:

"Oracle Forms Error-Message Handling—The Golden Rules." *RELATE, THE UK Oracle User Group Journal*, no. 36 (October 1999): 82–90.

"Forms 4.5/5.0 Error-Message Handling—Tricks of the Trade." *ODTUG Technical Journal* (September 1999): 37–39.

"Tips and Traps in Developer/2000 Forms Error-Message Handling." *SELECT Magazine, IOUG-A*, vol. 6, no. 3 (April 1999): 34–35.

"Advanced Application Development in Oracle Forms 4.5/5.0—More Tips." *RELATE, THE UK Oracle User Group Journal*, no. 35 (Spring 1999): 26–29.

"Forms 4.5 Error-Message Handling—Tricks of the Trade." *RELATE, THE UK Oracle User Group Journal*, no. 34 (Spring 1999): 45–46.

"Application Development Tips in Forms 4.5." *RELATE, THE UK Oracle User Group Journal*, Conference Edition, no. 33 (December 1998): 24–29.

"Forms 4.5—Tricks of the Trade." Proceedings of IOUG-A Live 98, Paper 417 (May 1998): 1038–47.

Dedication

With love to my wife, Anuradha.

Acknowledgments

I thank my lovely and sweet wife, Anuradha, for providing help in preparing part of the manuscript.

I thank my father, Professor B.S.K.R. Somayajulu, for his constant encouragement throughout.

I thank, as "a memory living," my brother, Bulusu Harihar Mallikarjuna, whose words still ring in my heart to ripple unto the chorus of my heartbeats.

I thank Mr. Paul Wu of the Associated Press, New York, New York, the client company for which I am consulting, for providing the necessary resources that enabled me to test part of the code.

I thank the publisher and various editors of Sams at Macmillan Computer Publishing for the golden opportunity to publish my first book and for steering its publication to see the light of day.

Some of the material of this book has been adapted from my technical papers, published in various journals and magazines, and from presentations given at numerous international and national conferences. My sincere gratitude goes to all concerned for their help, encouragement, and advice.

Tell Us What You Think!

As the reader of this book, *you* are our most important critic and commentator. We value your opinion and want to know what we're doing right, what we could do better, what areas you'd like to see us publish in, and any other words of wisdom you're willing to pass our way.

As an Associate Publisher for Sams, I welcome your comments. You can fax, email, or write me directly to let me know what you did or didn't like about this book—as well as what we can do to make our books stronger.

Please note that I cannot help you with technical problems related to the topic of this book, and that due to the high volume of mail I receive, I might not be able to reply to every message.

When you write, please be sure to include this book's title and author as well as your name and phone or fax number. I will carefully review your comments and share them with the author and editors who worked on the book.

Fax: 317-581-4770

Email: oracle_sams@macmillanusa.com

Mail: Angela Wethington
            Associate Publisher
            Sams
            201 West 103rd Street
            Indianapolis, IN 46290 USA

Introduction

Oracle Developer Forms is a robust front-end tool for developing second-generation client/server and Web-enabled applications. With the introduction of Oracle Developer 6.0, Oracle has elevated Forms to a level rich with GUI, beyond-GUI, and Web functionality—such as native hierarchical tree support, enhanced OO support, and Java-based component incorporation directly into forms.

Oracle Developer Forms Techniques provides the tricks of the trade involved in implementing quality front ends, taking the reader to a level "beyond-GUI." The book assists the reader in implementing techniques that are effective for real-world Forms applications. This will save the Forms developer time and effort, in addition to increasing his or her level to that of an advanced developer.

What's New

What is special about this book? Its primary focus is on invaluable techniques that will prove to be quintessential, some of which are *not* listed anywhere else, including Oracle documentation. What works and what doesn't are explained in detail. Techniques such as obtaining query count without actually executing a query, sharing record group data across forms, or handling errors in forms, such as errors that cannot be tracked by FORM-SUCCESS or FORM-FAILURE, might seem trivial at first glance. However, when it comes to implementation involving a real-world project, these are challenging tasks. The special emphasis is on the kinds of mind-boggling situations that, when encountered, can drag on the application development time.

The Structure of This Book

This book focuses on Oracle Developer Forms 6.0. However, the techniques described can be efficiently implemented on Forms versions 5.x and 4.5.x, also. The target database can be one of Oracle version 7.x, 8.x, or 8i. Stress has also been laid on features specific to Oracle 8 and 8i. At some points, I have provided alternatives for versions of Forms earlier than 6.0, to get around those features not supported.

Sample source code files illustrating examples found in the book are available for download from http://www.samspublishing.com. When you reach that page, click the Product Support link. On the next page, enter this book's ISBN number (0672318466) to access the page containing the code.

Intended Audience

The prerequisites for using this book are a working knowledge of Oracle RDBMS and SQL, the PL/SQL language, and Oracle Forms (at least, version 4.5.x). Various types of readers—such as experienced Oracle Forms developers, as well as those who have had some exposure, advanced programmers ready to jump to Forms 6.0, and consultants hunting for "pluggable" tips—can derive very useful information from this book. Also, IS managers, technical managers, system analysts, and DBAs will benefit from this book because they can learn readymade techniques useful at the design stage and afterwards.

Conventions Used in This Book

This book uses different typefaces to differentiate between code and regular English, and also to help you identify important concepts.

Text that you type and text that should appear on your screen is presented in monospace type.

```
It will look like this to mimic the way text looks on your screen.
```

Placeholders for variables and expressions appear in *monospace italic* font. You should replace the placeholder with the specific value it represents.

This arrow (➡) at the beginning of a line of code means that a single line of code is too long to fit on the printed page. Continue typing all characters after the ➡ as though they were part of the preceding line.

NOTE
A Note presents interesting pieces of information related to the surrounding discussion.

TIP
A Tip offers advice or teaches an easier way to do something.

GUI Development

IN THIS CHAPTER

This chapter describes some of the tips and techniques in Forms application development. The power of Forms can be leveraged fully when one moves from GUI to "beyond GUI"—that is, to GUI combined with programming. The tricks of the trade I explore in this chapter include quality-assured front ends such as implementing a standard toolbar, creating dynamic and floating toolbars, implementing timers, and displaying a clock. The chapter also provides special tips for list items, including simulating drill-down Lists of Values (LOVs), ordering by foreign key items, and implementing object-oriented methods in Forms. Finally, I'll present some tips for standard GUI practices. Wherever possible, code segments are provided to help you implement these techniques.

Standard Toolbar Implementation

A common application-specific feature is a standard iconic toolbar that provides icons to carry out common form functions such as Save, Undo, Enter Query, Execute Query, Next Block, Previous Block, Next Record, Previous Record, Insert Record, Delete Record, Exit, Clear, List Values, and Close Application. Toolbars also let users invoke functions such as Notepad, Diary, Calculator, and so on. Such a toolbar is useful especially when the application uses a customized menu bar to replace the default menu provided by Oracle Forms runtime. In addition, a toolbar enhances the GUI's look and feel.

In Forms 5.x and above, the default toolbar comes with Forms runtime (by adding the suffix &SMARTBAR to the DEFAULT value of the Menu Module property). However, think of a function like Close Application, mentioned earlier. This function might refer to closing all forms invoked in a multiform application—a task that cannot be achieved with the normal Exit toolbar icon unless it is clicked repeatedly.

In Forms 5.x and above, toolbars can be associated with a form at three levels at runtime:

- At the menu level—On an MDI platform, this toolbar is similar to the MDI toolbar in Forms 4.5. This toolbar also comes in an SDI platform. Forms supplies it by default with the name SMARTBAR with the DEFAULT menu.

- At the form level—This toolbar is new to Forms 5.x and above and is available for all windows within that form. It is not equivalent to the MDI toolbar.

- At the individual window level—This toolbar is specific to a particular window to which it is attached.

Displaying Menu-Level Toolbars

To create a menu-level toolbar, specify &SMARTBAR after the DEFAULT menu module name in the Form Module property palette. Dynamically hiding the menu using REPLACE_MENU('') in the WHEN_NEW_FORM_INSTANCE trigger will also suppress the display of the associated toolbar.

To create a menu-level toolbar for any customized menu, set either the Visible In Horizontal Menu Toolbar or Visible In Vertical Toolbar property to Yes for each menu item that should appear in the menu toolbar.

Figure 1.1 shows a menu-level toolbar.

Menu-level toolbar ——

FIGURE 1.1

A menu-level toolbar.

Displaying a Form-Level or Window-Level Toolbar

To create a form-level or window-level toolbar, you create a horizontal toolbar canvas view with iconic buttons. Then, specify it as the value for the Form Horizontal Toolbar property or the Window Horizontal Toolbar property. To do so, follow these steps:

1. Create a canvas view of type horizontal toolbar (that is, CANVAS_TOOLBAR).

2. Assign to the canvas view a property class specifying the standard canvas characteristics (such as PC_CANVAS). The height of the canvas should be just enough to enclose an iconic button of standard size. Set the Visible property of this canvas to Yes and the Bevel property to None.

3. Create a property class named PC_ICONIC_BUTTON with the following property values: Iconic set to Yes, Mouse Navigate set to Yes, Keyboard Navigable set to Yes, Width set to 10, Height set to 10, and ToolTip Visual Attribute Group set to DEFAULT.

4. Construct a block named TOOLBAR with items as iconified push buttons for each of the individual functions. The buttons inherit their properties from the PC_ICONIC_BUTTON property class.

5. A WHEN-BUTTON-PRESSED trigger for each of the buttons contains the appropriate Forms built in as arguments to the DO_KEY procedure. For example, the Save button can have the following line of code in its WHEN-BUTTON-PRESSED trigger:

```
WHEN-BUTTON-PRESSED
DO_KEY('COMMIT_FORM');
```

TIP

You can achieve the Close Application functionality described earlier by calling a procedure in the corresponding WHEN-BUTTON-PRESSED trigger. This technique is explained in the sub-section "Simulating a CLOSE ALL Forms" in Chapter 3, "Multi-form Applications."

6. ToolTips can be specified for each iconic button. This is done by specifying the respective text for the `ToolTip Text` property for each of the iconic buttons. For example, the ToolTip text for the iconic button corresponding to the `Save` function can be given in the button property palette by entering **Save Changes** in the `ToolTip Text` property.

NOTE

Specifying ToolTips provides a visual hint feature when the cursor enters the icon. This feature is available from Forms 5.x onwards. In Forms 4.5, this functionality has to be simulated with extra coding, as illustrated later in this section.

7. Specify this horizontal toolbar canvas `CANVAS_TOOLBAR` as the value for the `Form Horizontal Toolbar` property in Forms 5.x and above. In Forms 4.5, specify the `Horizontal MDI Toolbar` property in the Forms Module property sheet.

A sample toolbar constructed in this way looks like the one shown in Figure 1.2.

Form-level toolbar —

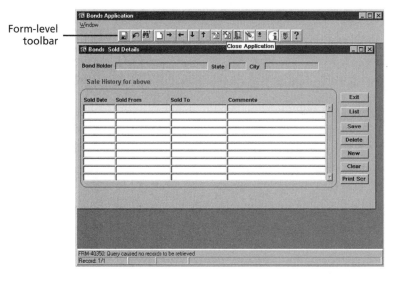

FIGURE 1.2
A form-level toolbar.

Simulating the ToolTip Feature in Forms 4.5

In Forms 4.5, you can display ToolTips by creating a display item, TOOLTIP_ITEM, with the following properties:

- Char data type
- The same visual attribute as the ToolTip visual attribute group
- The Bevel property set to None and Displayed property set to False
- Specify the ToolTip text as the value for the Label property for each iconic button

In addition, the property class PC_ICONIC_BUTTON discussed earlier can have the following two triggers attached to it: WHEN-MOUSE-ENTER and WHEN-MOUSE-LEAVE. The code for these triggers is explained in the steps that follow.

Dynamically populate this item with text equivalent to the Label in the WHEN-MOUSE-ENTER trigger, as follows:

WHEN-MOUSE-ENTER

```
DECLARE
  tooltip_x_pos NUMBER;
  tooltip_y_pos NUMBER;
  tooltip_text  VARCHAR2(30);
  item_id ITEM;
BEGIN
  tooltip_x_pos := GET_ITEM_PROPERTY(:SYSTEM.MOUSE_ITEM,X_POS);
  tooltip_y_pos := GET_ITEM_PROPERTY(:SYSTEM.MOUSE_ITEM,Y_POS);
  tooltip_text := GET_ITEM_PROPERTY(:SYSTEM.MOUSE_ITEM,LABEL);
  :toolbar.tooltip_item := tooltip_text;
  item_id := FIND_ITEM('TOOLBAR.TOOLTIP_ITEM');
  IF NOT ID_NULL(item_id) THEN
    SET_ITEM_PROPERTY(item_id, DISPLAYED, PROPERTY_TRUE);
    SET_ITEM_PROPERTY(item_id, POSITION tooltip_x_pos+10, tooltip_y_pos+10);
  ELSE
    MESSAGE('Invalid Tooltip Item');
    RAISE FORM_TRIGGER_FAILURE;
  END IF;
END;
```

A WHEN-MOUSE-LEAVE trigger will hide the dynamic ToolTip by setting its DISPLAYED property to FALSE as follows:

WHEN-MOUSE-LEAVE

```
DECLARE
  item_id ITEM;
```

```
BEGIN
  item_id := FIND_ITEM('TOOLBAR.TOOLTIP_ITEM');
  IF NOT ID_NULL(item_id) THEN
    :toolbar.tooltip_item := NULL;
    SET_ITEM_PROPERTY(item_id, DISPLAYED, PROPERTY_FALSE);
  END IF;
END;
```

In Forms 5.x and above, the ToolTip appears below the iconic button, whereas in Forms 4.5 it appears on the side. This has been intentionally done because the ToolTip in Forms 4.5 is attached to the MDI horizontal toolbar; there is no way to display it outside the toolbar canvas without making the canvas height more than the icons' height. This leaves a view space on the MDI toolbar.

Toolbar Tips

The following tips provide the tidbits often ignored while developing form-level and window-level toolbars. Also, the points to remember while associating toolbars with forms in multiform applications are highlighted.

The Toolbar Template Form

Use a source template form in which the toolbar can be constructed. Then, you can base customized forms on this template.

Common Form Toolbars

Toolbars attached at the form level are not available to all forms in an application. In a multiform application, especially when you're using OPEN_FORM, you can subclass the CANVAS_TOOLBAR from the source template form. Then, set the Form Horizontal Toolbar property to CANVAS_TOOLBAR for each form. Doing so creates an application with a common toolbar for each independent form.

To simulate the same functionality while using Forms 4.5, the CANVAS_TOOLBAR can be referenced from the source template form. Then, set the MDI Horizontal Toolbar property to CANVAS_TOOLBAR for each form.

Window-Specific Toolbars for Modal Windows

A modal window should have a window-level toolbar associated with it. Form-level toolbar icons are not accessible from a modal window. The same is true with toolbars associated with menu, SDI, or MDI windows. Figure 1.3 shows a form-specific toolbar with a Personal Info. icon. If you click on this icon, you get the window-specific toolbar for a modal window, shown in Figure 1.4.

FIGURE 1.3

A form-specific toolbar with a Personal Info. icon.

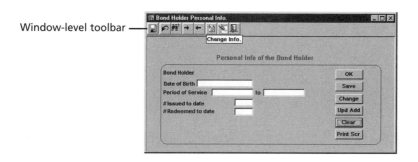

Window-level toolbar

FIGURE 1.4

A window-level toolbar.

Floating Toolbars

This section discusses the techniques to implement dynamic toolbars. It starts by looking at the various ways a toolbar can be "dynamic."

Dynamic toolbars can be implemented several ways. You can create toolbars that dynamically shrink or expand, based on the current mouse position or the current item, record, block, canvas, or form; you hide, unhide, and resize proportionately the toolbar's iconic buttons, depending on the current cursor position. Examples are as follows:

- Hiding (or disabling) the List button when the cursor is in a nonupdateable item or an item that has no LOV attached to it, and showing it otherwise.

- Hiding (or disabling) the Next Record button when the cursor is in the last record of a Query Only block, and showing it otherwise.

- Hiding (or disabling) the Enter Query and Execute Query buttons when a control block receives input focus, and showing them otherwise.

- Generating a new toolbar by selecting a subset of buttons from the original set when a form is being run in Query Only mode.

Other dynamic toolbars are scrollable for forms that require greater functionality to be provided by means of application-specific buttons. Floating toolbars can appear almost anywhere—that is, they "float" in an application or appear where you right-click. You can resize toolbars so that the icons fit proportionately. Finally, you can generate toolbars from a global set of iconic buttons, using point-and-click.

In this section, I will discuss the implementation of a floating toolbar. It has the flexibility of being able to *float*, or be displayed almost anywhere when initiated by a user action. It can also have dynamic resizing capability. It has the same functionality as a regular toolbar but remains displayed until closed by another user action. For example, the user action initiating the display of the toolbar can be a right mouse click on an empty part of the canvas (that's why it's floating), and the user action closing it can be a left mouse click in an empty area of the canvas.

> **TIP**
>
> The form objects including triggers can be included in an Object Group, which in turn can be included in an Object Library and shared (subclassed) across form modules.
>
> Alternatively, a template form can be created with the described objects, and customized application-specific forms can be based on this template form.

Follow these steps to create the floating toolbar:

1. Create a new WINDOW_FLOATING_TOOLBAR that is nonmodal and is not part of the normal windows being used in any form. Make this window's width and height the same as the canvas view width and height of the window-specific toolbar created in the last section's example.

2. Set the window's window style to Dialog, its Modal property to No, its Closeable property to Yes, its Minimizable and Maximizable properties to No, and its Bevel property to None.

3. Create a canvas named CANVAS_FLOATING_TOOLBAR. This canvas is created in the same manner as the standard toolbar described in the earlier example. The only difference is that the number of icons is less here. This number has been chosen at random and can be application specific. Note that this can also be a stacked canvas.

4. Specify the canvas view properties: Set the Window property to WINDOW_FLOATING_TOOLBAR, the Canvas Type to Horizontal Toolbar, the Visible property to No, and the Bevel property to None.

5. Set the Horizontal Toolbar property of the WINDOW_FLOATING_TOOLBAR window to CANVAS_FLOATING_TOOLBAR.

6. Initiate the window display by writing a WHEN-MOUSE-CLICK trigger at the form level and capturing the right mouse click event. The code for this trigger has the following logic:

- Check for the cursor not being positioned inside any item, including non–data-bearing items. This is done using the system variable :SYSTEM.MOUSE_ITEM.

- Check whether the mouse button pressed is not the left mouse button. This is done by checking that the value of the Forms system variable :SYSTEM.MOUSEBUTTON_PRESSED does not equal the constant 1. This system variable can take values 1, 2, or 3. The value 1 is for left, 2 for middle, and 3 for right mouse buttons. All these values are returned as character values. Checking for a value other than 1 ensures that the user-pressed mouse button is not the left one.

- Position the window WINDOW_FLOATING_TOOLBAR at the current (X,Y) position of the cursor. This is done by dynamically setting the X_POS and Y_POS properties of the window to the values :SYSTEM.MOUSE_X_POS and :SYSTEM.MOUSE_Y_POS, respectively, using SET_WINDOW_PROPERTY.

The WHEN-MOUSE-CLICK trigger code is as follows:

```
WHEN-MOUSE-CLICK

IF NAME_IN('SYSTEM.MOUSE_ITEM') IS NULL THEN
    IF NAME_IN('SYSTEM.MOUSEBUTTON_PRESSED') != '1' THEN
        SET_WINDOW_PROPERTY('WINDOW_FLOATING_TOOLBAR', X_POS,
                TO_NUMBER(NAME_IN('SYSTEM.MOUSE_X_POS')));
        SET_WINDOW_PROPERTY('WINDOW_FLOATING_TOOLBAR',Y_POS,
                TO_NUMBER(NAME_IN('SYSTEM.MOUSE_Y_POS')))
        SET_WINDOW_PROPERTY('WINDOW_FLOATING_TOOLBAR',
                VISIBLE,PROPERTY_TRUE);
    END IF;
END IF;
```

The floating toolbar will look like Figure 1.5.

TIP

The actual (X,Y) position of the displayed toolbar is an offset from the actual cursor (X,Y) position because the former is relative to the MDI Window and the latter is relative to the primary canvas of WINDOW0.

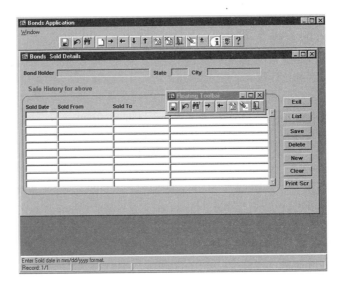

FIGURE 1.5

A floating toolbar.

You can initiate the window close in several ways. First, you can set the Hide On Exit property to Yes for this toolbar window. This is not a standard practice because the user might want to perform multiple functions in the form using this toolbar and would therefore want the toolbar to remain floating until explicitly closed. Applications demanding user-specific requests for such a feature are an exception to this rule.

Second, the window can close when the user clicks the upper-right ×. This is the recommended practice, unless a user requirement specifies a different approach. To use this technique, write a WHEN-WINDOW-CLOSED trigger at form level that checks for the currently active window and closes it if it is WINDOW_FLOATING_TOOLBAR:

WHEN-WINDOW-CLOSED

```
IF NAME_IN('SYSTEM.EVENT_WINDOW') = 'WINDOW_FLOATING_TOOLBAR' THEN
   SET_WINDOW_PEROPERTY('WINDOW_FLOATING_TOOLBAR', VISIBLE, PROPERTY_FALSE);
END IF;
```

Third, the window can be made to disappear by creating a timer at the time of window initiation and writing a WHEN-TIMER-EXPIRED trigger to hide it after a certain interval of time. You provide this second way of closing by specifying an appreciably large time interval—a minute, for example. Closing the floating toolbar by means of a timer involves the following steps:

1. Create a timer in the WHEN-MOUSE-CLICK trigger immediately before displaying the toolbar window. The modified WHEN-MOUSE-CLICK trigger is as follows:

```
WHEN-MOUSE-CLICK

DECLARE
    timer_id TIMER;
    one_minute NUMBER := 60000;
BEGIN
  IF NAME_IN('SYSTEM.MOUSE_ITEM') IS NULL THEN
    IF NAME_IN('SYSTEM.MOUSE_BUTTON_PRESSED') != '1' THEN
      SET_WINDOW_PROPERTY('WINDOW_FLOATING_TOOLBAR',
                  X_POS, NAME_IN('SYSTEM.MOUSE_X_POS'));
      SET_WINDOW_PROPERTY('WINDOW_FLOATING_TOOLBAR',
                  Y_POS, NAME_IN('SYSTEM.MOUSE_Y_POS'));
       BEGIN
          timer_id := FIND_TIMER('TIMER_HIDE_FT');
            IF ID_NULL(timer_id) THEN
              timer_id :=
                CREATE_TIMER('TIMER_HIDE_FT',one_minute, NO_REPEAT);
            END IF;
        END;
      SET_WINDOW_PROPERTY('WINDOW_FLOATING_TOOLBAR',
                  VISIBLE, PROPERTY_TRUE);
    END IF;
  END IF;
```

2. Write a WHEN-TIMER-EXPIRED trigger at the form level to close the window after the time period elapses, in one minute in this case:

```
WHEN-TIMER-EXPIRED

IF GET_APPLICATION_PROPERTY(TIMER_NAME) = 'TIMER_HIDE_FT' THEN
  IF GET_WINDOW_PROPERTY('WINDOW_FLOATING_FT', VISIBLE) = 'FALSE' THEN
    SET_WINDOW_PROPERTY('WINDOW_FLOATING_TOOLBAR',
                VISIBLE, PROPERTY_FALSE);
  END IF;
END IF;
```

Floating Toolbar Pop-Up Menus

Another convenient way of displaying a floating toolbar is by providing a pop-up menu on a right mouse button click. This pop-up can have at least two menu options: Show Toolbar and Hide Toolbar. This can be achieved by the following steps:

1. Create a pop-up menu in the Object Navigator with two items: SHOW_TOOLBAR (labeled Show Toolbar) and HIDE_TOOLBAR (labeled Hide Toolbar).

2. The WHEN-MOUSE-CLICK trigger is still necessary because the :system.mouse_x_pos for a pop-up menu is 0 when the cursor is in the pop-up. Therefore, you capture the (mouse_x_pos, mouse_y_pos) as soon as the user right-clicks to display the pop-up menu. You can write a WHEN-MOUSE-CLICK trigger, in addition to the menu item code, to capture the current (X,Y) of the cursor on right click before the cursor is positioned on one of the items of the pop-up menu:

WHEN-MOUSE-CLICK

```
IF :SYSTEM.MOUSE_BUTTON_PRESSED != '1' THEN
  IF  :SYSTEM.MOUSE_ITEM IS NULL THEN

    COPY(NAME_IN('SYSTEM.MOUSE_X_POS'), 'CTRL_BLK.MOUSEXPOS');
    COPY(NAME_IN('SYSTEM.MOUSE_Y_POS'), 'CTRL_BLK.MOUSEYPOS');

  END IF;
END IF;
```

Here, CTRL_BLK.MOUSEXPOS and CTRL_BLK.MOUSEYPOS are two control items to hold the current values of SYSTEM.MOUSE_X_POS and SYSTEM.MOUSE_Y_POS as defined in the preceding code snippet.

3. The menu item code for the SHOW_TOOLBAR item is as follows:

```
IF :SYSTEM.MOUSE_ITEM IS NULL THEN
  SET_WINDOW_PROPERTY('window_ft', X_POS,
            TO_NUMBER(:ctrl_blk.mousexpos));
    SET_WINDOW_PROPERTY('window_ft', Y_POS,
            TO_NUMBER(:ctrl_blk.mouseypos));
    SET_WINDOW_PROPERTY('window_ft', VISIBLE, PROPERTY_TRUE);
END IF;
```

4. The menu item code for the HIDE_TOOLBAR item is as follows:

```
SET_WINDOW_PROPERTY('window_ft', VISIBLE, PROPERTY_FALSE);
:ctrl_blk.mousexpos := NULL;
:ctrl_blk.mouseypos := NULL;
```

The pop-up menu appears somewhat like the one shown in Figure 1.6.

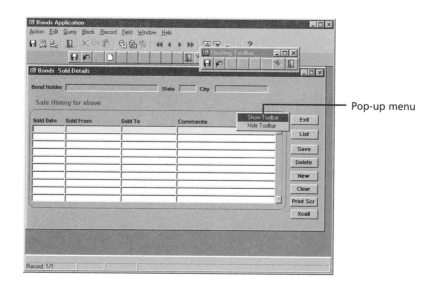

FIGURE 1.6

A pop-up menu to display a dynamic floating toolbar.

Timers and Displaying a Clock

An external clock can be constructed using timers. Timers correspond to internal clocks, which have a specific time period. When the specified duration expires, the timer can either perform an action once and stop or repeat the action regularly every time the timer expires. Timer duration is always in milliseconds. Timers are created using the CREATE_TIMER built in and require a WHEN-TIMER-EXPIRED trigger to be written at the form level. This trigger fires every time the timer expires.

Using REPEAT Timers

Let's create a display item, CURRENT_TIME, in the horizontal toolbar canvas CANVAS_TOOLBAR created earlier. This item shows the time in HH24:MI:SS format and updates itself every second (the timer duration).

In the WHEN-NEW-FORM-INSTANCE trigger, create a timer named CLOCK_TIMER, which iterates after every one second and populates the CURRENT_TIME item with the system date in HH24:MI:SS format. The code is as follows:

```
DECLARE
  timer_id TIMER;
  one_second NUMBER := 1000;
```

```
BEGIN
   timer_id := FIND_TIMER('CLOCK_TIMER');
   IF NOT ID_NULL(timer_id) THEN
     DELETE_TIMER(timer_id);
   ELSE
     timer_id := CREATE_TIMER('CLOCK_TIMER',one_second, REPEAT);
   END IF;
     SELECT  TO_CHAR(SYSDATE,'HH24:MI:SS')
     INTO    :toolbar.current_time
     FROM    DUAL;
   EXCEPTION WHEN OTHERS THEN
     MESSAGE(TO_CHAR(SQLCODE)¦¦' '¦¦SQLERRM);
END;
```

Create a WHEN-TIMER-EXPIRED trigger as follows:

```
DECLARE
   timer_name VARCHAR2(30);
BEGIN
   timer_name := GET_APPLICATION_PROPERTY(TIMER_NAME);
   IF  timer_name = 'CLOCK_TIMER'  THEN
      SELECT  TO_CHAR(SYSDATE,'HH24:MI:SS')
      INTO    :toolbar.current_time
      FROM    DUAL;
   END IF;
   EXCEPTION WHEN OTHERS THEN
      MESSAGE(TO_CHAR(SQLCODE)¦¦' '¦¦SQLERRM);
END;
```

Special Tips for List Items

In this section, I shall discuss some special tips and techniques offered by Forms with respect to lists and list items.

Populating List Items Dynamically

List items appear as either drop-down list boxes, T-lists, or combo boxes in Forms. Mostly, list items have static values as their elements, created during design time. However, there arises a need to populate a list item with elements based on runtime criteria or from a database table. For example, one might populate a drop-down list box with all the state codes from a look-up table named STATE_TAB. This can be done either using a query or adding elements one by one at runtime. This way of populating list items programmatically without hard-coding their values at design time is what is termed *dynamically* populating list items.

This technique involves populating the list with a query or without a query. I will discuss populating by means of a query because it is very powerful and efficient.

One elegant way to populate list items dynamically is to use programmatically created records groups. This record group should have a two-column structure, both being of character data type. The first column should correspond to the label of the list item, and the second column, to the corresponding value.

TIP

The record group has to be created programmatically. However, it can either query or nonquery as long as it follows the two-column structure mentioned here.

Never try to populate a list item using a query directly. Always create and populate a query record group, and use this record group to do the job.

The code performs these tasks:

- Create the record group using CREATE_GROUP_FROM_QUERY.
- Populate the record group using POPULATE_GROUP or POPULATE_GROUP_FROM_QUERY.
- Populate the list item using POPULATE_LIST.

The sample code is given here:

```
DECLARE
    rg_list_id RECORDGROUP;
    rg_name VARCHAR2(20) := 'RG_LIST';
    ret_code        NUMBER;
--The following holds a SELECT query from which the list elements are derived.
    v_select        VARCHAR2(300);
BEGIN
  v_select := 'SELECT state_code, state_code FROM state_tab ORDER BY 2';
  rg_list_id := FIND_GROUP(rg_name);
  IF NOT Id_Null(rg_list_id) THEN
     DELETE_GROUP(rg_list_id);
  END IF;
  rg_list_id := CREATE_GROUP_FROM_QUERY(rg_name, v_select);
  ret_code := POPULATE_GROUP(rg_list_id);
  POPULATE_LIST('LIST_ITEM','RG_LIST');
  DELETE_GROUP(rg_list_id);
END;
```

TIP

Use a form procedure, passing the input query and list item name as parameters.

A nonquery record group can also be used instead of a query record group, provided that it is created programmatically using CREATE_GROUP and populated using POPULATE_GROUP or POPULATE_GROUP_WITH_QUERY.

Populating a List Item with Date and Number Values

Sometimes, it might be necessary to populate NUMBER and DATE columns as list item element values. Because list items always retain character values only, for both the label and value, it is necessary to perform conversion to VARCHAR2 from NUMBER and DATE.

As an illustration, consider a drop-down list box showing all departments in an organization. You can assume that the DEPT table has the following structure:

```
CREATE TABLE DEPT
(ID NUMBER(6) PRIMARY KEY,
 NAME VARCHAR2(30) NOT NUL1);
```

The label column has its values derived from the NAME column. The value corresponding to each NAME is derived from the ID column and should be stored in the list item as a character value. This requires the use of TO_CHAR. Therefore, the query text in the preceding example changes to

```
v_select := 'SELECT name, TO_CHAR(id) FROM dept ORDER BY 1';
```

After populating the list, the value can be accessed by doing a reconversion to NUMBER using the TO_NUMBER function. The following shows how to access the ith element from the list discussed in the preceding example:

```
DECLARE
  v_id NUMBER;
  v_id_char VARCHAR2(6);
  item_id ITEM;

BEGIN
  item_id := FIND_ITEM('LIST_ITEM');
  IF ID_NULL(item_id) THEN
    MESSAGE('Invalid List');
    RAISE FORM_TRIGGER_FAILURE;
  END IF;
    FOR I IN 1..GET_LIST_ELEMENT_COUNT(item_id) LOOP
      v_id_char = GET_LIST_ELEMENT_VALUE(item_id, i);
      v_id := TO_NUMBER(v_id);
```

```
. . . . use this value for further processing
   END LOOP;
END;
```

> **TIP**
>
> Use conversion functions TO_CHAR, TO_DATE, and TO_NUMBER.
>
> On input to the list, use TO_CHAR for both date and numeric values that correspond to the Value column of the list.
>
> On output from the list, use TO_DATE and TO_NUMBER, respectively, for date and numeric values.
>
> Use these in the SELECT column list, which is used to populate the list.

Adding Items to the Beginning of a List

How many of you are aware of the fact that in Forms, you can add elements to the beginning of an already populated list item without repopulating it? This seems trivial at first thought but is a very powerful and flexible technique to be used in many demanding situations.

Use ADD_LIST_ELEMENT and specify the constant 1 for the element index. This displaces all the existing elements to one position below and makes room for the new element with index number 1. *Do not specify the constant 0 instead of 1.*

The code you will use is as follows:

```
ADD_LIST_ELEMENT(list_id, 1, <label>, <value>);
```

Adding Items in the Middle and to the End of a List

So far, I have discussed how to add elements dynamically to an empty list, how to access non-character list elements, and how to add to the beginning of an existing list. Now I will present a simple method to insert elements in the middle of an existing list and to append elements to the end of an existing list.

Use ADD_LIST_ELEMENT and specify the index number of the new element as

```
current element index + 1
```

where *current element* is the element after which the new element should be added. This displaces all the remaining elements to one position below and makes room for the new element.

To add to the end of the list, specify the constant returned by GET_LIST_ELEMENT_COUNT, which gives the number of existing elements, and then specify the index of the new element as the value of this constant incremented by 1.

The following is the code for this:

```
DECLARE
    cnt NUMBER := 0;
BEGIN
    cnt := GET_LIST_ELEMENT_COUNT(list_id);
        ADD_LIST_ELEMENT(list_id, (cnt+1), <label>, <value>);

END;
```

In this example, you take the count of the list elements and increment it by 1. This value serves as the index for the new list element to be added. This works even when the list is wholly empty, because you initialize the count to zero before incrementing it by 1. Therefore, it adds the first element in case of an empty list.

Simulating a Drill-Down and Drill-Up LOV Using T-Lists

LOV is the Forms acronym for *List of Values*. It functions in a manner similar to a pick list of choices. *Drill-down* LOV refers to descending through the LOV to its sublevels, starting from a highlighted element in the LOV.

Drill-down LOVs are very useful for tables involving recursive and/or parent-child relationships. Examples of such relationships are those involving a department and its employees, a manager and employees, or a company and its hierarchical representation.

In each of these cases, a foreign key is involved that is either self-referential or parent-referential. For example, the department-employee relationship involves a parent-referential foreign key from the Department table (the parent table). The manager-employees relationship is self-referential, with the primary and foreign keys being selected from the same table. Also, the information is hierarchical. The company information is another example of a hierarchical representation.

LOVs are a commonly required feature of any application involving this kind of look-ups. The features of LOVs supported by Forms are limited in the sense that

- There is no way to do multiselection from an LOV.
- There is no way to drill down an LOV into its sublevels.
- There is no way to add new rows to the look-up table using an LOV.

Out of these limitations, the most required functionality in case of parent-child relationships, especially tree-oriented, is the drill-down.

Drill-down functionality can be incorporated in an LOV directly using a Forms-provided LOV or using list items. This section discusses the implementation details of building a drill-down LOV using list items. The same method can be followed when using a Forms-supplied LOV.

You will use a T-list and dynamically populate it using a record group. The drill-down is achieved by dynamic replacement of the same record group query again and again till there is no further drill-down. Double-clicking a parent element will show this parent element and all its children one level below. The user "drills down" the LOV to reach a deeper level. The operation is repeatable until leaf elements are reached. The string ' - Parent' is appended to the parent element label to identify it as the parent. This element is always the first element of the list, irrespective of whether it has children.

Double-clicking a parent element will show its parent and all its children, that is, one level above. The user "drills up" the LOV to reach a higher level. The operation is repeatable until the root element is reached. Once at the root, the original list is restored; that is, all EMPNOs that exist as MGRs. The string ' - Parent' is still appended to the parent element label until the initial list is restored.

The same T-list and the same record group are reused for the drill-down and drill-up operations.

The selection of an element is done by pressing Shift and double-clicking on the element. The normal double-clicking being reserved for drill-down, the Shift+double-click is used as an alternative for selecting an element from the LOV.

1. Create a block, BLOCK2, having an item named LOV in it. The properties for the block are set as follows: Database Data Block property set to No, Number Of Records Displayed set to 1, Insert Allowed set to Yes, and Update Allowed set to Yes. The properties for the LOV item are as follows: Subclass Information property set to PC_TLIST (property class).

   The property class PC_TLIST has its properties set as shown in Figure 1.7.

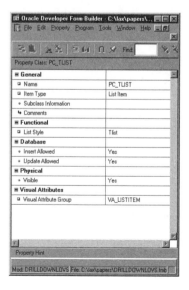

FIGURE 1.7

A property class named PC_TLIST for the T-list item LOV.

> **TIP**
>
> Remember to create a NULL list element; that is, both the label and its value are NULL. NULL means a null value, not the string 'NULL'.

2. The EMP table is used to project the hierarchical relationship between manager (MGR column) and employees (EMPNO column). Assume that the EMP table has the following structure:

```
CREATE TABLE EMP
(EMPNO    NUMBER(10) PRIMARY KEY,
 ENAME    VARCHAR2(30) NOT NULL,
 MGR      NUMBER(10) REFERENCES EMP (EMPNO),
 HIREDATE DATE,
 SAL      NUMBER(11,2),
 JOB      VARCHAR2(20),
 DEPTNO   NUMBER);
```

The LOV functions the following way. At first, all the employees at the parent level are displayed. The query for doing this follows:

```
SELECT ename, TO_CHAR(empno) empno FROM emp WHERE
                empno IN (SELECT mgr FROM  emp a)
```

This SELECT statement also guarantees that the first-level EMPNO is selected.

3. A dynamic record group, 'RG_'¦¦'LOV', is created from the preceding query and then populated and repopulated using rows returned by the query. The T-list is populated using this record group. You use a generic procedure for this step. The procedure is named p_populate_list:

```
PROCEDURE p_populate_list(item_name_in VARCHAR2,
                          query_in varchar2,
                          o_retcd OUT NUMBER)
IS
   rg_id RECORDGROUP;
   retcd NUMBER;
   rg_name VARCHAR2(100);
   item_id ITEM;
BEGIN
    item_id := FIND_ITEM(item_name_in);
    IF ID_NULL(item_id) THEN
            o_retcd := -1;
            RETRUN;
    END IF;
```

```
      rg_name :=
        'RG_'¦¦substr(item_name_in, INSTR(item_name_in, '.', 1)+1,
                      LENGTH(item_name_in));
    rg_id := FIND_GROUP(rg_name);
    IF NOT ID_NULL(rg_id) THEN
      DELETE_GROUP(rg_id);
    END IF;
    rg_id := CREATE_GROUP_FROM_QUERY(rg_name, query_in);
    retcd := POPULATE_GROUP(rg_id);
    IF (retcd <> 0) THEN
      o_retcd := retcd;
      RETURN;
    END IF;
    POPULATE_LIST(item_name_in, rg_id);
    IF NOT FORM_SUCCESS THEN
      o_retcd := -2;
    END IF;
    o_retcd := 0;
  END;
```

The appropriate trigger for calling the p_populate_list procedure is WHEN-NEW-FORM-INSTANCE:

WHEN-NEW-FORM-INSTANCE

```
DECLARE
    query_in VARCHAR2(32767) :=
                   'SELECT ename, TO_CHAR(empno) empno
                    FROM emp
                WHERE empno IN (SELECT mgr FROM emp);
    retcd NUMBER;
BEGIN
  p_populate_list('BLOCK2.LOV', query_in, retcd);
  IF (retcd <> 0) THEN
    MESSAGE('ERR: Could not populate list item.');
    RAISE FORM_TRIGGER_FAILURE;
  END IF;
END;
```

4. The right place for the drill-down code is the WHEN-LIST-ACTIVATED trigger:

```
DECLARE
    query_in VARCHAR2(32767);
    item_name VARCHAR2(100) := NAME_IN('SYSTEM.TRIGGER_ITEM');
    retcd NUMBER;
    current_rows_mgr NUMBER;
    current_rows_empno NUMBER;
```

```
BEGIN
  query_in :=
    ' select LPAD(ename, ((LEVEL-1)*4+LENGTH(ename)), '' '')¦¦
    DECODE(TO_CHAR(empno), '¦¦
  NAME_IN(item_name)¦¦', '' - Parent'' , NULL) ename, TO_CHAR(empno) '¦¦
  ' FROM   emp '¦¦' WHERE empno = '¦¦TO_NUMBER(NAME_IN(item_name))¦¦
          ' or mgr = '¦¦TO_NUMBER(NAME_IN(item_name))¦¦
  ' START WITH empno = '¦¦
TO_NUMBER(NAME_IN(item_name))¦¦' CONNECT BY PRIOR empno = mgr';


             ¦¦

  p_populate_list(item_name, query_in, retcd);
END;
```

5. The WHEN-LIST-ACTIVATED trigger is modified as follows (the following listing shows the
   complete code) to accomplish both drill-down and drill-up:

WHEN-LIST-ACTIVATED

```
DECLARE
    query_in VARCHAR2(32767);
    item_name VARCHAR2(100) := NAME_IN('SYSTEM.TRIGGER_ITEM');
    retcd NUMBER;
    current_rows_mgr NUMBER;
    current_rows_empno NUMBER;
BEGIN
  IF INSTR(GET_LIST_ELEMENT_LABEL(item_name, 1),'Parent', 1) = 0 THEN
  -- if current element is in the initial list
  query_in :=
    ' SELECT LPAD(ename, ((LEVEL-1)*4+LENGTH(ename)), '' '') ¦¦
      DECODE(TO_CHAR(empno), '¦¦
      NAME_IN(item_name)¦¦','' - Parent'',NULL) ename, TO_CHAR(empno)'¦¦
    ' FROM   emp '¦¦
    ' WHERE empno = '¦¦TO_NUMBER(NAME_IN(item_name))¦¦' or mgr = '¦¦
    TO_NUMBER(NAME_IN(item_name))¦¦
    ' START WITH empno = '¦¦TO_NUMBER(NAME_IN(item_name))¦¦
    ' CONNECT BY PRIOR empno = mgr ';
  ELSIF INSTR(GET_LIST_ELEMENT_LABEL(item_name, 1),'Parent', 1) > 0 and
    (TO_NUMBER(GET_LIST_ELEMENT_VALUE(item_name,1))
    != TO_NUMBER(NAME_IN(item_name))) THEN
  -- if current is a child of a parent
  query_in :=
      ' SELECT  LPAD(ename, ((LEVEL-1)*4+LENGTH(ename)), '' '') ¦¦
        DECODE(TO_CHAR(empno), '¦¦
  NAME_IN(item_name)¦¦', '' - Parent'' ,NULL) ename, TO_CHAR(empno)'¦¦
```

```
' FROM   emp '¦¦
' WHERE empno = '¦¦TO_NUMBER(NAME_IN(item_name))¦¦' or mgr = '¦¦
  TO_NUMBER(NAME_IN(item_name))¦¦
' START WITH empno = '¦¦TO_NUMBER(NAME_IN(item_name))¦¦
' CONNECT BY PRIOR empno = mgr ';
  ELSIF INSTR(GET_LIST_ELEMENT_LABEL(item_name, 1),'Parent', 1) > 0 AND
 (TO_NUMBER(GET_LIST_ELEMENT_VALUE(item_name,1))
    = TO_NUMBER(NAME_IN(item_name))) THEN
-- if current element is a parent
    BEGIN
                current_rows_empno := TO_NUMBER(NAME_IN(item_name));
                MESSAGE(TO_CHAR(current_rows_empno), ACKNOWLEDGE);
                SELECT mgr
                INTO   current_rows_mgr
                FROM   emp
                WHERE  empno = current_rows_empno;
                EXCEPTION WHEN NO_DATA_FOUND THEN NULL;
    END;
  IF current_rows_mgr IS NOT NULL THEN
     query_in :=
        ' SELECT LPAD(ename, ((LEVEL-1)*4+LENGTH(ename)), '' '') ¦¦
          DECODE(TO_CHAR(empno), '¦¦TO_CHAR(current_rows_mgr)¦¦
        ', '' - Parent'' , NULL) ename, TO_CHAR(empno) '¦¦
' FROM   emp '¦¦
' WHERE empno = '¦¦current_rows_mgr¦¦' or mgr = '¦¦current_rows_mgr¦¦
' START WITH empno = '¦¦current_rows_mgr¦¦
' CONNECT BY PRIOR empno = mgr ';
  ELSE
     query_in := 'SELECT ename, TO_CHAR(empno) empno FROM emp WHERE
                    empno IN (SELECT mgr FROM emp)';
     END IF;;
     END IF;
     p_populate_list(item_name, query_in, retcd);
END;
```

Figures 1.8 through 1.10 depict the drill-down operation on the sample list discussed here. The parent for the second level is suffixed with the phrase ' - Parent' to mark it as the parent element for the children displayed below it.

Oracle Developer Forms Techniques

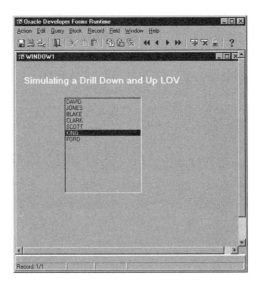

FIGURE 1.8

Original List before drill-down

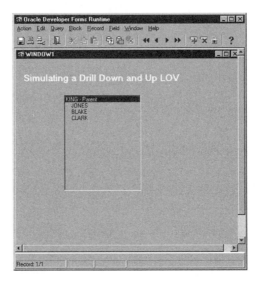

FIGURE 1.9

First Level LOV after drill-down

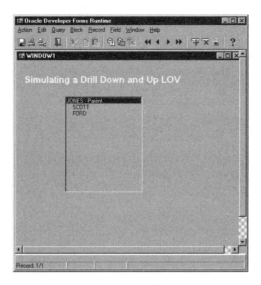

FIGURE 1.10
Second Level LOV after drill-down

Simulating the Find Feature of List of Values

The Find feature of LOVs enables you to enlarge or reduce the LOV list as the user types in characters of the LOV element value. This feature can be simulated using COMBO BOX and T-LIST type list items in Forms 4.5. Although it doesn't use the exact mechanism offered by LOVs, the method described here imitates the same functionality. You will assume that the list to be displayed is SITE_NAME, based on the SITE_TAB table. The SITE_TAB table has the following structure:

```
SITE_NO    NUMBER(6) NOT NULL,
SITE_NAME VARCHAR2(20) NOT NULL.
```

Follow these steps:

1. Create a combo box–type list item. Name it LIST_ITEM_COMBO. The trick lies in using a combo box so that as the user types in characters, the resulting list can be populated with a record group, which is created dynamically, based on user input. A WHEN-LIST-CHANGED trigger would suffice for this.

2. Create a T-list–type list item below LIST_ITEM_COMBO. Name it LIST_DEST_ITEM. This holds the destination list based on the characters the user types in LIST_ITEM_COMBO.

3. Create a WHEN-LIST-CHANGED trigger for LIST_ITEM_COMBO as follows:

```
DECLARE
    rg_list_id RECORDGROUP;
    ret_code        NUMBER;
BEGIN
    rg_list_id := FIND_GROUP('RG_LIST');
    IF NOT ID_NULL(rg_list_id) THEN
       DELETE_GROUP(rg_list_id);
    END IF;
    rg_list_id := CREATE_GROUP_FROM_QUERY('RG_LIST',
     'SELECT site_name, site_name
     FROM site_tab
     WHERE site_name LIKE '¦¦''''¦¦:LIST_ITEM_COMBO¦¦'%'¦¦'''');
    ret_code := POPULATE_GROUP(rg_list_id);
    POPULATE_LIST('LIST_DEST_ITEM','RG_LIST');
    DELETE_GROUP(rg_list_id);
END;
```

This reduces or enlarges the list, based on user input in LIST_ITEM_COMBO.

Ordering by Foreign Key Items in Forms

Items based on foreign key look-ups often figure in Forms applications. One of the features most admired in such applications is a sort order option for users to choose the data item to base the sorting order. This is often a feature required by end users and MIS managers alike. For example, an MIS manager might want to choose a sort order by the department name while tracking changes to his employees, department-wise. This seems so trivial on first thought but is not, when it comes to actual coding. The department name is generally a foreign key look-up item in the Employees screen and, therefore, a direct ORDER BY is not possible. This section presents a special technique to implement such ORDER-ing.

Use a stored function in the database, which retrieves the look-up value based on the foreign key column; specify this function in the ORDER BY clause for the corresponding block.

Consider a block based on the EMPLOYEE table with a nonbase table item DEPT_NAME in it. You want to order by DEPT_NAME, which is a look-up column (a nonbase table item in the block under consideration), from the DEPT table based on DEPT_ID in the EMPLOYEE table. The following steps will do the job:

1. CREATE a stored function named POPULATE_DEPT_NAME(ip_dept_id IN NUMBER) that returns the DEPT_NAME corresponding to the parameter ip_dept_id.

2. CREATE a nonbase item DEPT_NAME in the EMPLOYEE block (which is based on the EMPLOYEE table).

3. In the block properties, for the ORDER BY clause specify POPULATE_DEPT_NAME(DEPT_ID). Note that the argument passed is the actual column name (that is, DEPT_ID) in the DEPT table.

4. Create a POST-QUERY trigger for the EMPLOYEE block as follows:

```
:employee.dept_name := populate_dept_name(:employee.dept_id);
```

5. On querying, it can be seen that the records in the block are ordered by DEPT_NAME.

Querying by Nonbase Table Items

As a continuation to the sorting capability by foreign key look-up items discussed in the preceding section, I explore here the functionality of querying by nonbase items. The DEPT_NAME item in the EMPLOYEE block (illustrated in the preceding section) is a nonbase table, and Forms default query processing does not apply to it. A typical requirement would be to query on all employees belonging to a particular department, based on DEPT_NAME. The DEPT_ID is not as suggestive as the DEPT_NAME in identifying a department.

With the introduction of the capability to change the DEFAULT_WHERE of a base table block dynamically, querying by nonbase table items can be accomplished with a PRE-QUERY trigger containing an explicit cursor for determining the foreign key column values corresponding to the nonbase table item value.

> **TIP**
>
> An alternative way to order by foreign key items or query by nonbase table items involves specifying an inline SELECT in place of the base table for the block, based on a stored procedure returning a result set. See Chapter 2, "Advanced GUI Development: Developing Beyond GUI," for more details regarding this technique.

Consider the standard DEPT and EMP application. You will outline the technique of querying by DEPT_NAME that is a nonbase table item in the EMPLOYEE block. Follow these steps:

1. Set the Query Allowed property to YES/TRUE for the item DNAME.

2. Derive the foreign key item DEPT_ID based on the ad hoc query input of :EMPLOYEE.DEPT_NAME. Use the POPULATE_DEPT_NAME procedure to populate the DEPT_NAME item for every DEPT_ID retrieved. Use a POST-QUERY trigger on the EMPLOYEE block to do this:
POST-QUERY

```
:employee.dept_name := populate_dept_name(:employee.dept_id);
```

3. In the PRE-QUERY trigger, set the DEFAULT_WHERE of the EMP block dynamically based on the resulting DEPTNO:

PRE-QUERY

```
DECLARE
   v_dyn_where VARCHAR2(100) := NULL;
BEGIN
   v_dyn_where :=
     ' WHERE deptno IN
       (SELECT deptno FROM dept WHERE dname = NVL(:emp.dname, dname) ');
   SET_BLOCK_PROPERTY('EMP', DEFAULT_WHERE, v_dyn_where);
END;
```

4. Performing an Enter Query in the EMPLOYEE block and specifying a criteria like S% in the DEPT_NAME item followed by Execute Query would retrieve only those employees belonging to departments whose names start with uppercase *S*.

TIP

PRE-QUERY is fired even before the SELECT is constructed and is the best place to dynamically change the DEFAULT_WHERE and ORDER BY clauses. PRE-SELECT is fired after the SELECT is constructed and before it is issued for execution. The system variable :SYSTEM.LAST_QUERY holds this SELECT at this point in time. POST-SELECT fires after the SELECT has been executed but before records have been FETCHED. POST-FETCH fires repeatedly for each set of records fetched.

Tips for Standard GUI Practices and Forms Development

Any Forms application should conform to a specific set of GUI standards, which can be frozen for that application. The following serves as a selected list of guidelines that can prove helpful:

- Use a sign-on form for each application. A sign-on form helps in two ways. First, an added level of security can be provided. For example, in addition to the Oracle login and password, there can be a secret code for an application particular to each user. This second level of checking can be easily done using a sign-on form. Second, added functionality for the Oracle Forms login can be incorporated, for example, a pick-list of database names for the user to choose from.

- Use a standard iconic toolbar and button bar across forms by subclassing from a template form. You can have a vertical toolbar for function-specific buttons and a horizontal toolbar for application-specific or module-specific feature buttons. Also, common application-specific toolbars and common form-functionality toolbars can figure as menu-level toolbars for forms sharing common menus. Specific icons particular to a form can figure as form-level toolbars. Within a single form, window-specific icons can be organized as window-level toolbars.

- Use ToolTips or balloon help for iconic buttons. ToolTips provide onscreen visual hints and also improve the GUI look-and-feel.

- Highlight current and cursor records in multirecord blocks and blocks having master-detail relationships. This preserves the focus of the record the user is working on, as well as any of its related record(s).

- Use alerts, and standardize the alert categories. This provides a visual way of displaying messages, as well as a distinct categorization of messages according to which ones are real errors, which ones are warnings, and which ones are just informative. For example, it is worthwhile to display a save confirmation alert having Yes, No and Cancel buttons when the user is navigating out of a form or a subwindow.

- Use list items for more than five or six choices. Use radio groups in case of fewer choices.

- Leverage the full potential of List Items by populating list items dynamically. This helps in customizing the list choices according to user-input runtime criteria.

- Use drill-down LOVs in case of multiple levels of data in look-up tables, whether hierarchical or not. This eliminates the need for using multiple LOVs in case of multilevel look-ups.

- Take care of both keyboard navigation and mouse navigation.

- Control record access at the block level by specifying records-buffered and records-fetched properties for the block. This is a performance-related point and should be done with proper care. The cost of fetch time versus memory should be analyzed carefully. (This tip is not meant to be taken as a rule.)

- Exit child windows by means of buttons, such as OK or Close. Also, program the × for each window. This improves the flexibility, in addition to conforming to standard windows conventions.

- Use KEY triggers only to override default functionality of the corresponding physical function key. This is because KEY triggers are the only directly related components corresponding to a physical function key.

As an example, to check for user selection from an LOV, writing a KEY-LISTVAL trigger is recommended to redefine the List Values functionality. The following piece of code illustrates this:

```
KEY-LISTVAL

DECLARE
  Selected BOOLEAN := FALSE;
```

```
BEGIN
  LOOP
    Selected := SHOW_LOV('<lov_name');
    IF selected THEN
      EXIT;
    ELSE
      MESSAGE('A value has to be selected from the List of Values');
    END IF;
  END LOOP;
END;
```

The KEY-LISTVAL trigger can then be invoked using the DO_KEY built in at a single place or more than one place, if required. By doing this, you provide code that is both appropriate and sharable.

```
DO_KEY('LIST_VALUES');
```

- Use POST-QUERY to populate nonbase items during query time. This ensures that a database read is done only to query the look-up item based on the foreign key value and not also for the actual foreign key item.

- Use changing LOVs dynamically at runtime rather than creating multiple LOVs.

- Use Default Where and Order By to dynamically change query criteria rather than create multiple blocks for each criterion.

- Simulate the GUI window-specific standard functionality in forms wherever not supported—for example, closing a window using the × in the upper-right corner.

  As another example, you can use the Cut and Paste operations for duplicating an item, regardless of the instance of the record from where data is cut and pasted. The default Forms duplicate item functionality cuts data only from the immediately preceding record and pastes in the new (current) record. An easy way of implementing this is by means of pop-up menus.

- Implement multiform applications because they increase modularity and provide ease of use.

- Use timers for duration-specific applications such as balloon help.

- Implement object and code reusability. Make effective use of object groups and property classes.

- Do not set the Keyboard Navigable and Mouse Navigate properties to TRUE/YES for push buttons present in an exclusive BUTTON_PALETTE block. This prevents the control from shifting, that is navigating, to the buttons by using either the keyboard or the mouse. One very important reason for doing this is to prevent invalid operations in the button block.

  For example, assume that the BUTTON_PALETTE has a button labeled *List* to invoke the LOV corresponding to the cursor item, which is a text item. Specifying the Keyboard

Navigable and/or Mouse Navigate properties to Yes would shift the input focus from the cursor item to the List button. This causes Forms to invoke the LOV for the button instead, which does not make sense. As a result, you get the error FRM-41026: Field does not understand operation.

- Use text items with Insert Allowed and Update Allowed properties negated, to behave like display items for items with data length greater than the item width. This enables you to scroll to the end of the data present in the item. Secondly, it provides consistency by giving a standard look-and-feel to all data-bearing items.

- Do not set the current record attribute property for single record blocks and button-only blocks. There is no need to do so, because only one record is displayed at any point in time.

- Programmatically populating default values for items is a better practice than setting them through object properties, because it prevents the risk of messing up validation. Default values set through object properties in a record do not initiate validation unless there is either user input or a programmatic setting of some item in a record.

  Imagine a record with two items, BATCH_NO and BATCH_DATE, with BATCH_SEQNO being display only (because it will be populated through PRE-INSERT later on) and a default value of $$DATE$$ set for BATCH_DATE. Doing so ignores the default form-level valida-tion. As a consequence, consider a detail block for this master BATCH record, say, BATCH_ITEMS, where masterless operations are not allowed (because they should not be allowed). There is no way that the user can input data in this detail block unless there is user input—here it will be overwriting the same date. To control this programmatically, use WHEN-CREATE-RECORD. If there are items that can be entered besides the first item, use WHEN-DATABASE-RECORD. Alternatively, you can use WHEN-NEW-RECORD-INSTANCE with :SYSTEM.RECORD_STATUS = 'NEW'.

- Use standard form-specific libraries and application-specific libraries. Eliminate SQL from the Forms side as far as possible. This can be achieved by having a set of packaged procedures and functions, which can be called by the Forms Libraries.

Summary

The purpose of this chapter was to highlight some tips and techniques in Forms application development. The topics considered were standard toolbar implementation, including dynamic and floating toolbars, timers and a clock display, special tips for list items, querying and order-ing by foreign key items in Forms, and object-oriented methods in forms. Last, this chapter also touched on tips for standard GUI practices and forms development. The concepts were illustrated with examples, and alternatives to each concept were discussed. These tips are based on the author's individual experience in the related field, and any code segments presented herein are the author's own.

Advanced GUI Development: Developing Beyond GUI

IN THIS CHAPTER

As an integral component of Oracle Developer for second-generation client/server application development, Forms has rich capabilities that also extend beyond GUI by combining the GUI with programming. This chapter is a continuation of Chapter 1, "GUI Development." It highlights some advanced techniques in Forms programming for implementing quality-assured front ends, including dynamically changing relation properties to suppress master-detail behavior, toggling between Immediate and Deferred coordination, obtaining a query count before query execution, using form and global variables, and using base tables and record groups, including dynamic record groups. This chapter also touches on the differences between DO_KEY and the corresponding KEY- trigger. A customized sign form has been a long-felt need in Forms applications, and an elegant technique for the same is discussed. Finally, some cookies about Windows management are presented.

Playing with Relations

Relations are Forms internal objects that are created

- implicitly when a detail block is created and a master-detail relationship is specified between this detail block and an existing master block.
- explicitly using the Relations node in the Object Navigator.

The default behavior of a master-detail relation is as follows:

- When navigating to a different master record, clear the existing detail block(s), and then requery all its details automatically for the new master—that is, while scrolling through the master block records.
- Copy the master record primary key while creating a new detail record at commit time.
- Use the master record primary key to prevent deletion; delete the corresponding detail records when the master record is deleted.

These implicit actions are controlled by certain properties of a relation, which are

- Master-Deletes—It can take one of the values Non-isolated, Isolated, or Cascading. Specifying Non-isolated prevents the deletion of the master record if detail records exist. Isolated deletes the master record, leaving the detail records dangling. Cascading first deletes the detail records and then deletes the master record.
- Co-ordination—It can be either Immediate, meaning that the clearing and querying of the detail records happen as soon as the focus shifts to a new master record, or Deferred, meaning that this behavior can be postponed till a later point. Till what point is determined by the supplemental Auto-Query property. This property can be either Yes or No.

A Yes means that the process is delayed till the control navigates to the detail block, and a No delays it till the control navigates to the detail block and the user initiates an Execute Query using the physical function key.

- Prevent Master-less Operation—This prevents query or data entry in the detail block in the absence of a corresponding master record.

The first behavior is controlled by the Co-ordination property, the second by the Copy Value From Item property of the foreign key item in the detail block, and the third partly by the Copy Value From Item property and partly by the Master-Deletes property of a relation.

The techniques given in this section pertain to the following:

- Suppressing the default behavior as controlled by the Co-ordination property. Here we refer to Immediate coordination.
- Toggling between Immediate and Deferred coordination, that is, switching from Immediate to Deferred, and vice-versa, depending on what the current coordination is.

Suppressing Master-Detail Behavior

Suppressing master-detail behavior is a requirement when searching through the master block based on an item value. To speed the search process, it is worthwhile to suppress the automatic query of the detail block for every master record temporarily for the duration of the search.

You can do this by changing the master-detail relation properties dynamically before starting the search and by resetting them after the search is complete. The automatic clearing and querying of the detail block for every new master record are by means of the ON-CLEAR-DETAILS trigger at the form level and the ON-POPULATE-DETAILS trigger at the master-block level. This is due to the default Immediate coordination taking place when the master record changes. The firing of these two triggers can be suppressed by changing the Immediate coordination to Deferred with Auto-Query.

In the appropriate trigger, set the AUTOQUERY and DEFERRED_COORDINATION properties for the relation involved to TRUE before looping through the master block, and reset both of them to FALSE after the find is over. This delays the query of the detail block until the user does an explicit EXECUTE_QUERY and thus prevents automatic population of the detail block for every master record. The code involved is similar to the following:

```
WHEN-BUTTON-PRESSED trigger of search button.

DECLARE
  relation_id Relation;
BEGIN
/* Find the relation id corresponding to the relation name.
```

```
If the resulting ID is NULL, the given relation is invalid.
Otherwise, set its properties to DEFERRED with AUTOQUERY */

  relation_id := Find_Relation(<relation_name>);
  IF NOT Id_Null(relation_id) THEN
    SET_RELATION_PROPERTY(relation_id, AUTOQUERY, PROPERTY_TRUE);
    SET_RELATION_PROPERTY(relation_id, DEFERRED_COORDINATION,
                          PROPERTY_TRUE);  ELSE
    MESSAGE('InvalidRelation');
    RAISE FORM_TRIGGER_FAILURE;
  END IF;
/* Proceed with the search operation */
  <Code for search>
/* RE-query the detail block to ensure that it gets populated
after the search. This is required because no automatic query
of the detail block takes place due to DEFERRED coordination. */
  GO_BLOCK(<detail_block>);
  EXECUTE_QUERY;
  GO_BLOCK(<master_block>);
/* Reset the relation properties after the search is complete */
    SET_RELATION_PROPERTY(relation_id, AUTOQUERY, PROPERTY_FALSE);
  SET_RELATION_PROPERTY(relation_id, DEFERRED_COORDINATION,
                        PROPERTY_FALSE);
END;
```

The EXECUTE_QUERY for the detail block is necessary; otherwise, the detail block is left empty after the search is over.

Toggling Between Immediate and Deferred Coordination

This section presents a technique to toggle between immediate and deferred coordination. This is very useful in situations like the search operation discussed above. Before the search process, you switch to deferred coordination from the default immediate coordination. After the search is over, you can toggle back to immediate coordination.

You can toggle between the IMMEDIATE and DEFERRED coordination by dynamically changing the relation's Coordination property. To do so, you change the master-detail relation DEFERRED_COORDINATION property dynamically to the opposite of the current setting. The AUTOQUERY property has to be reset to TRUE if automatic requery is necessary after DEFERRED coordination is turned on. It is turned off automatically because of the cascading effect of DEFERRED coordination. This method can be implemented as a procedure p_toggle_ coordination given below. You can use code like the following in the actual trigger to make a call to the above mentioned procedure:

```
WHEN-BUTTON-PRESSED

DECLARE
  v_retcd NUMBER;
  v_errm VARCHAR2(100);
BEGIN

-- Call the togglre procedure before the search
  p_toggle_coordination(<relation_name>, v_retcd, v_errm);
  IF (v_retcd <> 0) THEN
    MESSAGE(v_errm);
    RAISE FORM_TRIGGER_FAILURE;
  END IF;

-- Search process

-- Call the toggle procedure after the search

END;
```

The code for the procedure p_toggle_coordination is given below:

```
PROCEDURE p_toggle_coordination(p_relation_name IN VARCHAR2,
                                retcd OUT NUMBER,
                                errm OUT VARCHAR2)
IS
relation_id RELATION;
BEGIN
  relation_id := FIND_RELATION(p_relation_name);
  IF NOT Id_Null(relation_id) THEN
    IF
     GET_RELATION_PROPERTY(relation_id, DEERRED_COORDINATION) = 'FALSE'
    THEN
      SET_RELATION_PROPERTY(relation_id, DEFERRED_COORDINATION,
                            PROPERTY_TRUE);
    ELSE
      SET_RELATION_PROPERTY(relation_id, DEFERRED_COORDINATION,
                            PROPERTY_FALSE);
    END IF;
    IF FORM_SUCCESS THEN
      retcd := 0;
    ELSE
      retcd := -1;
      errm  := 'Toggle Relation Failure';
  ELSE
    retcd := -1;
    errm := 'Invalid Relation';

  END IF;
END p_toggle_coordination;
```

2

ADVANCED GUI
DEVELOPMENT:
DEVELOPING BEYOND
GUI

Obtaining Query Count Without EXECUTE-ing a Query

Obtaining a count of records that will be retrieved by EXECUTE_QUERY before actually performing it in a database block is especially useful when the requirement is to prevent navigation to a block when query hits are zero. A typical scenario of such a situation is when the detail block records exist on a separate canvas not visible on Form startup and the user is required to click a Details button to see them. Giving an alert message such as No Details exist when the user clicks the Details button is more meaningful than displaying a blank details screen, when no details exist for the chosen parent record.

The technique given here avoids two performance issues. First, you do not want to perform a SELECT COUNT(*) from the corresponding base table mainly for performance reasons. Second, using :SYSTEM.LAST_QUERY and executing it dynamically using DBMS_SQL cause a bottleneck by executing the query on the server side explicitly, thus involving more trips.

The solution is to do a COUNT_QUERY and get the QUERY_HITS for the corresponding block immediately following the COUNT_QUERY. The following function does the job:

```
FUNCTION query_count (p_block_name VARCHAR2) RETURN NUMBER
IS
cnt NUMBER;
BEGIN
GO_BLOCK(p_block_name);
COUNT_QUERY;
cnt := GET_BLOCK_PROPERTY(p_block_name, QUERY_HITS);
IF FORM_SUCCESS THEN
    RETURN (cnt);
ELSE
    MESSAGE('Error in getting Query Hits for block '||:SYSTEM.CURRENT_BLOCK);
    RAISE FORM_TRIGGER_FAILURE;
END IF;
END;
```

The preceding function can be called in the appropriate trigger, such as WHEN-BUTTON-PRESSED, to achieve the desired functionality.

The following WHEN-BUTTON-PRESSED trigger is defined for the Details button. It initially invokes the above query_count function to obtain the count of detail records for a particular master record. If this count is zero it throws an alert to indicate No Details exist. Otherwise, control navigates to the detail block and does an EXECUTE_QUERY.

WHEN-BUTTON-PRESSED trigger of 'Details' button

```
DECLARE
    v_cnt NUMBER;
```

```
BEGIN
  v_cnt := query_count(<detail block name>);
  IF (v_cnt = 0) THEN
    p_show_alert('No Details exist.');
  ELSE
    GO_BLOCK(<detail block name>);
    EXECUTE_QUERY;
  END IF;
END;
```

This technique involves two tasks:

- COUNT_QUERY is necessary to initiate the QUERY_HITS property of the block and should be immediately before the GET_BLOCK_PROPERTY statement.
- Oracle Forms displays the message FRM-40355: Query will display 0 records when the query hits are zero as obtained by a call to COUNT_QUERY. This should be suppressed in an ON-MESSAGE trigger by using the following code:

```
if message_type = 'FRM' and message_code = 40355 then
   null;
else
   message(message_type¦¦'-'¦¦to_char(message_code)¦¦': '¦¦message_text);
end if;
```

Using Form and Global Variables

Proper use of form and global variables is indispensable for any Forms programming application, for both performance reasons and programming ability. When used improperly, they result in poor performance, as well as unintelligent programming. This section begins with tips on how to use form variables repeatedly.

> **TIP**
>
> To get the best results when working with variables, you should always assign a form or global variable to a local PL/SQL variable before using it, if it has to be used repeatedly in the same trigger or PL/SQL program unit.

Consider the following piece of code:

```
BEGIN
 IF :order_items.qty_on_hand  > 10000 THEN
    p_return_excess_quantity;
ELSIF :order_items.qty_on_hand  =  0 THEN
    p_order_quantity;
```

```
END IF;

END;
```

Here, `:ORDER_ITEMS.QTY_ON_HAND` is a Forms variable (in fact, a Forms item) that is referenced twice. Also, each time it is referenced, it has the same value. At first sight, this code seems all right. However, there is a hidden drawback here that hinders the performance, if not badly, at least to some extent. If this code is all the code in the trigger or PL/SQL program unit, the performance problems might not be so visible (it doesn't mean that there isn't performance; in fact, there is better performance), but think of one having the form variable repeated a large number of times.

You can make a small modification (remember, small doesn't necessarily mean less) to the code as follows:

```
DECLARE
      v_qty_on_hand NUMBER;
BEGIN
  v_qty_on_hand := NVL(:order_items.qty_on_hand,-1);
IF v_qty_on_hand  > 10000 THEN
     p_return_excess_quantity;
ELSIF v_qty_on_hand  =  0 THEN
      p_order_quantity;
END IF;

END;
```

The trick here is, PL/SQL is executed on the server side, and there will be trips from Oracle Server to Forms and back each time the PL/SQL engine encounters a Forms variable. Assigning the form item to a local PL/SQL variable costs only one trip. The PL/SQL engine then uses the value of the local variable on the server side, even if this local variable is repeated several times. The same holds true for a global variable.

Tips for Working with Variables

Here are some additional tips that will help as you work with variables:

- Use indirect referencing by using NAME_IN for read and COPY for write while referring to form item variables, form system variables, form global variables, and form parameter variables, in Object Libraries or Forms Libraries. This is because direct referencing with the colon (:) prefix is not allowed in libraries.

- Always "create" a global variable using DEFAULT_VALUE instead of explicit assignment. This not only creates, but also initializes the global variable. The COPY built-in doesn't create a variable.

- Always use indirect referencing when referring to a global variable. This preserves access control for these global variables and also improves code portability. Using routines such as `read_global_data()` and `write_global_data()`, which indirectly reference the global variables, can enhance reusability and the sharing capability of these routines across Forms applications.

- Create all global variables in a shared library packaged procedure, and call it once in the beginning of application startup, preferably after sign-on. In addition to providing the performance benefit provided by packages, this eliminates the problem of not creating those global variables that might be necessary from some point onward in a multiform application.

  An alternative for avoiding this problem is to use `DEFAULT_VALUE` in each required form.

Base Tables

This section explains techniques concerning base tables for a data block. It begins by explaining how to change the base table of a block at runtime. The subsequent subsections elaborate on the techniques for basing a block on a `FROM` clause query and on a stored procedure. The procedure for performing DML in each case is outlined.

Changing the Base Table of a Block Dynamically

That the base table of a block cannot be changed dynamically was really a hindrance to Forms development before version 5.0. Forms programmers had to rely on alternative methods like changing the `DEFAULT_WHERE` or creating multiple blocks and hiding or showing them at runtime. However, changing the `DEFAULT_WHERE` does not always accomplish the task, especially when there is no link between the current base table and the new base table. To avoid this, Forms 5.0 has provided two new attributes, `QUERY_DATA_SOURCE_NAME` and `DML_DATA_TARGET_NAME`, to the `SET_BLOCK_PROPERTY` built-in. This is an easy solution to the problem.

You use `SET_BLOCK_PROPERTY` and specify the base table/view/procedure name for the `QUERY_DATA_SOURCE_NAME` and `DML_DATA_TARGET_NAME`. You can also base a block on a stored procedure, a `FROM` clause `SELECT`, or a transactional trigger.

> **TIP**
>
> In Forms 5.x and above, a block can have separate sources for each of the `SELECT`, `INSERT`, `UPDATE`, `DELETE`, and `LOCK` DML operations, and each of these can be changed dynamically.
>
> In Forms 6.x, a block can be based on object tables, but cannot be based on nested tables and `VARRAYS`.

Basing a Block on a FROM Clause QUERY

This is a requirement when columns from multiple tables must be displayed in the block and the conditions for selecting the individual columns vary. Specifying a SELECT instead of a base table has the following advantages:

- A database view can be eliminated.

- Multilevel look-up columns and look-ups based on mutually non-related column sets can figure as part of the same record, thus eliminating the use of a POST-QUERY, which would have been costly otherwise.

- Sorting and ad hoc querying on foreign key look-up columns are easily implemented as a base table operation.

Although an explicit option in Forms 5.x and above, you could indirectly base a block on a FROM clause QUERY in Forms 4.5. In Forms 4.5, you specify a SELECT statement to substitute a table name as a base table (that is, in the FROM clause).

Specify a SELECT statement involving multiple table joins instead of a base table for a block, provided that the SELECT statement is specified within single parentheses. Column ambiguity is not automatically resolved. In Forms 4.5, enclose this SELECT statement within parentheses.

The Query Database Source columns have to be specified in the block's Property Palette. This can be done by using the Data Block Wizard or by using the block Property Palette when creating the block manually.

The WHERE condition has to be specified properly and should be contained as part of the INLINE query instead of the DEFAULT_WHERE for the block, especially when selecting mutually non-related column sets and joining on non–foreign key columns. Consider the SELECT statement:

```
SELECT DEPT.DEPTNO, DNAME, EMP.EMPNO, ENAME, JOB, HIREDATE, SAL
FROM   EMP, DEPT
WHERE EMP.DEPTNO = DEPT.DEPTNO)
```

This SELECT should be specified as it is (in Forms 4.5, also) rather than specifying EMP as the base table with DNAME as a foreign key look-up column. (This is the second method referred to in Chapter 1 for querying by nonbase table items.)

Here is an additional tip that will help as you work with base tables based on a FROM clause query:

- A FROM clause query specified as a base table for a data block is executed as an inline view and facilitates faster execution. Also, querying and ordering by foreign key look-up items are thus simplified, similar to querying and ordering in an ordinary base table block.

DML Operations on a Block Based on a FROM Clause Query

Because a FROM clause query is based on a SELECT statement and not on a database table, the default insertion, updating, deletion, and locking of records no longer hold good. These DML operations are carried out by writing ON-INSERT, ON-UPDATE, ON-DELETE, and ON-LOCK triggers for this block. These are similar to the INSTEAD-OF database triggers for doing DML on a view based on multiple tables in the database. These ON- transactional triggers replace the default processing of the respective DML operation, and the code inside each is executed instead.

A block based on a FROM clause query is treated as being based on a non-key preserved table, and no INSERT, UPDATE, or DELETE is allowed by default. Because no database table is involved and also multiple tables might be involved in the SELECT, the base table for the data block becomes one without a key column, therefore, the term non-key preserved. There is no rowid pre-reserved for each row.

The query operation is allowed by default, including the *ad hoc query*. An ad hoc query is the method by which users specify runtime criteria on which to base their queries. Querying records is similar to querying a view.

The sample form for this section's technique, FROMQUERY.FMB, is available online at this book's Web site. This technique is outlined in the following steps:

1. Consider the following query:

```
SELECT DEPT.DEPTNO, DNAME, EMP.EMPNO, ENAME, JOB, HIREDATE, SAL
FROM    EMP, DEPT
WHERE EMP.DEPTNO = DEPT.DEPTNO)
```

   Create a block named FROMCLAUSE_BLK based on this query. The columns in the SELECT statement automatically become items in the block.

2. The querying of records, including ad hoc querying, is taken care of by default.

3. To perform INSERT, UPDATE, and DELETE operations on the individual DEPT and EMP tables, you write ON-INSERT, ON-UPDATE, and ON-DELETE triggers.

   The code is as follows:

```
CREATE OR REPLACE PACKAGE PkgDeptEmp_fromclause AS

/* The following is a RECORD type having fields equivalent
to the FROM clause SELECT columns that the block is based on */

    TYPE Dept_Emp  IS RECORD (
     empno  NUMBER(4),
     ename        VARCHAR2(10),
     job   VARCHAR2(9),
     hiredate  DATE,
     sal          NUMBER(11,2),
```

```
        deptno  NUMBER(2),
        dname   NUMBER(14));
        SUCCESS  CONSTANT NUMBER := 0;

/* The following four procedures take care of the LOCK, INSERT,
UPDATE, and DELETE operations on the block */

    PROCEDURE lock_procedure  (lock_rec  IN OUT dept_emp,
                                  retcd OUT NUMBER,
                                  errm OUT VARCHAR2);
    PROCEDURE insert_procedure(insert_rec  IN OUT dept_emp,
                                  retcd OUT NUMBER,
                                  errm OUT VARCHAR2);
    PROCEDURE update_procedure(update_rec  IN OUT dept_emp,
                                  retcd OUT NUMBER,
                                  errm OUT VARCHAR2);
    PROCEDURE delete_procedure(delete_rec  IN OUT dept_emp,
                                  retcd OUT NUMBER,
                                  errm OUT VARCHAR2);
    FUNCTION get_success RETURN NUMBER;

END PKGDEPTEMP_FROMCLAUSE;

CREATE OR REPLACE PACKAGE BODY PKGDEPTEMP_FROMCLAUSE AS

/* The function below returns the constant SUCCESS */
    FUNCTION get_success RETURN NUMBER IS
    BEGIN
      RETURN(SUCCESS);
    END;

    PROCEDURE lock_procedure(lock_rec IN OUT  dept_emp,
                              retcd OUT NUMBER,
                              errm OUT VARCHAR2) IS

      v_temp NUMBER(4);
    BEGIN
/* Lock the row corresponding to the input EMPNO */
        SELECT empno
        INTO v_temp
        FROM emp
      WHERE empno=lock_rec.empno
       FOR UPDATE;
      retcd := SUCCESS;
  EXCEPTION WHEN OTHERS THEN retcd := SQLCODE;
     errm  := SQLERRM;
    END lock_procedure;
```

```
    PROCEDURE insert_procedure (insert_rec  IN OUT dept_emp,
                                 retcd OUT NUMBER,
                                 errm OUT VARCHAR2) IS
      CURSOR csr_deptemp IS       SELECT deptno
        FROM dept
        WHERE deptno=insert_rec.deptno;
      v_temp NUMBER(4);
    BEGIN
/* If input DEPTNO already exists, insert into EMP from input record;
else insert into both DEPT and EMP from input record */
        OPEN csr_deptemp;
        FETCH csr_deptemp  INTO v_temp;
        IF csr_deptemp%NOTFOUND THEN
          INSERT INTO dept(deptno,dname)
          VALUES (insert_rec.deptno, insert_rec.dname);
        END IF;
        CLOSE csr_deptemp;
         INSERT INTO emp (empno,ename, job,hiredate, sal, deptno)
         VALUES (insert_rec.empno, insert_rec.ename, insert_rec.job,
                 insert_rec.hiredate, insert_rec.sal, insert_rec.deptno);
        retcd := SUCCESS;
EXCEPTION WHEN OTHERS THEN
      retcd := SQLCODE;
      errm  := SQLERRM;
END insert_procedure;

  PROCEDURE update_procedure(update_rec IN OUT dept_emp,
                              retcd OUT NUMBER,
                              errm OUT VARCHAR2) IS
      CURSOR csr_dept IS       SELECT deptno
        FROM dept
        WHERE deptno=update_rec.deptno;
      v_temp NUMBER(4);
    BEGIN
/* If input DEPTNO already exists, then update EMP columns from
input record, or else insert into DEPT and update EMP from input record
based on EMPNO */
      OPEN csr_dept;
      FETCH csr_dept INTO v_temp;
      IF csr_dept%NOTFOUND THEN
         INSERT INTO dept(deptno,dname)
         VALUES(update_rec.deptno,update_rec.dname);
      END IF;
      CLOSE csr_dept;
      --
      UPDATE emp
```

```
          SET ename=update_rec.ename,
              job=update_rec.job,
              hiredate=update_rec.hiredate,
              sal    =update_rec.sal,
              deptno=update_rec.deptno
       WHERE empno=update_rec.empno;
      retcd := SUCCESS;
  EXCEPTION WHEN OTHERS THENretcd := SQLCODE;
     errm  := SQLERRM;
   END update_procedure;

    PROCEDURE delete_procedure(delete_rec IN OUT dept_emp,
                               retcd OUT NUMBER,
                               errm OUT VARCHAR2) IS
   BEGIN
/* Delete from emp based on input EMPNO. We do not delete from DEPT. */
    IF (delete_rec.empno IS NOT NULL)  THEN
       DELETE emp WHERE empno=delete_rec.empno;
    END IF;
     retcd := SUCCESS;
   EXCEPTION WHEN OTHERS THEN
     retcd := SQLCODE;
     errm  := SQLERRM;
   END delete_procedure;

END PKGDEPTEMP_FROMCLAUSE;

ON-INSERT trigger
DECLARE
   dept_emp_rec pkgdeptemp_fromclause.dept_emp;
   retcd NUMBER;
   errm VARCHAR2(100);
BEGIN
   dept_emp_rec.empno := :fromclause_blk.empno;
   dept_emp_rec.ename := :fromclause_blk.ename;
   dept_emp_rec.job := :fromclause_blk.job;
   dept_emp_rec.hiredate := :fromclause_blk.hiredate;
   dept_emp_rec.sal := :fromclause_blk.sal;
   dept_emp_rec.deptno := :fromclause_blk.deptno;
   dept_emp_rec.dname := :fromclause_blk.dname;
   Pkgdeptemp_fromclause.insert_procedure(dept_emp_rec, retcd, errm);
   IF (retcd != pkgdeptemp_fromclause.get_success) THEN
      MESSAGE(errm);
      RAISE FORM_TRIGGER_FAILURE;
   END IF;
END;
```

```
ON-UPDATE trigger
DECLARE
   dept_emp_rec pkgdeptemp_fromclause.dept_emp;
   retcd NUMBER;
   errm VARCHAR2(100);
BEGIN
   dept_emp_rec.empno := :fromclause_blk.empno;
   dept_emp_rec.ename := :fromclause_blk.ename;
   dept_emp_rec.job := :fromclause_blk.job;
   dept_emp_rec.hiredate := :fromclause_blk.hiredate;
   dept_emp_rec.sal := :fromclause_blk.sal;
   dept_emp_rec.deptno := :fromclause_blk.deptno;
   dept_emp_rec.dname := :fromclause_blk.dname;
   Pkgdeptemp_fromclause.update_procedure(dept_emp_rec, retcd, errm);
   IF (retcd != pkgdeptemp_fromclause.get_success) THEN
      MESSAGE(errm);
      RAISE FORM_TRIGGER_FAILURE;
   END IF;
END;


ON-DELETE trigger

DECLARE
   dept_emp_rec pkgdeptemp_fromclause.dept_emp;
   retcd NUMBER;
   errm VARCHAR2(100);
BEGIN
   dept_emp_rec.empno := :fromclause_blk.empno;
   dept_emp_rec.ename := :fromclause_blk.ename;
   dept_emp_rec.job := :fromclause_blk.job;
   dept_emp_rec.hiredate := :fromclause_blk.hiredate;
   dept_emp_rec.sal := :fromclause_blk.sal;
   dept_emp_rec.deptno := :fromclause_blk.deptno;
   dept_emp_rec.dname := :fromclause_blk.dname;
   Pkgdeptemp_fromclause.delete_procedure(dept_emp_rec, retcd, errm);
   IF (retcd != pkgdeptemp_fromclause.get_success) THEN
      MESSAGE(errm);
      RAISE FORM_TRIGGER_FAILURE;
   END IF;
END;


ON-LOCK_trigger

DECLARE
   dept_emp_rec pkgdeptemp_fromclause.dept_emp;
   retcd NUMBER;
```

```
    errm VARCHAR2(100);
BEGIN
    dept_emp_rec.empno := :fromclause_blk.empno;
    dept_emp_rec.ename := :fromclause_blk.ename;
    dept_emp_rec.job := :fromclause_blk.job;
    dept_emp_rec.hiredate := :fromclause_blk.hiredate;
    dept_emp_rec.sal := :fromclause_blk.sal;
    dept_emp_rec.deptno := :fromclause_blk.deptno;
    dept_emp_rec.dname := :fromclause_blk.dname;
    Pkgdeptemp_fromclause.lock_procedure(dept_emp_rec, retcd, errm);
    IF (retcd != pkgdeptemp_fromclause.get_success) THEN
        MESSAGE(errm);
        RAISE FORM_TRIGGER_FAILURE;
    END IF;
END;
```

Basing a Block on a Stored Procedure

As far as base tables are concerned, basing a block on a stored procedure is by far the most advanced extension of Forms over the earlier releases of 4.5 and below. The purpose of basing a block on a stored procedure is to provide user-defined logic for replacing the default functionality of SELECT, LOCK, INSERT, UPDATE, and DELETE. This is required when

- a block must be based on multiple tables tied together by complex application logic. In this case, a view or a FROM clause query cannot be used because of the complexity of the underlying logic involved.

- DML must be performed on the server side—either dynamic DML or DML encapsulating application logic.

This method of basing a block on a stored procedure involves getting and returning result sets of data rather than processing one record at a time, thus reducing network traffic. This is helpful especially when the network involved is a WAN.

To use this technique, follow these steps:

1. Define at least five stored procedures, which I recommend that you include as part of a package: one each for SELECT, INSERT, UPDATE, DELETE, and LOCK. The query procedure should pass and return a REFCURSOR or a table of records. The other four procedures should pass and return a table of records. A single record would do the job, but to involve multiple records, you should use a table of records.

    For this example, the database package PKGDEPTEMP uses the DEPT and EMP tables and contains the five required procedures pquery, pinsert, pupdate, pdelete, and plock. The code for the package appears in Listing 2.1.

> **TIP**
>
> Data blocks can be based on a stored procedure returning a REFCURSOR, an Index-by table of records, a record type, and an object REF.

2. The form uses a block named STPROC created using the Data Block Wizard. The five procedures are specified as the values for the Query procedure, Insert procedure, Update procedure, Delete procedure, and Lock procedure names in the Data Block Wizard. One such screen, for the Query procedure, appears in Figure 2.1.

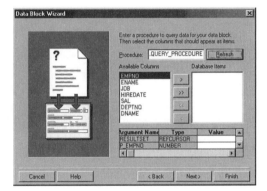

FIGURE 2.1
The Data Block Wizard shows how to specify values for the Query procedure.

The Available Columns box lists the result set columns. The argument names are carried over from the names of the procedure parameters. The extra parameter P_EMPNO is required for performing ad hoc queries and is explained at a later time.

3. Make the following changes to the property palette: Set the Query Data Source Procedure Name to QUERY_PROCEDURE, the query procedure name; set Query Data Source Columns to the result set columns, as shown in Figure 2.2. These columns also become the base table items in the block. Set Query Data Source Arguments to the Query procedure parameters, as shown in Figure 2.3.

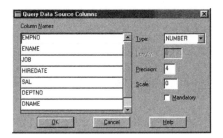

FIGURE 2.2

How to specify Query Data Source Procedure Name.

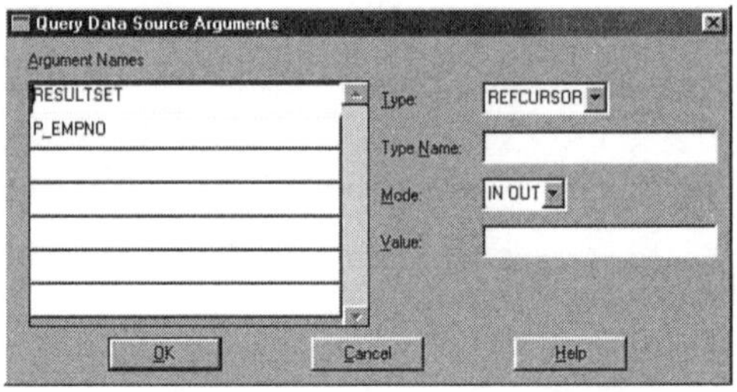

FIGURE 2.3

Specifying Query Data Source Arguments.

Similarly, in the Property Palette for the block, under the Advanced Database section, set the corresponding properties for Insert, Update, Delete, and Lock accordingly, as shown in Figure 2.4.

4. At the block level, Forms generates four triggers: INSERT-PROCEDURE, UPDATE-PROCEDURE, DELETE-PROCEDURE, and LOCK-PROCEDURE. These can be thought of as replacements for the ON-INSERT, ON-UPDATE, ON-DELETE, and ON-LOCK triggers for a base table block. The sample code for the INSERT-PROCEDURE appears in Figure 2.5.

TIP

Do not modify the code in the INSERT-PROCEDURE, UPDATE-PROCEDURE, DELETE-PROCEDURE, and LOCK-PROCEDURE triggers. Doing this will result in the corresponding operation (that is, Insert, Update, Delete, or Lock) functioning incorrectly. This trigger is not regenerated every time the Form is compiled; therefore, if modified, the customized code is executed, instead of default Forms written code, which might yield wrong results.

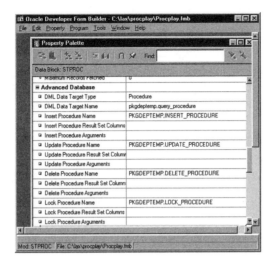

FIGURE 2.4

Specifying advanced database properties.

FIGURE 2.5

INSERT-PROCEDURE written by Forms for a block based on a stored procedure.

LISTING 2.1   The PKGDEPTEMP Package

```
CREATE OR REPLACE PACKAGE PkgDeptEmp AS

/* A REF cursor variable is used as an IN OIT parameter for the query
procedure, and recordtype variables are used as IN OUT variables
for the INSERT, UPDATE, DElETE, and LOCK procedures. These parameters
are IN OUT because they transfer data to and from the block
and the database. */

  TYPE Dept_Emp IS RECORD(
    empno        NUMBER(4),
    ename        VARCHAR2(10),
    job          VARCHAR2(9),
    hiredate     DATE,
    sal          NUMBER(11,2),
    deptno           NUMBER(2),
    dname            VARCHAR2(14));
  TYPE dept_emp_ref IS REF CURSOR RETURN dept_emp;
  TYPE dept_emp_tab IS TABLE OF dept_emp INDEX BY BINARY_INTEGER;
  PROCEDURE query_procedure  (resultset IN OUT dept_emp_ref,
                                p_empno IN NUMBER);
  PROCEDURE lock_procedure  (dmlset IN OUT dept_emp_tab);
  PROCEDURE insert_procedure(dmlset IN OUT dept_emp_tab);
  PROCEDURE update_procedure(dmlset IN OUT dept_emp_tab);
  PROCEDURE delete_procedure(dmlset IN OUT dept_emp_tab);
END PKGDEPTEMP;
/

CREATE OR REPLACE PACKAGE BODY PKGDEPTEMP AS
  PROCEDURE query_procedure(resultset IN OUT dept_emp_ref,
                              p_empno IN NUMBER)
  IS
  BEGIN

/* The code below selects from the EMP and DEPT tables into a REF cursor and
outputs the result to the block. A REF cursor is more efficient than a PL/SQL
record for the query operation because there is no PL/SQL involved. The
coordination and synchronization between the input dmlset and the
population of the block with these records are done by Forms
automatically */

    OPEN resultset FOR
      SELECT e.empno, e.ename, e.job, e.hiredate,
             e.sal, e.deptno, d.dname
      FROM  emp e, dept d
```

```
        WHERE e.deptno = d.deptno
          AND e.empno = NVL(p_empno, e.empno);
    END query_procedure;

    PROCEDURE lock_procedure(dmlset IN OUT dept_emp_tab) IS
        tempout NUMBER(4);
    BEGIN

/* The following locks each record in the input dmlset. The coordination
and synchronization between the input dmlset and the block's records that
have been marked for LOCKING are done by the  LOCK-PROCEDURE trigger
written by Forms */

FOR i IN 1..dmlset.COUNT LOOP
        SELECT empno
        INTO tempout
        FROM emp
        WHERE empno=dmlset(i).empno
        FOR UPDATE;
        END LOOP;
    END lock_procedure;

  PROCEDURE insert_procedure (dmlset IN OUT dept_emp_tab) IS
        CURSOR c_dept(i BINARY_INTEGER) IS
          SELECT deptno
          FROM dept
          WHERE deptno=dmlset(i).deptno;
        tempout NUMBER(4);
    BEGIN

/* The following inserts into the DEPT table if not found already.
It also inserts into the EMP table. Each record in the input dmlset
is inserted. The coordination and synchronization between the input dmlset
and the block's records that have been marked for INSERT are done by
the INSERT-PROCEDURE trigger written by Forms */

FOR i IN 1 .. dmlset.COUNT LOOP
        OPEN c_dept(i);
        FETCH c_dept INTO tempout;
        IF c_dept%NOTFOUND THEN
          INSERT INTO dept(deptno,dname)
          VALUES (dmlset(i).deptno,dmlset(i).dname);
        END IF;
        CLOSE c_dept;
        INSERT INTO emp(empno,ename, job,hiredate, sal, deptno)
```

2

ADVANCED GUI
DEVELOPMENT:
DEVELOPING BEYOND
GUI

continues

LISTING 2.1   Continued

```
      VALUES(dmlset(i).empno,dmlset(i).ename, dmlset(i).job,
            dmlset(i).hiredate, dmlset(i).sal, dmlset(i).deptno);
    NULL;
END LOOP;
  END insert_procedure;

  PROCEDURE update_procedure(dmlset IN OUT dept_emp_tab) IS
    CURSOR c_dept(i BINARY_INTEGER) IS
      SELECT deptno
      FROM dept
      WHERE deptno=dmlset(i).deptno;     tempout NUMBER(4);
  BEGIN

/* The following inserts into the DEPT table if not found already.
It also updates the EMP table. Each record in the input dmlset is updated.
The coordination and synchronization between the input dmlset and
the block's records that have been marked for UPDATE are done by
the  UPDATE-PROCEDURE trigger written by Forms */

FOR i IN 1..dmlset.COUNT LOOP
    OPEN c_dept(i);
    FETCH c_dept INTO tempout;
    IF c_dept%NOTFOUND THEN
       INSERT INTO dept(deptno,dname)
       VALUES(dmlset(i).deptno,dmlset(i).dname);
    ELSE
       UPDATE dept
          SET dname = dmlset(i).dname
        WHERE deptno = dmlset(i).deptno;
    END IF;
    CLOSE c_dept;
    --
    UPDATE emp
       SET ename=dmlset(i).ename,
           job=dmlset(i).job,
           hiredate=dmlset(i).hiredate,
           sal     =dmlset(i).sal,
           deptno=dmlset(i).deptno
      WWWHERE empno=dmlset(i).empno;
END LOOP;
  END update_procedure;

  PROCEDURE delete_procedure(dmlset IN OUT dept_emp_tab) IS
  BEGIN
```

```
/* The following  deletes from the EMP table. Each record in the input dmlset
is  deleted. The coordination and synchronization between the input dmlset
and the block's records that have been marked for DELETE are done by the
DELETE-PROCEDURE trigger written by Forms */

FOR i IN 1..dmlset.COUNT LOOP
     DELETE FROM emp WHERE empno=dmlset(i).empno;
END LOOP;
  END delete_procedure;

END PKGDEPTEMP;
```

Tips for Basing Blocks on Stored Procedures

Here are some additional tips that will help when you base blocks on stored procedures:

- There is no connection between a data block based on a stored procedure and the stored procedure itself, except for the following: The QUERY, INSERT, UPDATE, DELETE, and LOCK data source procedures specified are executed in response to the block QUERY, INSERT, UPDATE, and DELETE functions.

- As far as the query operation is concerned, all the triggers and system variables function in the same way as with a block based on a database table. Specifically, the PRE-QUERY, POST-QUERY, ON-SELECT, and ON-FETCH triggers fire by default (that is, without any extra code written), and the system variables, :SYSTEM.MODE, :SYSTEM.FORM_STATUS, : SYSTEM.BLOCK_STATUS, and :SYSTEM.RECORD_STATUS, return the same values as in the case of a base table block. Even ad hoc querying is possible, but with extra care taken. (Ad hoc querying is explained in the next section, "Specifying Ad Hoc Query Criteria.")

- Do not define ON-SELECT and ON-FETCH triggers for the block based on a procedure because it defies (and, in fact, replaces) the default selection procedure of returning a result set from the Query Data Source procedure.

- The ON-INSERT, ON-UPDATE, ON-DELETE, and ON-LOCK triggers do fire. Do not define these triggers for a data block based on a stored procedure.

Specifying Ad Hoc Query Criteria in Case of Blocks Based on Stored Procedures

As mentioned earlier, no connection exists between the data block and the DML procedures except for receiving and sending the data. Therefore, any additional functions must be taken care of explicitly. I have discussed the techniques for performing INSERT, UPDATE, DELETE, and LOCK operations in blocks based on stored procedures. The SELECT operation is possible by default, that is, by Forms, without writing code. However, one function pertaining to the selection of records is the specifying of ad hoc query criteria at runtime. This is an often-required feature because it provides the flexibility of querying on user-defined criteria, thus eliminating the need to search the entire result set for a specific subset of data. This section highlights the technique for ad hoc querying in a block based on a stored procedure.

To do so, follow these steps:

1. Specify extra parameters, one each for the items that are Query Allowed, to the Query Data Source procedure. This can be done while defining the stored package or at a later stage.

2. Specify the value clause for each parameter as the item name or form parameter name that supplies the IN value to each query procedure parameter defined in step 1. Again, this can be done while creating the block or later on, using the Data Block Wizard.

TIP

Creating the extra parameter(s) and specifying the value do not guarantee the query to be ad hoc. To take care of the desired functionality, the corresponding logic has to be coded in the body of the Query procedure by adding additional WHERE conditions.

The package code in Listing 2.1 already includes the extra parameter P_EMPNO for the PKGDEPTEMP.QUERY_PROCEDURE. The Data Block Wizard with the value modification appears in Figure 2.6.

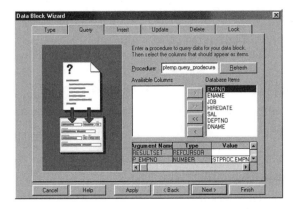

FIGURE 2.6

The Data Block Wizard shows the extra parameter P_EMPNO used for ad hoc querying.

Note that the value is specified as :STPROC.EMPNO (you must include the colon), which is the item name in the STPROC block. This value provides querying on the STPROC.EMPNO item in

Enter-Query mode. At runtime, the value of the user-entered EMPNO becomes the IN value of the P_EMPNO parameter. Completing these two steps will enable the user to query on a specific EMPNO.

Note that the technique described here works only for exact equality matches and without involving any other operators, such as >, <, and so on. For example, if the user enters > 1000 in the EMPNO item, an error occurs. Additional functionality for nonequality and LIKE matches should be coded explicitly in the Query procedure.

The Power of Record Groups

Since their inception in Forms 4.0, record groups have played a significant role in enhancing the development of forms, whether it be LOV manipulation, multiple selection, or intermediate sorting, to name a few uses. In this section, I will discuss techniques for

- changing a record group dynamically, for example, to repopulate it based on runtime criteria.
- adding rows to the beginning of a record group.
- adding rows anywhere in a record group and to the end of a record group.
- multiple selection.
- intermediate sorting.

Changing a Record Group Dynamically

Record groups can be created either at design time or programmatically at runtime (dynamically). Also, dynamically created record groups can be locally scoped or globally scoped. *Locally scoped* means that the data contained in such a record group is accessible to the particular form in which it is created. Therefore, such a record group is not sharable across forms in a multiform application. A *globally scoped* record group has its data sharable across all forms in a single multiform session.

There are varied uses for creating and manipulating record groups dynamically, the most common ones being

- populating list items dynamically.
- simulating multiselection pick lists.
- populating control blocks dynamically.
- performing intermediate actions such as sorting, searching, and computing, which require in-memory computations but are either not possible or not efficient when done using local or server-side PL/SQL.

I begin by providing a brief introduction to creating and manipulating dynamic record groups, both query and nonquery. In the subsequent subsections, I then discuss the techniques not often encountered in the normal creation and manipulation procedures.

Dynamically creating record groups involves creating a nonquery record group at runtime. This involves the following steps:

1. Creating the record group. This creates only the internal ID for the record group and is done using CREATE_GROUP.

2. Adding columns to the record group. This is done using ADD_GROUP_COLUMN.

3. Adding rows to the record group and setting the row-column cell values (populating the group). This is done in a loop, using ADD_GROUP_ROW and SET_GROUP_<datatype>_CELL, where <datatype> is one of NUMBER, DATE, and CHAR.

The following code illustrates this method:

```
DECLARE
   rg_id RECORDGROUP;
   rg_name VARCHAR2(20) := 'RG_DEPT';
   gc_id1 GROUPCOLUMN;
   gc_id2 GROUPCOLUMN;
   row_cnt NUMBER := 5;
BEGIN

/* First check whether the record group already exists.
If Yes, delete it. */

   rg_id := FIND_GROUP(rg_name);
   IF NOT ID_NULL(rg_id) THEN
     DELETE_GROUP(rg_id);
   END IF;

/* Create the record group to derive a handle or internal id */

   rg_id := CREATE_GROUP(rg_name);
   IF ID_NULL(rg_id) THEN
     MESSAGE('ERR: Creating Record Group '||rg_name);
     RAISE FORM_TRIGGER_FAILURE;
   END IF;

/* Add two group columns, deptno and dname */

   gc_id1 := ADD_GROUP_COLUMN(rg_id, 'deptno', NUMBER_COLUMN);
   gc_id2 := ADD_GROUP_COLUMN(rg_id, 'dname', CHAR_COLUMN, 20);
```

```
/* Create 5 rows and populate them in a loop. The constant 5 is chosen at
random to illustrate the concepts */

  FOR i in 1..row_cnt LOOP
    ADD_GROUP_ROW(rg_id, END_OF_GROUP);
    SET_GROUP_NUMBER_CELL(gc_id1, i, i);
    SET_GROUP_CHAR_CELL(gc_id2, i, 'Department '||TO_CHAR(i));
  END LOOP;

END;
```

Creating a query record group at runtime involves the following steps:

- Creating the record group based on a SELECT statement. This creates the internal ID for the record group, as well as the structure of the record group (that is, the columns). This is done using CREATE_GROUP_FROM_QUERY.

- Populating the record group with the rows retrieved by the query that was used in the CREATE_GROUP_FROM_QUERY built-in or a different query having one-to-one correspondence with this query. It automatically adds rows to it. This is done using POPULATE_GROUP if the query is the same as the one used to create the group or using POPULATE_GROUP_WITH_QUERY if the data is from a different query.

The following code implements this method:

```
DECLARE
  rg_id RECORDGROUP;
  rg_name VARCHAR2(20) := 'RG_DEPT';
  query_string := 'SELECT deptno,, dname FROM dept ORDER BY dname';
  ret_code NUMBER;
BEGIN

/* First check whether the record group already exists.
If Yes, delete it. */

  rg_id := FIND_GROUP(rg_name);
  IF NOT ID_NULL(rg_id) THEN
    DELETE_GROUP(rg_id);
  END IF;

/* Create the record group from an input query to derive a handle or
internal id, as well as the column structure */

  rg_id := CREATE_GROUP_FROM_QUERY(rg_name , query_string);
  IF ID_NULL(rg_id) THEN
    MESSAGE('ERR: Creating Record Group '||rg_name);
    RAISE FORM_TRIGGER_FAILURE;
```

```
  END IF;

/* Populate the created record group with data from the query used to
create the group. This need not be done in a loop. */
    ret_code := POPULATE_GROUP(rg_id);
    IF (ret_code <> 0) THEN
      MESSAGE('ERR: Populating Group');
      RAISE FORM_TRIGGER_FAILURE;
    END IF;

/* This line containing the call to POPULATE_GROUP can be replaced by
the following line if the query to populate the data is different.

    ret_code :=
      POPULATE_GROUP_WITH_QUERY(rg_id,
                                'SELECT deptno, dname
                                FROM dept
                                WHERE loc = ''NEW YORK''
                                ORDER BY dname');
  */

END;
```

Dynamically manipulating record groups amounts to adding, changing, and deleting row(s) in the following ways:

- At the beginning of an existing group
- At the end of an existing group
- Anywhere in the middle of an existing group, both query and nonquery
- Adding, changing, and deleting entire columns of a group, both query and nonquery

---

TIP

Here is an important tip that reminds us of an often-ignored point about creating record groups dynamically. You can change a record group dynamically only if it's created dynamically (query or nonquery) or if it's a query record group created at design time.

Changing GLOBAL_SCOPE record groups is discussed in Chapter 4, "Advanced Forms Programming" under the section "Sharing a Record Group across Forms."

Adding to the Beginning of a Record Group

How many of you are aware that in Forms 4.5 you can add rows to the beginning of an already created record group? This seems trivial at first thought, but is a powerful and flexible technique to be used in many demanding situations.

To do this, use `ADD_GROUP_ROW` and specify the constant 1 for the row index, as follows:

```
ADD_GROUP_ROW(rg_id, 1);
```

This displaces all the existing rows to one position below and makes room for the new row with row number 1. *Do not* specify the constant 0 instead of 1.

Adding in the Middle or at the End of a Record Group

To add a record in the middle of a record group, use `ADD_GROUP_ROW` and specify the index number of the new row as

```
current row index + 1
```

where *current row* is the row after which the new row should be added. This displaces all the remaining rows to one position below and makes room for the new row.

To add a record to the end of the record group, specify the constant `END_OF_GROUP` for the index number.

Multiple Selection

Multiple selection is a common requirement in almost all applications in which the user expects a choice of elements to choose from by click-and-highlight. The multiple selection is made possible by giving the user the flexibility of choosing from a `SELECT_ALL` list on the left. After the entire selection is made, an ADD button enables the selected records to be transferred to the right side. The question of retaining the selected records on the left hand side (LHS) is application and user-requirement specific. Here, I will retain the selected records from the LHS as soon as the user presses the ADD button.

Now I will discuss the technique of multiple selection by using dynamically created record groups and using Select and De-select toggle by click operation only.

To illustrate this technique, consider a payroll application in which users are presented with an initial selection screen displaying a list of all departments. Selection of multiple departments is allowed. The payroll must be processed for the employees of the multiple-selected departments.

The design is as follows:

- A multirecord ALL_DEPT block based on the DEPT table on the LHS. This block is a query-only block and will automatically display all records on screen startup. The items DEPTNO and DNAME are displayed.

- A multirecord SELECTED_DEPT control block on the right hand side (RHS) to hold the departments selected by the user. Here also the items DEPTNO and DNMAE are displayed.

  There will be no facility to perform INSERT, UPDATE, DELETE, or QUERY records in both the blocks.

- A CTRL_BLK control block with two items, ADD_COUNT and REMOVE_COUNT, to keep the count of records selected for either adding to or removing from LHS or RHS.

- Two push buttons, PB_ADD and PB_ADD_ALL, to enable transfer of some or all of the selected records from the LHS to the RHS.

- Two push buttons, PB_REMOVE and PB_REMOVE_ALL, to enable transfer of some or all of the selected records from the RHS to the LHS.

  These buttons belong to the control block.

- Two visual attributes, VA_SELECTED and VA_DESELECTED, to highlight and un-highlight the particular record when the user selects or deselects by clicking on a particular record.

- Selection and deselection are a toggle operation by point-and-click. This is the case when adding or removing records.

Figure 2.7 shows a typical multiselection functionality. To create it, follow these steps:

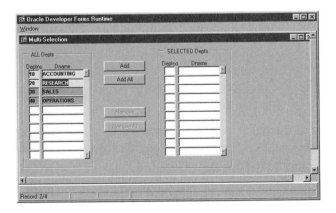

FIGURE 2.7

Multiple selection of departments.

1. The block ALL_DEPT has the following properties and their corresponding values set:

DATABASE BLOCK	YES
Number of Records Displayed	10
Query Allowed	Yes
Insert Allowed	No
Update Allowed	No
Delete Allowed	No
Query Data Source Type	TABLE
Query Data Source Name	DEPT
QUERY ALL RECORDS	YES

   Note the special property QUERY ALL RECORDS. This is set to YES to enable all the records to be fetched into the Forms buffer at the very beginning of the query.

2. The block SELECTED_DEPT has the following properties and their corresponding values set:

DATABASE BLOCK	NO
Number of Records Displayed	10
Query Allowed	No
Insert Allowed	Yes
Update Allowed	No
Delete Allowed	No

   The items DEPTNO and DNAME have the Insert Allowed and Update Allowed properties set to No. The block property Insert Allowed is set to Yes to enable programmatically creating a record while populating the selected records from the record group.

3. A WHEN-NEW-FORM-INSTANCE trigger queries the ALL_DEPT block on form startup:

```
GO_BLOCK('ALL_DEPT');
Check_package_failure;
EXECUTE_QUERY;
```

4. A POST-QUERY trigger on the ALL_DEPT block deselects all records whenever the ALL_DEPT block is queried. This block is requeried more than once, as will be evident from the steps that follow:

```
        SET_ITEM_INSTANCE_PROPERTY('ALL_DEPT.DEPTNO', CURRENT_RECORD,
                              VISUAL_ATTRIBUTE, 'VA_UNSELECTED');
        SET_ITEM_INSTANCE_PROPERTY('ALL_DEPT.DNAME', CURRENT_RECORD,
                              VISUAL_ATTRIBUTE, 'VA_UNSELECTED');
```

5. The WHEN-MOUSE-CLICK trigger for the ALL_DEPT block toggles between selection and deselection whenever the user clicks on a particular row:

```
DECLARE
    ret_code NUMBER;
BEGIN
    ret_code := selection_toggle('ALL_DEPT');
    :ctrl_blk.add_count := NVL(:ctrl_blk.add_count,0) + ret_code;
    IF :ctrl_blk.add_count > 0 THEN
      SET_ITEM_PROPERTY('CTRL_BLK.PB_ADD', ENABLED, PROPERTY_TRUE);
     IF :ctrl_blk.add_count > 1 THEN
       SET_ITEM_PROPERTY('CTRL_BLK.PB_ADD_ALL', ENABLED, PROPERTY_TRUE);
     END IF;
    ELSE
     SET_ITEM_PROPERTY('CTRL_BLK.PB_ADD', ENABLED, PROPERTY_FALSE);
     SET_ITEM_PROPERTY('CTRL_BLK.PB_ADD_ALL', ENABLED, PROPERTY_FALSE);
    END IF;
END;
```

6. The function SELECTION_TOGGLE has the following logic in it:

- A nonquery record group, RG_LHS, is created dynamically to populate each high-lighted record from the LHS. The record group has a selection feature in it to mark a record as selected or deselected. This will remove a very serious hazard in the process of record selection and deselection, as detailed in step 2. This record group is included as part of a package named rg_lhs that has the record group ID, the record group name, individual group column IDs and names, and the group row and selection counts. The advantage of choosing a package is twofold. It ensures, first, the availability of the preceding variables' retaining their global scope and, second, better performance.

- As the user clicks and highlights a record on the LHS, a row is fed into the record group and also into the group selection. If a record is deselected, the row is removed from the group selection, but *not from the record group.* This is because the user might click and select *n* of them at first and then deselect the *m*th one out of the *n* selected; this would involve a search from the record group. The records can be grouped as a selected group or a deselected group inside the same record group, but this is also a costly affair with respect to intergroup transfer. The selection in the record group saves the following important step: the process of keeping a third control item in the LHS block(s) and LOOPing through the blocks, which is not as efficient. You would have had to LOOP through the LHS block to get all the selected records when the user clicks the ADD button.

- This record group also has a third column to keep track of records that have already been added. This eliminates looping through the RHS block.

The function code is as follows:

```
FUNCTION selection_toggle(block_name VARCHAR2) RETURN NUMBER IS
   row_num Number;
   row_no Number;
   v_num    Number;
   v_added VARCHAR2(1);
   curr_rownum NUMBER;
   present_in_selection BOOLEAN := FALSE;
   present_in_group BOOLEAN := FALSE;
   already_added BOOLEAN := FALSE;
 BEGIN
IF GET_ITEM_INSTANCE_PROPERTY(block_name||'.'||
                              GET_BLOCK_PROPERTY(block_name, FIRST_ITEM),
      CURRENT_RECORD, VISUAL_ATTRIBUTE) = 'VA_UNSELECTED' THEN
   DISPLAY_ITEM(block_name||'.'||
      GET_BLOCK_PROPERTY(block_name, FIRST_ITEM), 'VA_SELECTED');
   DISPLAY_ITEM(block_name||'.'||
      GET_BLOCK_PROPERTY(block_name, LAST_ITEM), 'VA_SELECTED');

   -- Creating the Record Group
   rg_lhs.rg_id := FIND_GROUP(rg_lhs.rg_name);
   IF FORM_SUCCESS THEN
      IF ID_NULL(rg_lhs.rg_id) THEN
           rg_lhs.rg_id := CREATE_GROUP(rg_lhs.rg_name);
      IF FORM_SUCCESS THEN
        IF ID_NULL(rg_lhs.rg_id) THEN
           MESSAGE('ERR: Creating Group '||rg_lhs.rg_name);
           RAISE FORM_TRIGGER_FAILURE;
        END IF;
      END IF;
    END IF;
   END IF;
-- Add Group Columns
rg_lhs.gc_id1 :=
  FIND_COLUMN(rg_lhs.rg_name||'.'||rg_lhs.column_name1);
IF ID_NULL(rg_lhs.gc_id1) THEN
  rg_lhs.gc_id1 :=
   ADD_GROUP_COLUMN(rg_lhs.rg_id, rg_lhs.column_name1, NUMBER_COLUMN);
END IF;
rg_lhs.gc_id2 :=
  FIND_COLUMN(rg_lhs.rg_name||'.'||rg_lhs.column_name2);
IF ID_NULL(rg_lhs.gc_id2) THEN
  rg_lhs.gc_id2 :=
  ADD_GROUP_COLUMN(rg_lhs.rg_id, rg_lhs.column_name2, CHAR_COLUMN, 20);
END IF;
rg_lhs.gc_id3 :=
```

```
     FIND_COLUMN(rg_lhs.rg_name||'.'||rg_lhs.column_name3);
  IF ID_NULL(rg_lhs.gc_id3) THEN
    rg_lhs.gc_id3 :=
   ADD_GROUP_COLUMN(rg_lhs.rg_id, rg_lhs.column_name3, CHAR_COLUMN, 5);
  END IF;
  -- Getting group row count
  rg_lhs.row_cnt := get_group_row_count(rg_lhs.rg_id);

  -- current row num is row cnt incremented by 1
  row_num := NVL(rg_lhs.row_cnt,0) + 1;
  -- If rg cnt is 0, i.e., the very first time, add rg row.
  IF rg_lhs.row_cnt = 0 THEN
     Add_group_row(rg_lhs.rg_id, row_num);
     set_group_number_cell(rg_lhs.gc_id1, row_num,
                              TO_NUMBER(name_in('ALL_DEPT.DEPTNO')));
     set_group_char_cell(rg_lhs.gc_id2, row_num,
                            name_in('ALL_DEPT.DNAME'));
     set_group_char_cell(rg_lhs.gc_id3, row_num, 'N');
  END IF;
   -- Search if row already present in the record group.
     for i in 1 .. rg_lhs.row_cnt loop
     v_num := get_group_number_cell(rg_lhs.gc_id1, i);
      if :all_dept.deptno = v_num then
           curr_rownum := i;
        present_in_group := TRUE;
        exit;
      end if;
     end loop;
     if present_in_group then
           -- Search if row already selected.
           rg_lhs.sel_cnt := GET_GROUP_SELECTION_COUNT(rg_lhs.rg_id);
       for j in 1 .. rg_lhs.sel_cnt loop
         row_no := get_group_selection(rg_lhs.rg_id, j);
         v_num := get_group_number_cell(rg_lhs.gc_id1, row_no);
         if :all_dept.deptno = v_num then
               present_in_selection := TRUE;
               exit;
         end if;
       end loop;
       if not present_in_selection then
         set_group_selection(rg_lhs.rg_id, curr_rownum);
       end if;
     else -- not present in group, so add new row
       Add_group_row(rg_lhs.rg_id, row_num);
       set_group_number_cell(rg_lhs.gc_id1, row_num,
                                TO_NUMBER(name_in('ALL_DEPT.DEPTNO')));
```

```
            set_group_char_cell(rg_lhs.gc_id2, row_num,
                              name_in('ALL_DEPT.DNAME'));
            set_group_char_cell(rg_lhs.gc_id3, row_num, 'N');
            SET_GROUP_SELECTION(rg_lhs.rg_id, row_num);
          end if;
          Return(1);
    ELSIF GET_ITEM_INSTANCE_PROPERTY(block_name¦¦'.'¦¦
                              GET_BLOCK_PROPERTY(block_name,
    FIRST_ITEM),
              CURRENT_RECORD, VISUAL_ATTRIBUTE) = 'VA_SELECTED' THEN
    -- If already selected, de-select it
        rg_lhs.sel_cnt := GET_GROUP_SELECTION_COUNT(rg_lhs.rg_id);
        for idx in 1 .. rg_lhs.sel_cnt loop
              row_no := get_group_selection(rg_lhs.rg_id, idx);
              v_num := get_group_number_cell(rg_lhs.gc_id1, row_no);
              v_added := get_group_char_cell(rg_lhs.gc_id3, row_no);
          if :all_dept.deptno = v_num then
              if (v_added != 'Y') then
            unset_group_selection(rg_lhs.rg_id, row_no);
          end if;
            exit;
        else
          null;
        end if;
        end loop;
        DISPLAY_ITEM(block_name¦¦'.'¦¦
          GET_BLOCK_PROPERTY(block_name, FIRST_ITEM), 'VA_UNSELECTED');
        DISPLAY_ITEM(block_name¦¦'.'¦¦
          GET_BLOCK_PROPERTY(block_name, LAST_ITEM), 'VA_UNSELECTED');
        message(rg_lhs.sel_cnt);
        pause;
        Return (-1);
    END IF;
    END;
```

7. A WHEN-BUTTON-PRESSED trigger for the PB_ADD button has the following logic in it:

```
DECLARE
    row_no NUMBER;
    sl_cnt NUMBER;
BEGIN
    IF (:ctrl_blk.add_count > 0) THEN
          GO_BLOCK('SELECTED_DEPT');
          CLEAR_BLOCK(NO_VALIDATE);
    sl_cnt := GET_GROUP_SELECTION_COUNT(rg_lhs.rg_id);
    for idx in 1 .. sl_cnt loop
            row_no := get_group_selection(rg_lhs.rg_id, idx);
```

```
              COPY(GET_GROUP_NUMBER_CELL(rg_lhs.gc_id1, row_no),
                   'SELECTED_DEPT.DEPTNO');
              COPY(GET_GROUP_CHAR_CELL(rg_lhs.gc_id2, row_no),
                   'SELECTED_DEPT.DNAME');
              SET_GROUP_CHAR_CELL(rg_lhs.gc_id3, row_no, 'Y');
              CREATE_RECORD;
            end loop;
            go_block('ALL_DEPT');
            execute_query(no_validate);
    --      RESET_GROUP_SELECTION(rg_lhs.rg_id);
            :ctrl_blk.add_count := NULL;
            SET_ITEM_PROPERTY('CTRL_BLK.PB_ADD', ENABLED, PROPERTY_FALSE);
            SET_ITEM_PROPERTY('CTRL_BLK.PB_ADD_ALL', ENABLED, PROPERTY_FALSE);
          END IF;
        END;
```

8. The WHEN-BUTTON-PRESSED trigger for PB_ADD_ALL is done in a tricky way. Rather than loop through the LHS block, populating the record group and then populating the RHS block, you dynamically set the base table query source and query source name, query the SELECTED_ALL block, and reset their values to NULL after querying.

This method works well from Forms 5.x onwards. In Forms 4.5, you have three choices:

- Hide the RHS block and display a second base table block only when the user presses ADD ALL. Then, when all the records from RHS have been moved to LHS, hide this second base table block.

- Loop through the LHS block, highlighting each record. Populate the record group and then the RHS block so that no second base table block is involved.

- Use only one block for the RHS. Make it a base table block, and perform an EXECUTE_QUERY(ALL_RECORDS) in the WHEN-BUTTON-PRESSED trigger of ADD ALL. Remember, in this case, to set the record property to QUERY_STATUS in the code for PB_ADD, while populating the RHS from the record group as outlined earlier.

The actual code for WHEN-BUTTON-PRESSED of the ADD ALL button is as follows:

```
SET_BLOCK_PROPERTY('SELECTED_DEPT',QUERY_DATA_SOURCE_NAME, 'DEPT');
GO_BLOCK('ALL_DEPT');
CLEAR_BLOCK('NO_VALIDATE');
SET_BLOCK_PROPERTY('ALL_DEPT', CURRENT_RECORD_ATTRIBUTE,
                   'VA_UNSELECTED');
GO_BLOCK('SELECTED_DEPT');
EXECUTE_QUERY(ALL_RECORDS);
```

The WHEN-BUTTON-PRESSED trigger for PB_REMOVE_ALL is

```
GO_BLOCK('SELECTED_DEPT');
CLEAR_BLOCK(NO_VALIDATE');
```

```
SET_BLOCK_PROPERTY('SELECTED_DEPT', CURRENT_RECORD_ATTRIBUTE,
                   'VA_UNSELECTED');
GO_BLOCK('ALL_DEPT');
EXECUTE_QUERY(ALL_RECORDS);
```

9. The POST-QUERY is not necessary for the SELECTED_DEPT block because no query is involved here. The WHEN-MOUSE-CLICK trigger for this block is similar to the one for ALL_DEPT except that the block name ALL_DEPT is replaced by SELECTED_DEPT and the record group name RG_LHS is replaced by RG_RHS. The function selection_toggle is also similar except that the form variable CTRL_BLK.ADD_COUNT is replaced by CTRL_BLK.REMOVE_COUNT and the button names PB_ADD and PB_ADD_ALL are replaced by PB_REMOVE and PB_REMOVE_ALL.

Intermediate Sorting Using Record Groups

Imagine, in the preceding illustration, if the selected records in the intermediate record group were required to be sorted by DNAME before populating them to the RHS block. This could be a requirement if the user selects records from the LHS block at random.

The description of the bubble sort algorithm is as follows:

```
To sort an array of n integers, a1, a2, ..., aN,
For i in 1 to n loop
  For j in (i+1) to n-1 loop
    if a(i) > a(j) then
      temp = a(i)
      a(i) = a(j)
      a(j) = temp
    end if
  end loop
end loop
```

The following piece of code illustrates the preceding bubble sort algorithm for sorting rows in a record group:

```
DECLARE
      I NUMBER;
      J NUMBER;
      Row_count NUMBER;
      Rg_id recordGroup;
      Gc_id1 GroupColumn;
      Gc_id2 GroupColumn;
BEGIN

/* Check for the existence of the Record Group */
```

```
   Rg_id := FIND_GROUP('RG_LHS');
    IF ID_NULL(rg_id) THEN
      Return (-1);
      END IF;

/* Determine the sort columns */

    Gc_id1 := FIND_COLUMN(rg_id, 'deptno');
    Gc_id2 :=  FIND_COLUMN(rg_id, 'dname');

/* Get the Record Group Row Count */

    Row_count := GET_GROUP_ROW_COUNT(rg_id);

/* Implement the bubble sort algorithm */

    FOR i IN 1..(rg_lhs.sel_count - 1) LOOP
      FOR j in (i+1)..rg_lhs.sel_count  LOOP
    temp1_id := GET_GROUP_NUMBER_CELL(gc_id1,i);
    temp1_name := GET_GROUP_CHAR_CELL(gc_id2,i);
    temp2_id := GET_GROUP_NUMBER_CELL(gc_id1,j);
    temp2_name := GET_GROUP_CHAR_CELL(gc_id2,j);
    IF temp1_name > temp2_name THEN
      SET_GROUP_NUMBER_CELL(gc_id1,i, temp2_id);
      SET_GROUP_CHAR_CELL(gc_id2, i, temp2_name);
      SET_GROUP_NUMBER_CELL(gc_id1,j, temp1_id);
      SET_GROUP_CHAR_CELL(gc_id2, j, temp1_name);
    END IF;
  END LOOP;
END LOOP;

/* End of sorting */

<code for populating RHS block from record group follows>
END;
```

Creating a Customized Sign-on Form

A customized sign-on form has been a major requirement for Oracle Forms users in most of the client sites where I have worked. A typical requirement of such a customized logon screen is the capability to choose from the various databases available for the database string. The default logon screen for Forms doesn't provide this feature. This section presents an easy solution that I have discovered. Figure 2.8 shows an example of how such a screen would look.

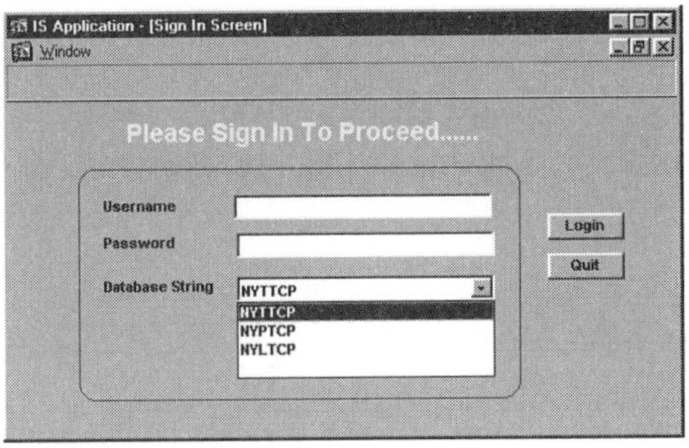

FIGURE 2.8

A customized sign-on form.

In this technique, you nullify the ON-LOGON trigger for the sign-on form conditionally and re-enable logging by using a call to LOGON with proper arguments, after the user completes data entry in the customized logon screen. The sign-on should be the very first form displayed in the application, even before the main menu. Invoke the sign-on form using Forms runtime in the normal manner, with username, password, and database string specified.

This design can be implemented with the following steps:

1. Create a control block named CTRL_BLK with two text items, USERNAME and PASSWORD; a pop-up list, DATABASE_STRING; and two push buttons, PB_LOGIN and PB_QUIT.

2. The desired functionality can be achieved by writing an ON-LOGON trigger at the form level and a WHEN-BUTTON-PRESSED trigger for the Login button. The ON-LOGON code is as follows:

```
ON-LOGON
DEFAULT_VALUE('', 'GLOBAL.tologin');
IF NAME_IN('GLOBAL.tologin') IS NULL THEN NULL;
ELSE
DECLARE
  ret_err_code NUMBER;
  ret_err_text VARCHAR2(1000);
BEGIN
  p_logon(:ctrl_blk.username,
          :ctrl_blk.password,
          :ctrl_blk.database_string,
          ret_err_code,
          ret_err_text);
  IF (ret_err_code <> 0) THEN
    p_show_alert(ret_err_text);
    RETURN;
```

```
    END IF;
END;
END IF;
```

The WHEN-BUTTON-PRESSED trigger for the Login button would consist of the following code:

```
BEGIN
  ENTER;
  IF FORM_SUCCESS THEN
    LOGON(NULL, NULL, FALSE);
      END IF;
END;
```

The code for p_logon is as follows:

```
PROCEDURE p_logon(un VARCHAR2,
                  pw VARCHAR2,
                  dcs VARCHAR2,
                  o_err_code OUT NUMBER,
                  o_err_text OUT VARCHAR2) IS
  v_err_code NUMBER;
  v_err_text VARCHAR2(1000);
BEGIN
  IF dcs IS NOT NULL THEN
    LOGON(un,pw¦¦'@'¦¦dcs, FALSE);
    IF NOT FORM_SUCCESS THEN
      v_err_code := DBMS_ERROR_CODE;
      v_err_text := DBMS_ERROR_TEXT;
    END IF;
  ELSE
    LOGON(un,pw, FALSE);
    IF NOT FORM_SUCCESS THEN
      v_err_code := DBMS_ERROR_CODE;
      v_err_text := DBMS_ERROR_TEXT;
    END IF;
  END IF;
  IF v_err_code IS NULL THEN
    v_err_code := -1;
  END IF;
  o_err_code := v_err_code;
  o_err_text := v_err_text;
END;
```

3. The logic for the Quit button is a simple call to EXIT_FORM.

A few points should be noted here:

- The use of the global variable. This is done to disable the login for the initial run form but enable subsequent logins.

- The NULL arguments to the LOGON built-in. This is done only to make the ON-LOGON trigger fire the subsequent times.

- FORM_TRIGGER_FAILURE is not raised so that repeated clicks of the Login button behave the same as the very first click. Raising FORM_TRIGGER_FAILURE would freeze the login screen until the user corrects the error. This is fine but would defy the functionality of the default Oracle Forms login screen. The customized form would behave exactly as the default one would, but with more features.

On logon failure, the DBMS_ERROR_TEXT captures the error from the database side, and the procedure p_show_alert throws up this message in the form of an alert. For example, in the case of an invalid username or password, you would receive the alert shown in Figure 2.9.

FIGURE 2.9

This alert message is displayed in the case of an invalid username or password.

The code for the procedure p_show_alert is as follows:

```
PROCEDURE p_show_alert
                    (ip_errm    VARCHAR2)
IS
    alert_id  ALERT;
    alert_button  NuMBER;
    error_msg   VARCHAR2(32767);
BEGIN
    alert_id := FIND_ALERT('ALERT_ERROR');
    error_msg := ip_errm;
    SET_ALERT_PROPERTY(alert_id, ALERT_MESSAGE_TEXT, error_msg);
    alert_button  := SHOW_ALERT(alert_id);
END p_show_alert;
```

An alternative way of implementing a customized sign-on form without using an ON-LOGON trigger is to LOGOUT first and then LOGON. Then, the only trigger required is WHEN-BUTTON-PRESSED for the Login button, with code modified as follows:

```
BEGIN
  ENTER;
  IF FORM_SUCCESS THEN
    LOGOUT;
    p_logon(:ctrl_blk.username,
            :ctrl_blk.password,
```

```
            :ctrl_blk.database_string,
            ret_err_code,
            ret_err_text);
    IF (ret_err_code <> 0) THEN
      p_global_alert(NULL, ret_err_text, 'E', FALSE);
      Return;
    END IF;
  END IF;
END;
```

Avoiding Confusion Between DO_KEY and the Corresponding KEY- Trigger

Built-ins in Forms control various user actions at runtime. These actions are nothing but the logical Forms functions that happen at runtime. User navigation or invoking list values for a data-bearing item are examples of such actions. Corresponding to each of these actions or logical functions are physical function keys that can initiate these actions, in addition to the programmatic control through built-ins. Also, for each of these physical function keys, there is a KEY- trigger to customize physical its default action. For example, writing a KEY-LISTVAL trigger can replace the default function of LIST_VALUES with more advanced code.

Forms has provided a common built-in named DO_KEY to customize these actions, irrespective of whether these actions were initiated by a built-in or a physical function key. This section attempts to highlight the subtle differences of using a KEY- trigger, a corresponding built-in, and the DO_KEY built-in with examples. Also, it goes a little beyond this to pinpoint the use of EXECUTE_TRIGGER in reference to the earlier ones.

Table 2.1 gives a clear picture of the differences among the following:

- A Logical Function key
- The corresponding physical key (on Windows NT as an example)
- The KEY- trigger associated with the logical key
- The corresponding built-in
- The use of the built-in as a parameter to the DO_KEY and EXECUTE_TRIGGER built-ins

TABLE 2.1 Correspondence between Logical Function Key, Physical Function Key, KEY- trigger, built-in and DO_KEY.

Item	Item Value	Item Description
Logical Function key	List of Values	The logical key to pop up an LOV for an item.
Physical key	F9	The physical hot key for invoking an LOV when the cursor is inside an item.
KEY- trigger	KEY-LISTVAL	The KEY trigger to add logic to the default process of popping up an LOV (for example, to check runtime conditions). Fires only when the user presses the hot key.
Built-in	LIST_VALUES	The Forms built-in to invoke an LOV. Can be called from any trigger that allows it.
DO_KEY	DO_KEY('LIST_VALUES')	Checks whether a KEY-LISTVAL trigger is defined. If Yes, executes this KEY trigger; if No, executes just the built-in. Can be called from any trigger including KEY-LISTVAL; when called from KEY-LISTVAL, has the same effect as LIST_VALUES. Takes a valid KEY-trigger–related built in as an argument.
EXECUTE_TRIGGER	EXECUTE_TRIGGER ('KEY-LISTVAL')	Takes any trigger name as an argument, provided that the scope of the trigger supplied as theparameter makes sense. For example, EXECUTE_TRIGGER ('MY_TRIGGER'), where MY_TRIGGER is a user-defined trigger. If, instead of a user-defined trigger, a Forms predefined trigger is being called using EXECUTE_TRIGGER, the scope of the trigger calling the EXECUTE_TRIGGER and the scope of the parameter trigger should match.

As an example of EXECUTE_TRIGGER (the last item in the above table), the following code, although commonly written in the KEY-NEXT-ITEM trigger,

```
EXECUTE_TRIGGER('WHEN-VALIDATE-ITEM');
IF FORM_SUCCESS THEN
    <a sequence of actions?
END IF;
```

can be called from any trigger, such as WHEN-BUTTON-PRESSED, keeping in mind the restriction just mentioned.

TIP

Use DO_KEY by default whenever there is a need to execute a function corresponding to a KEY- trigger.

The DO_KEY built-in executes the function key trigger associated with the built-in specified as its argument, irrespective of the trigger in which it is specified.

For example, the code

```
DO_KEY('NEXT_RECORD');
```

behaves in the following way. If a separate KEY-NXTREC trigger is written, the built-in executes this trigger; otherwise, it executes the function NEXT_RECORD (that is, it just navigates to the next record). It doesn't matter whether the user presses the <Next Record> function key. In fact, pressing the function key is not mandatory. On the other hand, for KEY-NXTREC to execute without the DO_KEY, the user must explicitly press <Next Record>. Otherwise, KEY-NXTREC is called as an argument to EXECUTE_TRIGGER, in which case it fires even without the user pressing <Next Record>.

TIP

There is a significant difference between DO_KEY and EXECUTE_TRIGGER. The former fires even when <Next Record> is pressed and the latter doesn't, which defeats the purpose of writing a KEY-NXTREC trigger when an action is required on user navigation.

In addition, the EXECUTE_TRIGGER takes any name, not only predefined trigger names.

Window Management in Forms

This section presents two very useful techniques of windows management: closing an active window by clicking the upper-right × icon and resizing, repositioning, and closing any open active window in a form. The former is a much appreciated user requirement that Oracle Forms lacks; it is in strict conformity with any standard Windows application. The second technique is a generic routine to minimize programming effort, as well as end-user effort, in closing each open window individually.

Closing a Window with the × Icon

Closing a window by clicking the × icon in the upper-right corner is an often required feature and also standard Windows functionality. Although this technique is ignored by Forms, you can achieve it by means of a few lines of code.

To do so, write a WHEN-WINDOW-CLOSED trigger, and navigate out of the window or exit the form as necessary by checking for :SYSTEM.EVENT_WINDOW. For example, to exit a form by clicking × when the active window is the console window (which is generally WINDOW1), the procedure p_close_window can be coded as follows:

```
PROCEDURE p_close_window(p_window_name  VARCHAR2,
                         console_window VARCHAR2,
                         ret_code OUT NUMBER)
IS
   Win_id Window;
BEGIN
Win_id := FIND_WINDOW(p_window_name);

   IF ID_NULL(win_id) THEN
      Ret_code := -1;
      Return;
    END IF;

   IF NAME_IN('SYSTEM.EVENT_WINDOW') = p_window_name THEN
      IF console_window = 'Y' THEN
         DO_KEY('EXIT_FORM');
      ELSE
       SET_WINDOW_PROPERTY(win_id, VISIBLE, PROPERTY_FALSE);
      END IF;
      IF FORM_SUCCESS THEN
        Ret_code := 0;
      ELSE
        Ret_code := -1;
      END IF;
   END IF;

END;
```

This procedure is generic in the sense that it can be used to close any window, not just the console window.

A form-specific key exit can be written to take care of any special checking before closing that particular form by clicking the × icon.

Resizing, Repositioning, and Closing Any Window

Child windows holding stacked canvases are very often required in a form to display information that becomes part of the primary window. For example, a selection list might be displayed in the primary window, and subsequent details and subdetails might figure in one or more stacked canvases held by child windows. Dynamically resizing, repositioning, or closing each of these windows is essential when multiple windows must be displayed at the same time. This requires a significant amount of code. This technique provides a generic routine to resize, reposition, and close any given window in a single form, thus saving the programmer the time and effort necessary to write the substantial code required.

> **TIP**
>
> The event window should have the `close_allowed`, `resize_allowed`, and `move_allowed` properties set to Yes/True at design time. This is necessary to enable the default closing, resizing and repositioning features.

Procedures for resizing and repositioning any window can be written on similar lines:

```
PROCEDURE p_resize_window(p_window_name  VARCHAR2,
                          console_window VARCHAR2,
                          width NUMBER,
                          height NUMBER,
                          ret_code OUT NUMBER)
IS
   Win_id Window;
BEGIN

/* The window name, its target width, and its height are passed
as input parameters. Also, an additional parameter to identify whether
the window under consideration is a console window is passed as input. */

   Win_id := FIND_WINDOW(p_window_name);
/* If input window does not exist, exit the procedure and return -1 */

   IF ID_NULL(win_id) THEN
      Ret_code := -1;
      Return;
   END IF;
```

```
/* If the input window is the active window and is not the console window,
resize it to the specified width and height */

   IF NAME_IN('SYSTEM.EVENT_WINDOW') = p_window_name THEN
      IF console_window = 'Y' THEN
        NULL; /* CANNOT RESIZE CONSOLE WINDOW */
      ELSE
        RESIZE_WINDOW(win_id, WIDTH, HEIGHT);
      END IF;
      IF FORM_SUCCESS THEN
        Ret_code := 0;
      ELSE
        Ret_code := -1;
      END IF;
   END IF;

END;

PROCEDURE p_reposition_window(p_window_name VARCHAR2,
                             console_window VARCHAR2,
                             xpos number,
                             ypos NUMBER,
                             ret_code OUT NUMBER)
IS
   Win_id Window;
BEGIN
/* The window name and its target (x,y) position are passed as
input parameters. Also, an additional parameter to identify whether the window
under consideration is a console window is passed as input. */

    Win_id := FIND_WINDOW(p_window_name);

/* If the input window does not exist, exit the procedure and return -1 */

   IF ID_NULL(win_id) THEN
      Ret_code := -1;
      Return;
   END IF;

/* If the input window is the active window and is not the console window,
resize it to the specified width and height */

   IF NAME_IN('SYSTEM.EVENT_WINDOW') = p_window_name THEN
      IF console_window = 'Y' THEN
        NULL; /* CANNOT RESIZE CONSOLE WINDOW */
      ELSE
```

```
        MOVE_WINDOW(win_id, xpos, ypos);
      END IF;
      IF FORM_SUCCESS THEN
        Ret_code := 0;
      ELSE
        Ret_code := -1;
      END IF;
    END IF;

END;
```

The preceding two procedures and the one given in the preceding section can be generalized into one by adding an extra parameter named action_type:

```
PROCEDURE p_action_window(p_window_name VARCHAR2,
                          console_window VARCHAR2,
                          action_type VARCHAR2,
        Width number, height number, xpos number, ypos number,
        ret_code OUT NUMBER,
)
IS
   Win_id Window;
   V_window_name VARCHAR2(40);
BEGIN

/* This procedure takes the action type (CLOSE, RESIZE or REPOSITION )
as an input parameter and calls the corresponding procedure
(p_close_window,
 p_rresize_window or p_reposition_window ) to perform that action.
Initially, it checks for the existence of the input window name */

Win_id := FIND_WINDOW(NAME_IN(p_window_name));

    IF ID_NULL(win_id) THEN
        Ret_code := -1;
        Return;
      END IF;
      IF (action_type = 'CLOSE') THEN
          P_close_window(p_window_name, console_window, ret_code);
        ESLIF (action_type = 'RESIZE') THEN
          P_resize_window(p_window_name, console_window, ret_code);
        ELSIF (action_type = 'REPOSITION')
          P_reposition_window(p_window_name, console_window, ret_code);
      END IF;
      IF FORM_SUCCESS THEN
          ret_code := 0;
```

```
        ELSE
            (ret_code = -1);
        END IF;
    END IF;

END;
```

The call to p_close_window can be replaced by p_action_window as follows:

```
WHEN-WINDOW-CLOSED

DECLARE
    ret_code NUMBER;
BEGIN

p_action_window('WINDOW0'), 'Y','CLOSE', ret_code);
IF (ret_code <>  0) THEN
    MESSAGE('Error closing Console Window!');
    RAISE FORM_TRIGGER_FAILURE;
END IF;
END;
```

The code for each of the three procedures p_close_window, p_resize_window, and p_reposition_window can be customized to handle application-specific logic. For example, the code for the p_close_window procedure can be customized to contain calls to initiate explicit navigation out of the respective window, such as GO_ITEM or GO_BLOCK, which will enable that window to close and also throw a Do you want to save? alert in case of pending database changes. Also, as seen in the example of closing the console window, EXIT_FORM can be helpful in closing all windows that initiate exiting a particular form.

TIP

The call to the built-in SET_WINDOW_PROPERTY with the property VISIBLE set to FALSE closes (hides) the window only if the window has no navigable items in it or the window style is Document. If the window has at least one navigable item in it, or the window style is Dialog, the window remains displayed unless and until the user explicitly navigates out of the window. Also, if the window is modal, the only way to exit is by means of explicit navigation. This can be taken care of by customization of the p_close_window procedure as outlined in the preceding example.

Summary

The purpose of this chapter was to highlight some tips and techniques for advanced Forms GUI programming. The topics under discussion were the suppressing of default master-detail behavior, toggling between Immediate and Deferred coordination, preventing a query in a block from execution if it returns no records, using form and global variables, base tables, and record groups, and the persistent confusion between DO_KEY and the corresponding KEY- trigger. This chapter also presented a simple solution for creating a customized sign-on form. Last, I discussed Windows management with regard to standard window operations such as Resize, Reposition, and Close.

Multi-form Applications

IN THIS CHAPTER

Multi-form applications are almost a mandatory feature in any software system that handles multiple logical units. A multi-form application also provides a concise integration of the various logical subunits and allows proper break-up of functionality. For example, such an application might display an initial selection screen showing all customers who have placed orders; it would then invoke order-related form(s) for the particular customer highlighted. Other features, such as comparing the orders of two customers, can be achieved by calling a separate form when the order-related information is displayed.

This chapter presents techniques concerning the management of multi-form applications, including techniques for bidirectional sharing of data between forms, interform navigation, commit processing, and exiting sequence in multi-form applications. An important technique for tracking the query-only mode of a called form is explained. The chapter begins by highlighting the theory behind the form filename, form module name, and form ID, along with the method to read and write their values.

Myths About the Form Filename, Form Module Name, and Form ID

Any Oracle Form that is stored as an operating system file has three values associated with it: the form filename, the form module name, and the form ID. The third value is invisible to the developer and can be obtained only by using Forms' supplied built-ins for that purpose. The first two seem to be closely related, but an in-depth analysis reveals that they are two entirely different values. This section exposes the theory hidden behind these three variables and presents tips to read and write their values.

The form filename is the actual operating system filename representing the binary .FMX. It can be obtained by using `GET_APPLICATION_PROPERTY(CURRENT_FORM)` or `GET_FORM_PROPERTY(FILE_NAME)`.

The form module name is the name of the form module (which appears as the very first name under the Forms node in the Object Navigator), irrespective of whether the form is stored in the file system or database. This is obtained by `GET_APPLICATION_PROPERTY (CURRENT_FORM_NAME)` and `GET_FORM_PROPERTY(FORM_NAME)`. The form system variables `:SYSTEM.CURRENT_FORM` and `:SYSTEM.LAST_FORM` also give the value of the form module name.

The form ID is an internal ID assigned to each form presently open (active or inactive) in a run-form session. This is of the composite data type `FORMMODULE` and can be obtained by using the `FIND_FORM` function. The parameter to be passed to this function can be one of the values specified in the preceding paragraph:

```
DECLARE
  form_id FORMMODULE;
BEGIN
  form_id := FIND_FORM(NAME_IN('SYSTEM.CURRENT_FORM'));
  form_id := FIND_FORM(GET_APPLICATION_PROPERTY(CURRENT_FORM_NAME)
END;
```

Also, the parameters for GO_FORM in an OPEN_FORM configuration can be either the form module name or form_id. I recommend using form_id because referencing by internal IDs saves an extra evaluation of the form_id each time the form is referenced.

Multiple instances of the same form result in different form IDs, even if the form module name is the same. This is because form_id is a composite structure that includes an id column—meaning that each instance of the same form has a different form_id.id stored in it. The use of form_id.id is illustrated in the "Form Management in an OPEN_FORM Configuration" section later in this chapter.

Passing Data from the Called Form to the Calling Form

Any multi-form application involves at least two forms: a calling form and a called form. Parameters help a lot in passing data from the calling form to the called form, that is, in the forward direction. Sometimes there is a requirement to pass data from the called form to the calling form.

As an example, consider an employee-department screen that lists the employee information for each department in an organization, including each employee's address. Because the address information is display only, the address of an employee is changed by means of a link to a separate address screen. Therefore, the new address must be selected in the address screen (the called form) to be populated in the employee screen (the calling form) when the address screen is exited. This data transfer in the reverse direction, that is, passing data from the called form to the calling form, can be done using global variables only.

TIP

Use parameters for passing data across two forms in the forward direction and global variables for passing data in the reverse direction, unless the same data has to be shared across multiple forms. In this case, use global variables.

Form Management in an OPEN_FORM Configuration

Form management in an OPEN_FORM configuration requires special attention, especially when there is a chain of OPEN forms and each of these, in turn, has detail forms OPEN. For example, consider the multi-form situation described in the introduction to this chapter. It can be implemented by using OPEN_FORM to invoke multiple instances of ORDER form, with each instance displaying order information about each customer. The ORDER form might then invoke an ORDER DETAILS form that is particular to the current ORDER. Four critical issues must be taken care of:

- Proper navigation between the various forms
- Proper commit in the various forms
- Proper exiting sequence of the various forms
- Simulating a CLOSE ALL FORMS

Ensuring these will guarantee that the data, as well as the functionality, are in sync. I will discuss each of these in the following sections.

Proper Navigation Between Forms

You can navigate properly between forms by tracking the form_id. Consider the application cited earlier. Three forms are involved: CUSTOMER_SELECTION, CUSTOMER_ORDERS, and CUSTOMER_ORDER_DETS. The CUSTOMER_SELECTION form calls the CUSTOMER_ORDERS form using OPEN_FORM. It uses OPEN_FORM to enable multiple instances of the CUSTOMER_ORDERS form to be opened in order to compare the order information of two or more customers. The CUSTOMER_ORDERS form, in turn, uses OPEN_FORM to call the CUSTOMER_ORDER_DETS form, because the main CUSTOMER_SELECTION form is being called from a menu using CALL_FORM. No subsequent calls to CALL_FORM are allowed in the form chain, after using OPEN_FORM initially.

TIP

When opening multiple instances of the same form in OPEN_FORM configuration, especially in an OPEN_FORM chain, ensure correct navigation from the subform to its parent form. This can be done using GO_FORM(form_id) in the WHEN-WINDOW-ACTIVATED trigger of the calling form.

The desired functionality can be achieved in three steps:

1. In the CUSTOMER_ORDERS form, write a WHEN-BUTTON-PRESSED trigger that keeps track of the form ID of the current particular instance of the form and then invokes the

CUSTOMER_ORDER_DETS form using OPEN_FORM. The global variable CUSTOMER_ORDER_
DETS_PRESSED is initialized in the WHEN-NEW-FORM-INSTANCE trigger as follows:

```
DEFAULT_VALUE('','global.customer_order_dets_pressed');
WHEN-BUTTON-PRESSED trigger of CUSTOMER_ORDERS form.

BEGIN
  :global.customer_order_dets_pressed := 'Y';
  SET_ITEM_PROPERTY('BUTTON_PALETTE.PB_CUST_ORD_DETS',
                    ENABLED, PROPERTY_FALSE);
  form_id := FIND_FORM('CUSTOMER_ORDERS');
  :global.form_id := TO_CHAR(form_id.id);
END;
```

The global variable is necessary to prevent pressing of the button to invoke
CUSTOMER_ORDER_DETS a second time while it is already open. An alternative way is to
follow the same tracking by form_id for this form, also, and control it. This is not necessary if a need exists to compare the order details of two orders, such as the order information of two customers.

2. In the CUSTOMER_ORDERS form, write a WHEN-WINDOW_ACTIVATED trigger that forces navigation to this form after the CUSTOMER_ORDER_DETS is exited:

```
DECLARE
  form_id FORMMODULE;
BEGIN
  IF :SYSTEM.EVENT_WINDOW = 'WINDOW0' THEN
    IF :global.customer_order_dets_pressed = 'N' THEN
      IF :global.form_id IS NOT NULL THEN
        form_id.id := TO_NUMBER(:global.form_id);
        GO_FORM(form_id);
        :global.form_id := NULL;
      END IF;
    END IF;
  END IF;
END;
SET_ITEM_PROPERTY('BUTTON_PALETTE.PB_CUST_ORD_DETS',
                  ENABLED, PROPERTY_TRUE);
```

The last line re-enables the button after correct navigation has taken place.

3. Reset the value of the global variable to 'N' while exiting the CUSTOMER_ORDER_DETS
   form:

```
POST-FORM trigger of CUSTOMER_ORDER_DETS form
:global.customer_order_dets_pressed := 'N';
```

Proper COMMIT

Proper COMMIT in the various forms is automatically ensured by forms, depending on whether the child forms are invoked in the same session or a different session. In such a case of multiple open forms,

- Call all forms in the same session.

- As a general rule of thumb, invoke the child forms after saving pending database changes in the calling forms. An alert similar to 'Do you want to save the changes you have made?' with three choices—Yes, No, and Cancel—can be displayed whenever the form status is changed. A Yes saves the pending changes and invokes the child forms, a No undoes the pending changes and invokes the child form, and a Cancel does a NULL operation.

TIP

Pending changes in the calling form invoke the called form in POST ONLY mode, which enables the form to only POST and NOT COMMIT, pending changes in the called form.

Proper Exiting Sequence

A proper exiting sequence makes sure that all child forms are exited before exiting the parent forms. (Do not exit parent forms before exiting child forms, unless otherwise specifically required.) This is done by writing a KEY-EXIT trigger for the CUSTOMER_ORDERS and CUSTOMER_SELECTION forms. If the CUSTOMER_ORDER_DETS form calls child forms, you must exit those forms properly, also. The following shows code for a KEY-EXIT for the CUSTOMER_ORDERS form. A similar KEY-EXIT can be written for the CUSTOMER_SELECTION form by replacing the module name.

```
KEY-EXIT for the CUSTOMER_ORDERS form

DECLARE
  form_id FORMMODULE;
  v_msg VARCHAR2(1000);
BEGIN
  form_id := FIND_FORM('CUSTOMER_ORDER_DETS');
  IF NOT ID_NULL(form_id) THEN
   v_msg := 'There are instance(s) of the Customer Order Details Open.';
   v_msg := v_msg||' Please close them first!';
   MESSAGE(v_msg);RAISE FORM_TRIGGER_FAILURE;
  END IF;
```

```
  IF FORM_SUCCESS THEN
    EXIT_FORM;
  END IF:
END;
```

If the form is being exited by means of an Exit button or using the × box of the main window, use DO_KEY('EXIT_FORM') in the WHEN-BUTTON-PRESSED trigger of the Exit button or WHEN-WINDOW-CLOSED of the main window, respectively, to invoke the preceding code without repeating it.

Simulating a CLOSE ALL FORMS

When multiple forms are open in a single run-form session, exiting the application requires each open form to be exited individually. However, providing a single function to close all open forms in one shot gives greater flexibility to the end user. It calls for some amount of coding on the part of the developer. You can implement a trick of the trade to simulate a CLOSE ALL FORMS using the WHEN-WINDOW-ACTIVATED trigger. This section presents this technique, which is both elegant and efficient.

TIP	
	Set a global variable like global.close_all to 'Y'. Use CLOSE_FORM to close the currently activated form.

A WHEN-WINDOW-ACTIVATED trigger can be written for each and every form invoked, either by using CALL_FORM or by independently using OPEN_FORM, and its code is based on the following algorithm. Declare a global variable to initiate CLOSE ALL FORMS. Set its value to 'Y'. If the value of this global variable is 'Y', close the currently active form.

The algorithm is given below:

```
if <global_variable_value> = 'Y' then
        if <current form = <active form> then
          close form;
        end if;
      end if;
```

The WHEN-WINDOW-ACTIVATED trigger calls a procedure p_close_all_forms whose logic is based on the above algorithm. The code for this procedure follows this trigger code:

```
WHEN-WINDOW-ACTIVATED
p_close_all_forms;
```

The code for the procedure p_close_all_forms is as follows:

```
PROCEDURE p_close_all_forms IS
  form_id FORMMODULE;
BEGIN
  IF NAME_IN('global.close_all') = 'Y' THEN
    form_id := FIND_FORM(NAME_IN('SYSTEM.CURRENT_FORM'));
    IF NOT ID_NULL(form_id) THEN
      CLOSE_FORM(form_id);
    END IF;
  END IF;
END;
```

The global global.close_all can be set in an iconic button on a toolbar, in a trigger for a hot key, or in a menu option common to all forms. The disadvantage of this method is that any nonactive forms are still left open until the user clicks on a particular form. To enhance the functionality to accommodate this feature, use :SYSTEM.MOUSE_FORM and the WHEN-MOUSE-ENTER trigger at the form level of each independent form. Then the user can just move the mouse around, and the CLOSE ALL FORMS magic follows. The corresponding procedure is named xclose_all_forms.

```
WHEN-MOUSE-ENTER
xclose_all_forms;
```

The code for the procedure is as follows:

```
PROCEDURE xclose_all_forms IS
  form_id FORMMODULE;
BEGIN
  IF NAME_IN('global.close_all') = 'Y' THEN
    form_id := FIND_FORM(NAME_IN('SYSTEM.MOUSE_FORM'));
    IF NOT ID_NULL(form_id) THEN
      CLOSE_FORM(form_id);
    END IF;
  END IF;
END;
```

This method is more user friendly than the first because it saves the many extra clicks required in the former.

TIP

CLOSE_FORM is equivalent to EXIT_FORM(ASK_COMMIT). If other parameters such as NO_COMMIT, DO_COMMIT or NO_VALIDATE are required, use EXIT_FORM instead.

Tracking QUERY_ONLY Mode

There is no easy way to track whether a form is being called in query-only mode. Of course, the easiest way of using global variables works, but calling too many forms means too many global variables just for tracking the QUERY_ONLY mode. A more elegant way of doing this is by building a wrapper over CALL_FORM or NEW_FORM that returns the query-only mode of the called form.

This way, two problems are solved:

- You can check for QUERY_ONLY without worrying about Forms' internal data structures, such as the break-up of FORMMODULE, and so on.

- You avoid the use of too many global variables and their names or, if using parameters, the process of creating them in each called form. The technique also takes care of setting them in the called form and referencing them in the calling form.

You will use the names XCALL_FORM and XNEW_FORM for the wrapper procedures. Capture the constants QUERY_ONLY or NO_QUERY_ONLY that are passed to CALL_FORM or NEW_FORM, and return them using OUT variables to the wrapper procedure. Then call the wrapper procedure rather than using CALL_FORM or NEW_FORM. Finally, check for QUERY ONLY in the called form by a simple call to the function XQUERY_ONLY, as in

```
IF Xquery_only(<formmodule_name>) THEN
      ......
      END IF;
```

The value of the parameter formmodule_name actually refers to the form filename of the form stored in the file system. If the form is stored in the database, it refers to the form module name. This is similar to that specified in CALL_FORM and NEW_FORM. That is why the function XQUERY_ONLY also takes as input the actual filename and not the module name. This means that you cannot check query-only using :SYSTEM.CURRENT_FORM. As outlined in the "Myths About the Form Filename, Form Module Name, and Form ID" section, you can always get the form filename from the form module name and then use XQUERY_ONLY to check it. If the form module name is to be passed, the parameter formmodule_name has to be of type FORMMODULE.

You achieve the desired functionality in the following steps:

1. The procedures XCALL_FORM and XNEW_FORM return the query mode of the input form. The choice to use XCALL_FORM or XNEW_FORM depends on whether the functionality desired is similar to CALL_FORM or NEW_FORM. If a CALL_FORM functionality is desired, a call to XCALL_FORM can be made—similarly for NEW_FORM, which should be done in the calling form.

2. A call to the function XQUERY_ONLY can be made in the called form to check whether it was called with the QUERY_ONLY parameter on.

3. A third function, XQUERY_ONLY, returns Boolean values TRUE or FALSE, depending on whether the calling form is being called in QUERY_ONLY mode.

The code is as follows:

```
PACKAGE Xcallform IS
  PROCEDURE XCALL_FORM(formmodule_name      VARCHAR2,
                       display              NUMBER DEFAULT HIDE,
                       switch_menu          NUMBER DEFAULT NO_REPLACE,
                       query_mode  IN OUT NUMBER DEFAULT NO_QUERY_ONLY,
                       data_mode NUMBER DEFAULT NO_SHARE_LIBRARY_DATA,
                       paramlist_id         PARAMLIST DEFAULT NULL);

  PROCEDURE XNEW_FORM(formmodule_name      VARCHAR2,
                      rollback_mode        NUMBER DEFAULT TO_SAVEPOINT,
                      query_mode   IN OUT NUMBER DEFAULT NO_QUERY_ONLY,
                      data_mode    NUMBER DEFAULT NO_SHARE_LIBRARY_DATA,
                      paramlist_id         PARAMLIST DEFAULT NULL);

  FUNCTION XQUERY_ONLY(FormModule_name VARCHAR2) RETURN BOOLEAN;

END Xcallform;


PACKAGE BODY Xcallform IS
  TYPE xcallform_rec is RECORD (formmodule_name VARCHAR2(40),
                                queryonly NUMBER);
  TYPE Xcallform_tab IS TABLE OF xcallform_rec INDEX BY BINARY_INTEGER;
  Xcallform_stack xcallform_tab;

  FUNCTION getstackcount RETURN NUMBER
  IS
  BEGIN
    RETURN(xcallform_stack.count);
  END;

  Procedure XCALL_FORM(formmodule_name      VARCHAR2,
                       display              NUMBER DEFAULT HIDE,
                       switch_menu          NUMBER DEFAULT NO_REPLACE,
                       query_mode  IN OUT NUMBER DEFAULT NO_QUERY_ONLY,
                       data_mode NUMBER DEFAULT NO_SHARE_LIBRARY_DATA,
                       paramlist_id         PARAMLIST DEFAULT NULL)
```

```
IS
   cnt BINARY_INTEGER := getstackcount;
   current_form_before FORMMODULE;
   current_form_after FORMMODULE;

 BEGIN

   /* Populate the next element of this array */
   xcallform_stack(cnt+1).formmodule_name := formmodule_name;
   xcallform_stack(cnt+1).queryonly := query_mode;
   current_form_before := FIND_FORM(NAME_IN('SYSTEM.CURRENT_FORM'));
   CALL_FORM(formmodule_name,
             display,
             switch_menu,
             query_mode,
             data_mode,
             paramlist_id);
   current_form_after := FIND_FORM(NAME_IN('SYSTEM.CURRENT_FORM'));
   /* If call_form is not a success, delete added stack element */
   IF (current_form_before.id = current_form_after.id ) THEN
     xcallform_stack.delete(cnt+1);
   END IF;

END;

PROCEDURE XNEW_FORM(formmodule_name      VARCHAR2,
                    rollback_mode        NUMBER DEFAULT TO_SAVEPOINT,
                    query_mode   IN OUT NUMBER DEFAULT NO_QUERY_ONLY,
                    data_mode     NUMBER DEFAULT NO_SHARE_LIBRARY_DATA,
                    paramlist_id         PARAMLIST DEFAULT NULL)
IS
   cnt BINARY_INTEGER := getstackcount;
   current_form_before FORMMODULE;
   current_form_after FORMMODULE;
BEGIN
   /* Populate the next element of this array */
   xcallform_stack(cnt+1).formmodule_name := formmodule_name;
   xcallform_stack(cnt+1).queryonly := query_mode;

   NEW_FORM(formmodule_name,
            rollback_mode,
            query_mode,
            data_mode,
            paramlist_id);
   current_form_after := FIND_FORM(NAME_IN('SYSTEM.CURRENT_FORM'));
   /* If new_form is not a success, delete added stack element */
```

3

MULTI-FORM
APPLICATIONS

```
    IF (current_form_before.id = current_form_after.id) THEN
      xcallform_stack.delete(cnt+1);
    END IF;

  END;

  FUNCTION XQUERY_ONLY(formmodule_name VARCHAR2) RETURN BOOLEAN
  IS
    queryonly NUMBER;
  BEGIN
    FOR I IN 1..getstackcount LOOP
      IF xcallform_stack(i).formmodule_name = formmodule_name THEN
        queryonly := xcallform_stack(i).queryonly;
      END IF;
    END LOOP;
    IF queryonly = 501 THEN
      RETURN TRUE;
    ELSIF queryonly = 502 THEN
      RETURN FALSE;
    END IF;
  END;

END Xcallform;
```

You can also use XCALL_FORM or XNEW_FORM to call forms using CALL_FORM or NEW_FORM, respectively. This is in the calling form, for example, in the appropriate WHEN-BUTTON-PRESSED trigger in the calling form:

```
XCALL_FORM(<formmodule_name>, NO_HIDE, NO_REPLACE, QUERY_ONLY);
```

You call the function XQUERY_ONLY passing the called form module name in the called form. The return values of this function will determine whether the form is in query-only mode. For example, in the WHEN-NEW-FORM-INSTANCE of the called form, a warning message can be displayed to notify users of the query-only mode, even before they start working on it:

```
WHEN-NEW-FORM-INSTANCE

DECLARE
   v_msg  VARCHAR2(1000);
BEGIN  IF XQUERY_ONLY(:SYSTEM.CURRENT_FORM) THEN
    v_msg := 'This form is running in Query Only mode, ';
    v_msg := v_msg||'cannot make database changes!';
    p_show_alert(v_msg);
  END IF;
```

This package should be included in a Forms PL/SQL library or an object library and attached to both the calling and called forms. The calls to CALL_FORM and NEW_FORM should be made

with the data_mode parameter set to SHARE_LIBRARY_DATA. If the call to CALL_FORM or
NEW_FORM is being made with the data mode parameter set to NO_SHARE_LIBRARY_DATA (which
is the default), and this package is included in a library attached to both the calling form and
called form, then instead of the PL/SQL table of records, use a GLOBAL_SCOPE record group.
The package XCALLFORM with such an implementation is given here:

```
PACKAGE Xcallform IS

   PROCEDURE XCALL_FORM(formmodule_name       VARCHAR2,
                        display               NUMBER DEFAULT HIDE,
                        switch_menu           NUMBER DEFAULT NO_REPLACE,
                        query_mode  IN OUT NUMBER DEFAULT NO_QUERY_ONLY,
                        data_mode NUMBER DEFAULT NO_SHARE_LIBRARY_DATA,
                        paramlist_id          PARAMLIST DEFAULT NULL);

   PROCEDURE XNEW_FORM(formmodule_name       VARCHAR2,
                       rollback_mode         NUMBER DEFAULT TO_SAVEPOINT,
                       query_mode   IN OUT NUMBER DEFAULT NO_QUERY_ONLY,
                       data_mode  NUMBER DEFAULT NO_SHARE_LIBRARY_DATA,
                       paramlist_id          PARAMLIST DEFAULT NULL);

   FUNCTION XQUERY_ONLY(formmodule_name VARCHAR2) RETURN BOOLEAN;

END Xcallform;

PACKAGE BODY xcallform IS
   rg_id RECORDGROUP;
   gc_id1 GROUPCOLUMN;
   gc_id2 GROUPCOLUMN;

   PROCEDURE p_global_record_group IS
   BEGIN
     rg_id := FIND_GROUP('RG_GLOBAL');
     IF NOT ID_NULL(rg_id) THEN
       DELETE_GROUP(rg_id);
     END IF;
     rg_id := CREATE_GROUP('RG_GLOBAL', GLOBAL_SCOPE);
     IF ID_NULL(rg_id) THEN
       MESSAGE('ERR: XQUERY_ONLY failure.!');
       RAISE FORM_TRIGGER_FAILURE;
     END IF;
     gc_id1 := ADD_GROUP_COLUMN(rg_id, 'formmodule_name', CHAR_COLUMN, 40);
     gc_id2 := ADD_GROUP_COLUMN(rg_id, 'queryonly', NUMBER_COLUMN);
   END;
```

```
FUNCTION getrgcount(i_rg_id RECORDGROUP) RETURN NUMBER
IS
BEGIN
  p_global_record_group;
  RETURN(GET_GROUP_ROW_COUNT(i_rg_id));
END;

PROCEDURE XCALL_FORM(formmodule_name      VARCHAR2,
                     display              NUMBER DEFAULT HIDE,
                     switch_menu          NUMBER DEFAULT NO_REPLACE,
                     query_mode  IN OUT NUMBER DEFAULT NO_QUERY_ONLY,
                     data_mode NUMBER DEFAULT NO_SHARE_LIBRARY_DATA,
                     paramlist_id         PARAMLIST DEFAULT NULL)
IS
  cnt NUMBER := NVL(getrgcount(rg_id),0);
  current_form_before FORMMODULE;
  current_form_after FORMMODULE;

BEGIN

  /* Populate the next element of this array */
  ADD_GROUP_ROW(rg_id, cnt+1);
  SET_GROUP_CHAR_CELL(gc_id1, cnt+1, formmodule_name);
  SET_GROUP_NUMBER_CELL(gc_id2, cnt+1, query_mode);
  CALL_FORM(formmodule_name,
            display,
            switch_menu,
            query_mode,
            data_mode,
            paramlist_id);
  /* If call_form is not a success, delete added stack element */
  IF (current_form_before.id = current_form_after.id ) THEN
    DELETE_GROUP_ROW(rg_id, cnt+1);
  END IF;

END;

PROCEDURE XNEW_FORM(formmodule_name      VARCHAR2,
                    Rollback_mode        NUMBER DEFAULT TO_SAVEPOINT,
                    query_mode   IN OUT NUMBER DEFAULT NO_QUERY_ONLY,
                    data_mode      NUMBER DEFAULT NO_SHARE_LIBRARY_DATA,
                    paramlist_id         PARAMLIST DEFAULT NULL)
IS
  cnt NUMBER := NVL(getrgcount(rg_id),0);
  current_form_before FORMMODULE;
  Current_form_after FORMMODULE;
```

```
BEGIN
  /* Populate the next element of this array */
  ADD_GROUP_ROW(rg_id, cnt+1);
  SET_GROUP_CHAR_CELL(gc_id1, cnt+1, formmodule_name);
  SET_GROUP_NUMBER_CELL(gc_id2, cnt+1, query_mode);
  NEW_FORM(formmodule_name,
           rollback_mode,
           query_mode,
           data_mode,
           paramlist_id);
  /* If new_form is not a success, delete added stack element */
  IF (current_form_before.id = current_form_after.id) THEN
    DELETE_GROUP_ROW(rg_id, cnt+1);
  END IF;

END;


FUNCTION XQUERY_ONLY(FormModule_name VARCHAR2) RETURN BOOLEAN
IS
  queryonly NUMBER;
BEGIN
  FOR I IN 1 .. getrgcount(rg_id) LOOP
    IF GET_GROUP_CHAR_CELL(gc_id1, I) = formmodule_name THEN
      queryonly := GET_GROUP_NUMBER_CELL(gc_id2, I);
    END IF;
  END LOOP;
  IF queryonly = 501 THEN
    RETURN TRUE;
  ELSIF queryonly = 502 THEN
    RETURN FALSE;
  END IF;
END;

END Xcallform;
```

Special Tips for Working with Multi-form Applications

The following is a list of pointers to have at your fingertips when developing multi-form applications. These are not hard and fast rules, but rules of thumb that, when followed, make the resulting application error-proof. Some of the pointers are based on the techniques in the preceding sections.

- Use CALL_FORM to run forms in modal mode. The calling form remains inactive till the called form is exited.

3

MULTI-FORM
APPLICATIONS

- Use NEW_FORM to close the calling form, and then invoke the called form.

- Use OPEN_FORM for interform navigation or interform sessions. Multiple instances of the called form can be opened in this case.

- Share data forward across forms by means of parameters and parameter lists, and reserve global variables to share data from the called to the calling forms.

- When using timers, create timers in each form independently, and delete the respective timer when exiting the particular form. Doing so maintains used timers and discards unused ones. Also, this reduces unnecessary faults such as network errors, which might otherwise crop up, especially when running applications on the Web.

- When opening multiple instances of the same form in OPEN_FORM configuration, especially in an OPEN_FORM chain, ensure correct navigation from subform to its parent form. This can be done in the WHEN-WINDOW-ACTIVATED trigger of the calling form using GO_FORM(form_id).

- Invoke the child forms after saving pending database changes in the calling forms. Particular requirements due to the user or to the demands of the application are the only exclusions to this rule.

- Do not exit parent forms before exiting child forms, unless otherwise specifically required. This avoids a random disorder of active forms left open. Also, it maintains an application's logical functional order.

- Writing a generic procedure for simulating a CLOSE ALL FORMS provides extra flexibility to close a multi-form application in one shot.

- Be careful about the data mode parameter of CALL_FORM, NEW_FORM, and OPEN_FORM. Use GLOBAL_SCOPE record groups as an alternative. This enables the sharing of global data among all forms with ease. For example, using a global scope record group can avoid the use of too many global variables.

Summary

This chapter highlighted some advanced tips and techniques in multi-form application development. The topics considered were data sharing forwards and backwards, form management in an OPEN_FORM configuration with particular reference to proper navigation, committing, and exiting sequence, and simulating a CLOSE ALL FORMS. Of special mention was the technique described for checking the query-only mode of a called form. The code presented can be directly incorporated into a Forms library and used as such.

Advanced Forms Programming

IN THIS CHAPTER

This chapter describes useful tips and techniques in Forms advanced programming (Forms 5.x and above). The chapter starts with the work-around for PL/SQL limitations in Forms 4.5. It then goes on to detail these techniques: populating a PL/SQL table from a block using Forms' implicit populating method, taking advantage of PL/SQL 2.x in Forms and how it can be used as an elegant alternative to a major Find requirement, file output from a block, how to get the query count without executing the query, and two powerful techniques for exclusive server-side commit and intersession and interdatabase connection from forms. Sharing data by means of record groups has been a long-felt need and is finally possible, as discussed in the final section.

The Work-around for PL/SQL 2.x Limitations in Forms 4.5

PL/SQL in Forms 4.5 is limited to version 1.x and poses certain limitations to application development. Forms 5.x has lifted these limitations by supporting PL/SQL2.x, which has significant advantages in the programming constructs that can be used. Also, from Forms 5.x onwards, some of the DBMS packages supplied by Oracle can be directly called from Forms. Regarding the former, the use of PL/SQL tables, especially a PL/SQL table of records, eliminates the need for temporary blocks. As an example of the latter, PL/SQL 1.x prohibits the direct referencing of package variables in Forms 4.x. I will discuss the limitations of PL/SQL in Forms 4.x and also discuss their work-around.

PL/SQL in Forms 4.5 has two limitations:

- PL/SQL 2.x features such as PL/SQL tables cannot be used in Forms 4.x. The record types %ROWTYPE and %TYPE can be used.
- Public package variables cannot be directly referenced in Forms 4.x

Both these limitations can be solved by placing PL/SQL 2.x structures inside a package as public variables and by having stored (not public packaged) functions return their values. This is because Forms looks for the validity of the package specification and not the body.

The package PkgDeptEmp_fromclause, used for performing DML in a block based on a FROM CLAUSE query (described in the "Basing a Block on a FROM CLAUSE Query" section in Chapter 2, "Advanced GUI Development: Developing Beyond GUI"), contains procedures that return a public record type variable and cannot be directly called from Forms 4.5 triggers or program units. The package can be modified as follows using the technique I've described.

Follow these steps:

1. Replace the code for ON-INSERT, ON-UPDATE, and ON-LOCK triggers with stored procedures, named p_on_insert, p_on_update, and p_on_lock, taking the individual record fields as parameters. These procedures also have two more OUT parameters having RETCD

and ERRM to return. RETCD returns the success or failure of the procedure, which is 0 on success and the corresponding SQLCODE on failure. ERRM is the SQLERRM exception error message corresponding to the SQLCODE returned. It is NULL in case of a success.

2. Call the created wrapped procedures with the respective block item values, in the ON-INSERT, ON-UPDATE, and ON-LOCK triggers.

3. There is no need for a p_on_delete procedure because the original delete procedure takes EMPNO as an argument that is not referenced by a packaged public variable.

The following code eliminates the drawback of directly referencing the packaged variable pkgdeptemp_fromclause.dept_emp by wrapping around the code contained in the ON_INSERT, ON-UPDATE, and ON-LOCK triggers in the form of stored procedures p_on_insert, p_on_update, and p_on_lock. The record type fields are passed as individual parameters to these procedures. The direct reference to the dept_emp packaged variable is made in these wrapper procedures. The code is as follows:

```
CREATE OR REPLACE PROCEDURE p_on_insert
    (p_empno NUMBER,
     p_ename VARCHAR2,
     p_job   VARCHAR2,
     p_hiredate DATE,
     p_sal      NUMBER,
     p_deptno   NUMBER,
     p_dname    VARCHAR2,
     retcd OUT NUMBER,
     errm  OUT VARCHAR2)
IS

/* The following line shows how the packaged public variable dept_emp
can be directly referenced in the wrapper procedure instead of directly
in Forms 4.x */
   dept_emp_rec pkgdeptemp_fromclause.dept_emp;
BEGIN

/* The individual parameters are assigned to their counterparts in the
local record type variable dept_emp_rec declared to be of type dept_emp,
the one defined in the package */

   dept_emp_rec.empno := p_empno;
   dept_emp_rec.ename := p_ename;
   dept_emp_rec.job    := p_job;
   dept_emp_rec.hiredate := p_hiredate;
   dept_emp_rec.sal    := p_sal;
   dept_emp_rec.deptno := p_deptno;
   dept_emp_rec.dname  := p_dname;
```

4

ADVANCED FORMS
PROGRAMMING

```
    Pkgdeptemp_fromclause.insert_procedure(dept_emp_rec, retcd, errm);
END p_on_insert;
/

ON-INSERT trigger

DECLARE
  Retcd NUMBER;
  Errm  VARCHAR2(100);
BEGIN

/* The ON-INSERT trigger directly calls this wrapper procedure and
compiles successfully */

  P_on_insert(:fromclause_blk.empno, :fromclause_blk.ename,
  :fromclause_blk.job, :fromclause_blk.hiredate,
  :fromclause_blk.sal, :fromclause_blk.deptno,
  :fromclause_blk.dname, retcd, errm);
  IF (retcd <> pkgdeptemp_fromclause.get_success) THEN
    MESSAGE(errm);
    RAISE FORM_TRIGGER_FAILURE;
  END IF;
END;
```

The code for the procedures p_on_update and p_on_lock and the corresponding ON-UPDATE and ON-LOCK triggers is similar to the code for the p_on_insert wrapper procedure and the preceding ON-INSERT trigger.

```
CREATE OR REPLACE PROCEDURE p_on_update
  (p_empno NUMBER,
  p_ename VARCHAR2,
  p_job   VARCHAR2,
  p_hiredate DATE,
  p_sal      NUMBER,
  p_deptno   NUMBER,
  p_dname    VARCHAR2,
  retcd OUT NUMBER,
  errm  OUT VARCHAR2)
IS
  dept_emp_rec pkgdeptemp_fromclause.dept_emp;
BEGIN
  dept_emp_rec.empno := p_empno;
  dept_emp_rec.ename := p_ename;
  dept_emp_rec.job    := p_job;
  dept_emp_rec.hiredate := p_hiredate;
  dept_emp_rec.sal    := p_sal;
```

```
  dept_emp_rec.deptno := p_deptno;
  dept_emp_rec.dname  := p_dname;
  Pkgdeptemp_fromclause.update_procedure(dept_emp_rec, retcd, errm);
END p_on_update;
/


ON-UPDATE trigger


DECLARE
  Retcd NUMBER;
  Errm  VARCHAR2(100);
BEGIN
   P_on_update(:fromclause_blk.empno, :fromclause_blk.ename,
   :fromclause_blk.job, :fromclause_blk.hiredate,
   :fromclause_blk.sal, :fromclause_blk.deptno,
   :fromclause_blk.dname, retcd, errm);
   IF (retcd <> pkgdeptemp_fromclause.get_success) THEN
     MESSAGE(errm);
     RAISE FORM_TRIGGER_FAILURE;
   END IF;
END;


ON-DELETE trigger


BEGIN
   Pkgdeptemp_fromclause.delete_procecdure(:fromclause_blk.empno);
END;


CREATE OR REPLACE PROCEDURE p_on_lock
  (p_empno NUMBER,
   p_ename VARCHAR2,
   p_job   VARCHAR2,
   p_hiredate DATE,
   p_sal      NUMBER,
   p_deptno   NUMBER,
   p_dname    VARCHAR2,
   retcd OUT NUMBER,
   errm  OUT VARCHAR2)
IS
   dept_emp_rec pkgdeptemp_fromclause.dept_emp;
   retcd number;
   errm varchar2(100);
BEGIN
   dept_emp_rec.empno := p_empno;
   dept_emp_rec.ename := p_ename;
   dept_emp_rec.job := p_job;
```

```
      dept_emp_rec.hiredate := p_hiredate;
      dept_emp_rec.sal := p_sal;
      dept_emp_rec.deptno := p_deptno;
      dept_emp_rec.dname := p_dname;
      Pkgdeptemp_fromclause.lock_procedure(dept_emp_rec, retcd, errm);
  END p_on_lock;


  ON-LOCK_trigger


  DECLARE
    Retcd NUMBER;
    Errm  VARCHAR2(100);
  BEGIN
      P_on_lock(:fromclause_blk.empno, :fromclause_blk.ename,
      :fromclause_blk.job, :fromclause_blk.hiredate,
      :fromclause_blk.sal, :fromclause_blk.deptno,
      :fromclause_blk.dname, retcd, errm);
      IF (retcd <> pkgdeptemp_fromclause.get_success) THEN
        MESSAGE(errm);
        RAISE FORM_TRIGGER_FAILURE;
      END IF;
  END;
```

Populating a PL/SQL Table from a Block

A PL/SQL table can be populated from a block using Forms' implicit populating built-in
TABLE_FROM_BLOCK. This very handy feature eliminates your having to loop through the block
explicitly. The following procedure illustrates the concept:

```
PROCEDURE populate_plsql_table(my_table1 my_table, cnt OUT NUMBER)
IS

/* Define a PL/SQL record with two fields code and name */

   TYPE state_rec IS RECORD (code varhcar2(2), name varhcar2(30));

/* Define a PL/SQL table of the record defined above */

   TYPE my_table IS TABLE OF state_rec INDEX BY BINARY_INTEGER;
    my_table1 my_table;

/* Define a variable of type ITEMS_IN_BLOCK. ITEMS_IN_BLOCK is a
Forms-defined table */
    Item_data ITEMS_IN_BLOCK;
    Cnt NUMBER;
BEGIN
```

```
    Item_data(1) := 'STATE_CODE';
     item_data(2) := 'STATE_NAME';
```

/* The call to the Forms built-in TABLE_FROM_BLOCK retrieves the records
from the block and populates the my_table1 table of records */

```
    TABLE_FROM_BLOCK(my_table1, 'STATE',1, ALL_RECORDS, item_data);
    -- The SUCCESS or FAILURE of this built-in can be assessed
    -- with FORM_SUCCESS, just like any other built-in

    IF NOT FORM_SUCCESS THEN
        RAISE FORM_TRIGGER_FAILURE;
    END IF;
     Cnt := my_table1.COUNT;
END populate_plsql_table;
```

To use this technique, follow these steps:

1. Define a PL/SQL record to be equivalent to the record structure to be passed as input. In this case, it is state_rec and constitutes the two items CODE and NAME corresponding to STATE_CODE and STATE_NAME.

2. Define the PL/SQL table to be a table of records of the type defined in step 1. In this case, it is my_table.

NOTE

The Oracle documentation defines the PL/SQL table to be of type PLITBLM.TABLE_OF_ANY, but defining the PL/SQL table in the manner I've described works well.

3. Define a variable of type ITEMS_IN_BLOCK (a table of VARCHAR2) and set its individual elements to be the names of the block item names whose values figure as elements of the record type defined in step 1.

4. Call the built-in TABLE_OF_ANY with the defined PL/SQL table, input block name, start record number, end record number, and the variable defined in step 3 passed as parameters.

TIP

To pass all the records in the block, specify 1 as the starting record number and the constant ALL_RECORDS as the end record number.

4

ADVANCED FORMS
PROGRAMMING

The Success or Failure of TABLE_FROM_BLOCK

The success or failure of TABLE_FROM_BLOCK can in most cases be trapped by FORM_SUCCESS. However, there are exceptions. One such exception is the error FRM-40733: PL/SQL built-in TABLE_FROM_BLOCK failed.

In this case, it is not one of FORM_SUCCESS, FORM_FAILURE, or FORM_FATAL. ON-ERROR is often a handy alternative to FORM_SUCCESS for tracking the success or failure of TABLE_FROM_BLOCK and in this example, too, helps us in trapping this error. The preceding error occurs when a nonexistent block name is passed or negative values are passed for the starting or starting and ending record positions.

> **TIP**
>
> Another important point to note is that TABLE_FROM_BLOCK implicitly loops through the block, so POST-QUERY is executed for each record. However, it's faster than the manual looping. For a result set of 3,300 records, it was seen to be 3.5 times faster than the manual looping with Oracle 8.0.5 running on Windows NT.

Taking Advantage of PL/SQL 2.x in Forms

In many applications, getting a huge number of records into a base-table block becomes necessary, especially when a search based on user criteria is involved. *Search* here means locating a particular record in the entire result set with the usual functions of KEY-UP and KEY-DOWN, and Find First and Find Next in case of multiple matches (for example, when the user types in **S%** for the search). This search should not be confused with a filter, which involves a dynamically shrinking or expanding result set. Even a filter may return a large result set. The usual procedure is to do an EXECUTE_QUERY in the block and to loop through until a match is found. In a client/server environment, it involves buffering of disk space, as well as a time delay in locating the desired record. For example, locating a record after the 7000th in a result set of 10,000 could cause buffer allocation if the record-size is large and client-side disk space is insufficient. It also has a significant time delay.

A more elegant solution to this problem is to replace the normal Forms buffering and fetching process and manually control record fetching and block population. That Forms 5.0 supports PL/SQL 2.x is an advantage in this kind of a situation. The trick lies in using a PL/SQL table of records in Forms 5.0. The search process then follows a new algorithm that saves disk buffering, as well as improves location time significantly.

The new algorithm works as follows:

- No EXECUTE_QUERY is done.

- A Find essentially involves a filter with the result set containing only those records that match the Find criteria.

- At any point of time, only *n* number of records are brought into the block. This involves fetching all records into a PL/SQL table of records and populating the block with these *n* records manually. If the number of database trips is not a problem, even records can be fetched in chunks of *n*.

- A Find Next operation essentially involves navigating to the next record in the block until the *n* records are exhausted, then fetching the next chunk, clearing the block, and repopulating the block with this new chunk.

- A Find First operation involves populating the block with the very first set of *n* records that match the Find criteria.

- KEY-UP and KEY-DOWN work fine for the *n* records in the block, and choosing the value of *n* to be a large number, say 100, will suffice (assuming that any user will navigate within a block, either up or down, not more than 100 times at any time). Also, beyond this range, it should not be a problem because you have the whole result set in the PL/SQL table and keeping track of the indexes in the current result set will help in getting the preceding or next record.

You implement this technique with these steps:

1. Declare a PL/SQL cursor with a SELECT statement selecting all the base table columns in the block and having a WHERE clause specifying the Find criteria and an ORDER BY clause. When the WHERE and ORDER BY clauses are dynamic, the whole algorithm has to be implemented using dynamic SQL.

2. Declare at least two PL/SQL tables of records, with each element being a record type similar to the declared cursor record type. Populate one of these tables (say, FIRST_SET) with the very first set of *n* records for the Find First function and another table (say, WHOLE_SET) with the entire result set from the cursor.

3. Loop through the PL/SQL table WHOLE_SET iterating from index to (index+n–1), where index equals 1 for the very first set and index equals n+1 for the subsequent sets. Do a CLEAR_BLOCK first. Then, using CREATE_RECORD, populate the block with the table element values and use

```
SET_RECORD_PROPERTY(:SYSTEM.CURSOR_RECORD, <block_name>,
                    STATUS, QUERY_STATUS)
```

to ensure that record status is QUERY for each record populated.

4. In step 3, for index = 1, populate the table `FIRST_SET` using `TABLE_FROM_BLOCK` immediately after populating the block. This will store the first set of records for the Find First function.

5. `KEY-UP` and `KEY-DOWN` should not be a problem beyond the amplitude of (index, index+n-1) because all the records are in the `WHOLE_SET` index-by table. You have to keep track only of the PL/SQL table index for the current set to get the preceding or next record.

File Output from a Block

The technique I describe in this section provides a convenient method for outputting the records in a block without having to write code using the `TEXT_IO` package supplied by Forms. The advantages are a more elegant implementation. Also the option for outputting `ALL`, `VIEWED` or `DISPLAYED` records eases the effort of putting in extra logic for getting `ALL` and `VIEWED` records. It does loop through the block implicitly and `POST-QUERY` is executed for each record.

The `F50WRITE.WRITE_BLOCK` does the job and has the following definition:

```
FUNCTION F50WRITE.WRITE_BLOCK(block_name VARCHAR2,
                             output_file VARCHAR2
                             output_mode VARCHAR2,
                             column_align BOOLEAN,
                             sep_char VARCHAR2,
                             rec_option VARCHAR2,
                             displayed_only BOLEAN) RETURN NUMBER;
```

The elements of this definition are as follows:

- `OUTPUT_FILE` requires the full path to be specified, including the extension.
- `OUTPUT_MODE` is either `W` (for write) or `A` (for append).
- `COLUMN_ALIGN` specifies whether the columns should be aligned.
- `SEP_CHAR` is the interfield separator in the output file.
- `REC_OPTION` is either `ALL`, `VIEWED`, or `DISPLAYED`. `VIEWED` refers to the records to which the user has navigated.
- `DISPLAYED_ONLY` refers to output-only `DISPLAYED` items or all items (null canvas items, nondisplayed items).

You can use `F50WRITE.WRITE_BLOCK` to do file output from a block, as follows:>

```
FUNCTION write_to_file    (ip_block_name IN VARCHAR2,
                          op_file_name IN VARCHAR2,
                          op_mode IN VARCHAR2,
                          ip_sep_char IN VARCHAR2,
                          ip_rec_option IN VARCHAR2)
```

```
RETURN NUMBER
IS
   v_column_align BOOLEAN := TRUE;
   v_displayed_only BOOLEAN := FALSE;
ret_code NUMBER;
BEGIN
      ret_code := F50WRITE.WRITE_BLOCK(ip_block_name,
                                       op_file_name,
                                       op_mode,
                                       v_column_align,
                                       ip_sep_char,
                                       ip_rec_option,
                                       v_displayed_only);

      RETURN (ret_code);
END write_to_file;
```

Here is a generic function named write_to_file that wraps the call to
F50WRITE.WRITE_BLOCK and returns the constant 0 on success and -1 on failure. A wrapper
procedure like this helps in modularization of the code, as well as giving the capability of
encapsulating it as part of a more generic package. The important thing to note here is that the
wrapper subprogram is a function that returns the success or failure of the code within it and
hence has greater flexibility of being used everywhere a function can be used.

Now, use the following function to perform the operation. Remember to check the return value
for success. This function returns 0 on success and -1 on failure:

```
DECLARE
      ip_block_name VARCHAR2(30);
      op_file_name  VARCHAR2(30);
      op_mode VARCHAR2(30);
      ip_sep_char VARCHAR2(3);
      ip_rec_option VARCHAR2(10);
      v_column_align BOOLEAN := TRUE;
      v_displayed_only BOOLEAN := FALSE;
      Ret_Code NUMBER;
BEGIN
      ret_code := write_to_file(ip_block_name,
                                op_file_name,
                                op_mode,
                                v_column_align,
                                ip_sep_char,
                                ip_rec_option,
                                v_displayed_only);

      IF (ret_code <> 0) THEN
         RAISE FORM_TRIGGER_FAILURE;
         END IF;
END write_to_file
```

4

**ADVANCED FORMS
PROGRAMMING**

Note that the function's parameters have no default values: Specifying null values for rec_option and output mode results in an error. Also, if sep_char is omitted, a single blank is not taken as a field separator.

This technique is useful for data loading using SQL*Loader—for example, from production to test environments. Create a test form that runs against the production database, do a simple EXECUTE_QUERY to the corresponding block, and then execute the preceding procedure to get the loader data file created.

Note that the output file is created on the client machine and not on the server.

An Exclusive Server-Side Commit from Forms

Generally, committing in Forms at runtime performs a form-level commit of all pending changes to the database. This commit takes into account all records in all data blocks that have been reserved for an insert, an update, or a delete operation. Specifically, issuing a COMMIT, COMMIT_FORM, or DO_KEY('COMMIT_FORM') will commit any DML present within the Forms triggers, as well as any records in the form that have been marked for the insert, update, or delete operations in the form. Sometimes, there might be a need to commit only the DML present in form triggers such as INSERT, UPDATE, or DELETE statements and ignore all other pending database changes in the form. In other words, ignore the default insertion, update, or deletion taken care of by Forms. Nullifying these forms operations in ON-INSERT, ON-UPDATE, or ON-DELETE triggers disables the default committing for good.

To commit only on the server side from Forms, there is a simple but powerful trick of the trade: Use FORMS_DDL('COMMIT'), as follows (do not place a semicolon after the COMMIT):

```
BEGIN
    FORMS_DDL('COMMIT');
    IF NOT FORM_SUCCESS THEN
        MESSAGE(TO_CHAR(DBMS_ERROR_CODE)¦¦' '¦¦DBMS_ERROR_TEXT);
    END IF;
END;
```

This code commits exclusively on the server side, and any pending changes in the form are unsaved. To check the success or failure of the COMMIT, the code after the FORMS_DDL does the job.

TIP

Any INSERT, UPDATE, or DELETE operations can be carried out using FORMS_DLL in addition to DDL.

> **TIP**
>
> Anonymous PL/SQL blocks and stored subprograms can be executed by placing them within a BEGIN and END. Do place a semicolon at the end of END while doing PL/SQL.

Intersession and Interdatabase Communication from Forms

Before Oracle Developer Forms 6, in order to output a current set of records from a block, developers had to resort to one of the following methods:

- Loop through the block, and insert into a destination table in the same schema.
- Loop through the block, and insert into a destination table in a different schema in the same database, with privileges granted.
- Write to an O/S file using the TEXT_IO API.
- In dynamic SQL, use DBMS_SQL to perform the task.
- Pass data to another form that inserts into a destination table in a different session, but the same schema, using a GLOBAL_SCOPE record group, a packaged PL/SQL table of records, or global variables.

The limitations of these methods are as follows:

- There is no way to open a separate database connection from Forms that enables you to communicate with a different schema on the same server or an altogether different database server, that is, connections to multiple databases.
- The schema and database server names have to be hard-coded inside the code.
- DBMS_SQL executes with creator rights, and dynamic SQL is limited to this restriction.
- To communicate between two sessions, you must rely on the DBMS_PIPE package and/or DBMS_AQ package, each of which has its own limitations.

Oracle Forms 6 facilitates intersession (interschema) and interdatabase connection from Forms using the EXEC_SQL package. EXEC_SQL is asynchronous in the sense that it is independent of pending database changes in the form.

You can use EXEC_SQL as follows:

- To populate a database table in a different database from a Forms block based on a database table in a source connection, such as BLOCK_TO_TABLE.
- To eliminate file I/O for purposes such as Forms error logging.

- To simulate a FORMS PIPING mechanism.

- To execute common application logic in multiple schemas in multiple databases from a single form.

TIP

You can simulate a FORMS PIPING mechanism to send and receive data using EXEC_SQL. Think of the error-logging using DBMS_PIPE or sending priority messages using DBMS_AQ. These applications can be implemented using a source form sending data directly to multiple user connections. A destination form can output this data by simply picking up. In fact, there is no need for a pipe or queue because no delay time is involved in transfer of the data till somebody receives it.

A time-out interval can be set to synchronize transfer of the data to the target database or schema.

TIP

Using OPEN_FORM with the SESSION parameter specified will create a separate session using the current schema and the current database only. Of course, Forms error logging can be done using OPEN_FORM in a different session.

Similarities between DBMS_SQL and EXEC_SQL are as follows:

- Like DBMS_SQL, SQL statements are constructed at runtime. Also, both DML and DDL can be issued using EXEC_SQL.

- EXEC_SQL has the following procedures in similarity to DBMS_SQL:

```
EXEC_SQL.OPEN_CURSOR
EXEC_SQL.PARSE
EXEC_SQL.DESCRIBE_COLUMN
EXEC_SQL.BIND_VARIABLE
EXEC_SQL.DEFINE_COLUMN
EXEC_SQL.EXECUTE
EXEC_SQL.EXECUTE_AND_FETCH
EXEC_SQL.FETCH_ROWS
EXEC_SQL.COLUMN_VALUE
EXEC_SQL.VARIABLE_VALUE
EXEC_SQL.IS_OPEN
EXEC_SQL.CLOSE_CURSOR
```

Differences between EXEC_SQL and DBMS_SQL are as follows:

- EXEC_SQL directly executes in the connection specified, so creator and invoker rights do not come into the picture. This means that it doesn't matter whether the owner of the database objects or a different user is executing the EXEC_SQL package.

- There is no concept of array processing in EXEC_SQL, so there are no EXEC_SQL.DEFINE_ARRAY and EXEC_SQL.BIND_ARRAY procedures.

- EXEC_SQL uses bind by value, in contrast to the bind by address used by DBMS_SQL.

- EXEC_SQL requires the use of EXEC_SQL.VARIABLE_VALUE to retrieve the value of a bind parameter that is an OUT parameter.

- EXEC_SQL requires the use of EXEC_SQL.COLUMN_VALUE to retrieve values in a result set.

- EXEC_SQL has no need for indicator variables because NULLs are handled just like PL/SQL variables.

- EXEC_SQL does not support PL/SQL tables and record types in PL/SQL and CHAR, RAW, LONG, and ROWID in SQL. Therefore, there are no EXEC_SQL.DEFINE_COLUMN_LONG and EXEC_SQL.COLUMN_VALUE_LONG procedures.

- EXEC_SQL has the following extra procedures and/or functions defined as part of the package:

```
EXEC_SQL.OPEN_CONNECTION
EXEC_SQL.CURR_CONNECTION
EXEC_SQL.DEFAULT_CONNECTION
EXEC_SQL.MORE_RESULT_SETS
EXEC_SQL.IS_CONNECTED
EXEC_SQL.IS_OCA_CONNECTION
EXEC_SQL.CLOSE_CONNECTION
EXEC_SQL.LAST_ERROR_CODE
EXEC_SQL.LAST_ERROR_MESG
```

- EXEC_SQL has the following exceptions as part of its specification:

```
EXEC_SQL.PACKAGE_ERROR
EXEC_SQL.INVALID_CONNECTION
EXEC_SQL.INVALID_COLUMN_NUMB
EXEC_SQL.VALUE_ERROR
```

4

ADVANCED FORMS PROGRAMMING

TIP

The functions EXEC_SQL.LAST_ERROR_CODE and EXEC_SQL.LAST_ERROR_MESG return the error code and error message text of the last occurred error. This error code is different from EXEC_SQL.LAST_SQL_FUCTION_CODE.

TIP

EXEC_SQL.LAST_ERROR_CODE returns 0 on success.

In this section, I will discuss the first of the preceding examples: outputting a current block of records to a different schema in the same database, dynamically creating the destination table.

To do this, follow these steps:

1. Open source connection (defaults to the primary Oracle Developer connection—the DEFAULT_CONNECTION). This is done by creating connection handles using EXE_SQL.OPEN_CONNECTION or EXEC_SQL.DEFAULT_CONNECTION.

2. Open a destination connection (defaults to the current connection). You can also do this by using EXEC_SQL.OPEN_CONNECTION or EXEC_SQL.CURR_CONNECTION.

3. Open a source cursor for the source connection. Create cursor handles for the corresponding connection handles using EXEC_SQL.OPEN_CURSOR. No parameters specified to EXEC_SQL.OPEN_CURSOR will default both the source and destination connections to the current connection.

4. Parse the source cursors with the SQL and/or PL/SQL statements, either static or dynamic. Use EXEC_SQL.PARSE, passing the dynamically constructed SQL or PL/SQL statements.

5. Execute the source cursor. Use EXEC_SQL.EXECUTE or EXEC_SQL.EXECUTE_AND_FETCH.

6. Repeat steps 3, 4, and 5 for the destination cursor.

7. For retrieving result sets, it is necessary to define columns, fetch in a loop, and get column values. Use EXEC_SQL.DEFINE_COLUMN for defining columns, EXEC_SQL.FETCH_ROWS in a loop for fetching, and EXEC_SQL.COLUMN_VALUE for getting column values.

8. For other SQL and/or PL/SQL operations, binding variables and retrieving OUT bind variable values are required before and after step 5. Use EXEC_SQL.BIND_VARIABLE and/or EXEC_SQL.VARIABLE_VALUE.

9. Close the destination and source cursors. The order is important. Use EXEC_SQL.CLOSE_CURSOR.

10. Close the destination and source connections. The order is important. Use EXEC_SQL.CLOSE_CONNECTION.

Your source form contains the following elements:

- A DEPT block based on the DEPT table—After querying using user-specific criteria, which varies from user to user, the records have to be transferred to region-specific DEPT tables, created dynamically as <region>_DEPT_FROM_BLOCK.

- A control block CTRL_BLK with a push button PB_SQLEXEC—When clicked, the data is transferred to the destination table.

You use a generic procedure BLOCK_TO_TABLE to do this, and you call this procedure in the WHEN-BUTTON-PRESSED trigger of PB_SQLEXEC:

```
PROCEDURE BLOCK_TO_TABLE
PROCEDURE block_to_table(source_block_name IN VARCHAR2,
                         destination_table_name IN VARCHAR2,
                         destination_connection IN VARCHAR2,
                         retcd OUT NUMBER)
IS
  deptno NUMBER;
  dname  VARCHAR2(20);
  loc    VARCHAR2(20);
  destination_connid EXEC_SQL.CONNTYPE;
  destination_cursor EXEC_SQL.CURRTYPE;
  ret_cd PLS_INTEGER;
BEGIN
destination_connid := EXEC_SQL.OPEN_CONNECTION(destination_connection);
destination_cursor := ExEC_SQL.OPEN_CURSOR(destination_connid);
  destination_cursor := EXEC_SQL.OPEN_CURSOR(destination_connid);
  EXEC_SQL.PARSE(destination_connid, destination_cursor,
  'CREATE TABLE '||destination_table_name||' ( DEPTNO NUMBER(2),
                  DNAME VARCHAR2(14), LOC VARCHAR2(13))');
ret_cd := EXEC_SQL.EXECUTE(destination_connid, destination_cursor);
EXEC_SQL.PARSE(destination_connid, destination_cursor,
  'INSERT INTO '||destination_table_name||
              ' (deptno,dname,loc) VALUES (:deptno, :dname, :loc)');
  GO_BLOCK(source_block_name);
  FIRST_RECORD;
  LOOP
  deptno := :dept.deptno;
  dname := :dept.dname;
  loc := :dept.loc;

    EXEC_SQL.BIND_VARIABLE(destination_connid, destination_cursor,
                           ':deptno', deptno);
    EXEC_SQL.BIND_VARIABLE(destination_connid, destination_cursor,
                           ':dname', dname);
    EXEC_SQL.BIND_VARIABLE(destination_connid, destination_cursor,
```

4

```
                                        ':loc', loc);
        ret_cd := EXEC_SQL.EXECUTE(destination_connid, destination_cursor);
            IF :SYSTEM.LAST_RECORD = 'TRUE' THEN
                    EXIT;
            ELSE
                    NEXT_RECORD;
            END IF;
    END LOOP;
    EXEC_SQL.PARSE(destination_connid, destination_cursor, 'COMMIT');
    ret_cd := EXEC_SQL.EXECUTE(destination_connid, destination_cursor);
    EXEC_SQL.CLOSE_CURSOR(destination_cursor);
    EXEC_SQL.CLOSE_CONNECTION(destination_connid);
    retcd := 0;
    EXCEPTION
        WHEN EXEC_SQL.PACKAGE_ERROR THEN
          MESSAGE('ERROR ('||
                  TO_CHAR(EXEC_SQL.LAST_ERROR_CODE(destination_connid))||
                  ' ): '||
          EXEC_SQL.LAST_ERROR_MESG(destination_connid));
          IF EXEC_SQL.IS_CONNECTED(destination_connid) THEN
            IF EXEC_SQL.IS_OPEN(destination_connid, destination_cursor)
                THEN
                  EXEC_SQL.CLOSE_CURSOR(destination_connid,
                                             destination_cursor);
                END IF;
                EXEC_SQL.CLOSE_CONNECTION(destination_connid);
          END IF;
          retcd := EXEC_SQL.LAST_ERROR_CODE(destination_connid);
END;


WHEN-BUTTON-PRESSED

declare
      retcd number;
      destination_block_name VARCHAR2(100);
      region_name VARCHAR2(20) := 'REGION1';
begin
      destination_block_name := region_name||'_DEPT_FROM_BLOCK';
  block_to_table('DEPT',destination_block_name, 'user1/user1', retcd);
  IF (retcd <> 0) THEN
       MESSAGE('ERR: BLOCK to TABLE failed with return code'||to_char(retcd));
       RAISE FORM_TRIGGER_FAILURE;
  END IF;
end;
```

> **TIP**
>
> EXEC_SQL is an Oracle Forms package. Thus, the direct referencing of the package variables like EXEC_SQL.ConnType and EXEC_SQL.CursType is possible in Forms. This is in contrast to database packages, including DBMS_SQL.

Always include the following exception-handling section when using EXEC_SQL. Repeat the IF statements for each connection opened, either by default (either unspecified or using EXEC_SQL.DEFAULT_CONNECTION or EXEC_SQL.CURR_CONNECTION) or explicitly, using EXEC_SQL.OPEN_CONNECTION:

```
EXCEPTION
  WHEN EXEC_SQL.PACKAGE_ERROR THEN
    IF (EXEC_SQL.LAST_ERROR_CODE(connection_handle>) <> 0) THEN
      MESSAGE('ERROR ('¦¦
              TO_CHAR(EXEC_SQL.LAST_ERROR_CODE(<connection_handle>) ¦¦
              ' ): '¦¦
        EXEC_SQL.LAST_ERROR_MESG(<connection_handle>));
    END IF;
    IF EXEC_SQL.IS_CONNECTED(connection_handle>) THEN
      IF EXEC_SQL.IS_OPEN(<connection_handle>, <cursor_handle>) THEN
        EXEC_SQL.CLOSE_CURSOR(<connection_handle>, <cursor_handle>);
      END IF;
      EXEC_SQL.CLOSE_CONNECTION(<connection_handle>);
    END IF;
```

Sharing a Record Group Across Forms

Before Forms 5.0, there was no way to share data by means of record groups across forms in a multiform application. Such a requirement arises when a result set is to be shared. The only way to do this is either by means of a PL/SQL table of records defined in a package or by means of too many global variables. The former requires additional code to be maintained outside Forms or to-and-fro round trips from Forms to server, and vice-versa, if maintained in the database.

The following tips are worth noting:

- Sharing a record group by passing it as a parameter to the called form is not allowed.

- Copying or subclassing a record group across other forms shares only the structure and not the data.

4

ADVANCED FORMS PROGRAMMING

- Referencing a record group does not share data in the record group. Only the structure is carried over.

- Record groups created dynamically and placed in a library do not share data contained in them.

From Forms 5.0 onwards, there is a way to share the data in record groups across forms in the same run-form session—by creating the record group dynamically and specifying GLOBAL_SCOPE for the scope parameter.

Consider two forms, A and B. Create a record group RG_LIST in form A with the scope parameter specified as GLOBAL_SCOPE. Form A is the calling form that calls form B. The following code segment illustrates this concept:

```
DECLARE
   rg_id    RECORDGROUP
   rg_name VARCHAR2(30);
   ret_code  NUMBER;
BEGIN
   rg_name := 'RG_LIST';
   rg_id := FIND_GROUP(rg_name);
   IF NOT ID_NULL(rg_id) THEN
      DELETE_GROUP(rg_id);
   END IF;

The constant GLOBAL_SCOPE is specified to indicate global scope.
The default scope is FORM_SCOPE, which is for the current form only */
   rg_id :=
     CREATE_GROUP_FROM_QUERY( rg_name,
       'SELECT state_code, state_name from state order by 1', GLOBAL_SCOPE);
   ret_code := POPULATE_GROUP( rg_id );
   IF (ret_code <> 0) THEN
      MESSAGE('ERR: Populating Record Group '¦¦rg_name);
      RAISE FORM_TRIGGER_FAILURE;
   END IF
END;
```

In form B, the data in this record group can be assessed by a call to the GET_GROUP_...._CELL as follows:

```
DECLARE
  v_state_name VARCHAR2(30);
BEGIN
  FOR i IN 1..GET_GROUP_ROW_COUNT LOOP

/*  The column state_name of the record group rg_list created in form A
is directly accessible in form B */
```

```
     v_state_name := GET_GROUP_CHAR_CELL('RG_LIST.STATE_NAME', i);
fsEND LOOP;
END;
```

Note how a call to GET_GROUP_CHAR_CELL makes the value of a cell of the record group created in form A, directly available.

Additional Tips for Sharing Record Groups

The following points provide a list of useful tips to be kept in mind while sharing record groups across forms:

- To share record groups across forms, create them programmatically with GLOBAL_SCOPE specified.

- Records groups created at design time cannot be shared across forms.

- A record group created with GLOBAL_SCOPE can be either query or nonquery. However, if a query record group contains local bind variable references, it is automatically converted into a nonquery record group, with the data retained after the current form is exited.

- Data shared by means of record groups in this way is also available in the called forms when invoked by means of OPEN_FORM in a different session. As long as the run-form session is the same, it doesn't matter, even if the called form is running in a different session.

- Repopulating a GLOBAL_SCOPE record group is possible while it is being shared. The news data is available only when the record group is accessed the subsequent time. The data is not available live.

- GLOBAL_SCOPE record groups, when placed in libraries and attached to two or more forms, enable the data to be shared even if the target forms are the result of calls to CALL_FORM or OPEN_FORM with the data_mode parameter set to NO_SHARE_LIBRARY_DATA.

- The need to use PL/SQL 2.x and 8.x features such as packaged index-by tables, tables of records, cursor variables, object types, and so on, is eliminated by using GLOBAL_SCOPE record groups. This avoids unnecessary trips to the database. Also server memory is saved significantly.

4

ADVANCED FORMS
PROGRAMMING

Summary

This chapter dealt with some advanced Forms 5.x programming concepts and their implementation. The areas explored were a work-around for PL/SQL 2.x in Forms 4.5, populating a PL/SQL table from a block, utilizing PL/SQL 2.x features to implement an efficient Find capability, a method for OS File Output from a block, and tips for getting the query count without executing a query. Finally, two powerful techniques, for performing a server-side exclusive commit from Forms and intersession and interdatabase communication from Forms, were discussed. Last, sharing of record groups across forms was highlighted.

Error-Message Handling

IN THIS CHAPTER

Error-message and exception handling are part and parcel of any quality software application, and Oracle Forms is no exception. This chapter provides the tricks of the trade for error-message handling in Forms programming and describes techniques required to augment the default Forms error-messaging capabilities.

Basically, the errors raised in Forms can be classified in the following broad categories:

- Errors raised out of failure of Forms built-ins (FRM errors)

- Errors raised out of failure of Forms object properties (also, FRM errors)

- Errors raised out of exceptions from triggers and program unit code—that is, failure of DML statements or PL/SQL errors

- Errors raised on the server side and propagated to Forms as a failure of integrity constraints, insufficient privileges on base tables, and so on (ORA-ERRORS)

All these types of errors can be tracked either by default Forms error-messaging capabilities or by augmenting these capabilities with customized code. I will discuss the various techniques to handle each of these types of errors, along with special cases involved.

The Basics of Error-Message Handling

All Forms errors belong to a standard type of FRM and are characterized by

- *Error type*—Whether the error is an informative message or an actual error message

- *Error code*—An integer indicating the error number

- *Error text*—The text of the error message

- *Error severity level*—The classification of the error message

Error Type

An *informative*-type error message results from an error caused by some missing data or insufficient data and is not an error in the strict sense. No action is necessary by default, and further processing can be resumed after the occurrence of the error.

Examples are

```
FRM-40350: Query caused no records to be retrieved.
FRM-40353: Query Cancelled.
```

However, these types of errors can be tracked and replaced by customized messages to improve readability to the end user.

An *error*-type error message results from an error in the strict sense, which must be rectified before further processing can resume.

Examples are

```
FRM-40202: Field must be entered.
FRM-40360: Cannot Query Records here.
FRM-40600: Record has already been inserted.
```

In Forms, few error-type error messages occur for which no action is required. A commonly occurring example is

```
FRM-40100: At first record.
```

When the cursor is in the first record in a block and the user presses the <Previous Record> or <Up> key, this error is raised and requires no action to be taken. However, the same error resulting from the built-in FIRST_RECORD is a genuine failure, and the code following this built-in is executed after the FRM-40100 error message is displayed. The latter error might result when the user presses the Enter key and the corresponding KEY-NEXT-ITEM trigger has a call to FIRST_RECORD in it:

```
KEY-NEXT-ITEMFIRST_RECORD;
--- <perform some action>
......
```

In this case, if the cursor is in the first record in the block, the code following the FIRST_RECORD built-in is executed after the error message FRM-40100 is displayed.

The only way to distinguish between an informative error message and an actual error message is by further processing, usually at runtime, without correcting the error. (Of course, the easy way is to look at the online help.)

> **TIP**
>
> Failure of built-ins or form object properties can be the cause of both informative-type and error-type error messages.

Error Severity Level

Most error messages, whether informative or error, are assigned a severity level. The severity level of an error message determines the damage caused by that error and whether that message can be suppressed. The severity level can be one of 0, 5, 10, 15, 20, 25, and greater than 25, which includes 99. Table 5.1 shows some examples.

TABLE 5.1   Error Messages and Severity Levels

Error Number	Error Message	Level
FRM-40100	At first record.	5
FRM-40513	ORACLE error: Unable to get date/time from database.	10
FRM-40202	Field must be entered.	15
FRM-40602	Cannot insert into or update data in a view.	20
FRM-40355	Query will retrieve 1 record.	25
FRM-40007	Invalid user identifier or password. Re-enter.	25
FRM-40109	Cannot navigate out of current block in enter-query mode.	99

TIP

Not every message with a severity level less than or equal to 25 can be suppressed. Error messages can be suppressed only for errors in which Forms can do away with the damage caused by the resulting error.

As an example, consider the message

```
FRM-40202: Field must be entered.
```

This message has a severity level of 15 and cannot be suppressed at all. The reason is that a mandatory item in a form should always have a value, irrespective of whether the resulting error message is suppressed.

Built-ins, Triggers, System Variables, and Exceptions

Oracle Forms has a set of built-ins, triggers, system variables, and exceptions to handle errors.

- *Built-ins*—FORM_SUCCESS, FORM_FAILURE, FORM_FATAL, MESSAGE_TYPE, MESSAGE_CODE, MESSAGE_TEXT, ERROR_TYPE, ERROR_CODE, ERROR_TEXT, DBMS_ERROR_CODE, DBMS_ERROR_TEXT, SQLCODE, and SQLERRM (the standard PL/SQL functions to catch exceptions)
- *Triggers*—ON-MESSAGE and ON-ERROR
- *System Variables*—:SYSTEM.MESSAGE_LEVEL and :SYSTEM.SUPPRESS_WORKING
- *Exceptions*—FORM_TRIGGER_FAILURE (to be raised explicitly with the RAISE built-in)

I will elaborate on each of these as we progress through the chapter. More specifically, I will address issues such as how to trap (suppress) informative and error messages using these different methods (that is, how to use the various system variables and triggers to trap messages).

Handling Errors

Now you will learn how to handle errors raised by each of the four categories.

FORM_SUCCESS and FORM_TRIGGER_FAILURE

Either the FORM_SUCCESS built-in or the FORM_TRIGGER_FAILURE exception must be used to handle all Forms errors. FORM_SUCCESS is a Boolean function that evaluates to TRUE or FALSE depending on the success or failure of a Forms built-in. FORM_TRIGGER_FAILURE is an exception that has to be raised to stop further processing whenever an error occurs or FORM_SUCCESS evaluates to FALSE. The following sections describe their use in error-message handling.

Suppressing Errors Using ON-ERROR and ON-MESSAGE Triggers

The two triggers ON-ERROR and ON-MESSAGE can be used to suppress unnecessary messages of both error and informative types. Here, I will elaborate on the examples discussed earlier in the "Error Type" section.

Consider the following informative-type error messages:

```
FRM-40350: Query caused no records to be retrieved.
FRM-40353: Query Cancelled.
```

These messages can be suppressed by means of an ON-MESSAGE as follows:

```
ON-MESSAGE

IF MESSAGE_TYPE = 'FRM' AND MESSAGE_CODE IN (40350, 40353) THEN
    NULL;
ELSE
    MESSAGE(MESSAGE_TYPE||'-'||TO_CHAR(MESSAGE_CODE)||': '||MESSAGE_TEXT);
END IF;
```

This is how informative messages are trapped: You use the ON-MESSAGE trigger with MESSAGE_TYPE, MESSAGE_CODE, and MESSAGE_TEXT. Note the ELSE part. This is a very important part because it ensures that other genuine messages are not suppressed.

Now consider these error-type messages:

```
FRM-40202: Field must be entered.
FRM-40360: Cannot Query Records here.
```

```
FRM-40600: Record has already been inserted.
FRM-40100: At first record.
```

An ON-ERROR trigger along similar lines as the preceding example can be written with ERROR_TYPE, ERROR_CODE, and ERROR_TEXT to suppress unnecessary error-type errors:

```
ON-ERROR
IF ERROR_TYPE = 'FRM' AND ERROR_CODE = 40401 THEN
   NULL;
ELSE
    MESSAGE(ERROR_TYPE||'-'||TO_CHAR(ERROR_CODE)||': '||ERROR_TEXT);
END IF;
```

With ON-MESSAGE and ON-ERROR, you can suppress errors at any severity level because you are trying to replace the default functionality of Forms error-message handling. However, the trigger does not suffice for the purpose of capturing the error unless it is handled.

> **TIP**
>
> The rule of the thumb is to raise FORM_TRIGGER_FAILURE for error-type error messages except those that are being suppressed.

As mentioned earlier, you should always include an ELSE part, such as

```
ELSE
    MESSAGE(MESSAGE_TYPE||'-'||TO_CHAR(MESSAGE_CODE)||': '||MESSAGE_TEXT);
```

in ON-MESSAGE and ON-ERROR triggers to prevent other genuine messages from being suppressed.

Errors Raised from the Failure of Forms Built-Ins

FRM errors are errors raised by the failure of Forms built-ins used in trigger or program unit code. An example is the failure of the GO_BLOCK built-in. The code

```
GO_BLOCK('CUST_ORDERS');
```

causes the error

```
FRM-40104: No such block CUST_ORDERS.
```

All errors occurring because of built-in failures should be trapped by using FORM_SUCCESS followed by a RAISE FORM_TRIGGER_FAILURE. Check form success and form failure for any built-ins by means of the following general procedure, and call this procedure after the call to the built-in:

```
PROCEDURE check_package_failure
IS
IF NOT FORM_SUCCESS THEN
    RAISE FORM_TRIGGER_FAILURE;
END IF;
END check_package_failure;
```

Note how FORM_SUCCESS is negated to cover both FORM_FAILURE and FORM_FATAL caused by internal errors (such as memory failures, and so on). Using only FORM_FAILURE and omitting the negation would have served the purpose but not fully, because FORM_FATAL would have been ignored.

The one line of code containing the GO_BLOCK call can be replaced by a line segment as follows:

```
GO_BLOCK('CUST_XX');
CHECK_PACKAGE_FAILURE;
```

Errors Raised from the Failure of Forms Object Properties

These FRM errors are caused by form, block, object, or item property failures. A very common example is the error

```
FRM-40202: Field must be entered.
```

which is caused by a null value in a mandatory form item, specified by setting the Required item property to True.

Normally, Forms causes an input lockout until the item is filled in with a value, and there is no way to continue further processing except by entering a valid value or exiting the form.

Always, as far as possible, track errors raised by form object properties by simulating them with a WHEN-VALIDATE-<object> trigger (if applicable) rather than specifying them in the object properties. Otherwise, track them in an ON-ERROR trigger. The former might seem too redundant a task, to write code for what is available ready-made, but the later sections "Errors That Cannot Be Tracked by FORM_SUCCESS or FORM_FAILURE" and "The Inability of the ON-ERROR Trigger to Track Forms Errors" explain the disastrous consequences that can result from the insufficiency of the ON-ERROR trigger and FORM_SUCCESS.

As an example, the substituted code for tracking the preceding error can be written as

```
WHEN-VALIDATE-ITEM

IF NAME_IN('SYSTEM.CURSOR_VALUE') IS NULL THEN
  MESSAGE('This Item Value must be entered.');
  RAISE FORM_TRIGGER_FAILURE;
END IF;
```

This code can be used to validate any number of NOT NULL items in the form, irrespective of the data type.

Take a look at another typical example. Consider the error

```
FRM-40505: ORACLE error, unable to perform query.
```

At first, this might seem the result of one of the following:

- The base table doesn't exist.
- One or more of the base table items do exist, such as an invalid column name.
- Either one or both of the WHERE and ORDER BY clauses is wrong.
- Insufficient privileges.

Of course, it *is* one of these, but how do you figure out which one?

At first sight, capturing this error might seem as trivial as getting the DBMS_ERROR_TEXT in the ON-ERROR trigger (as explained in the "Errors Raised on the Server Side and Propagated to Forms" section later). Fine. This helps to unearth the actual error message.

The error is a server error propagated to Forms, and it shows up as

```
ORA-00904: Invalid column name.
```

Now, what is the cause? All items in the block seem to be valid column names in the underlying base table.

It is surprising to note that the error message and the cause of it seem to be totally unrelated when you see the error message alone. It is very difficult to figure out that one peculiar cause of this error can be the failure of the Forms block property Include REF Item set to YES. The world of objects seems to cause problems for querying.

The Include REF Item property is valid only for blocks having object tables as base tables and not for blocks having items corresponding to OBJECT REFS or column objects.

After all, the error was due to incorrect setting of a block object property.

The Proper Use of FORM_TRIGGER_FAILURE

This section points out a common use of FORM_TRIGGER_FAILURE, which might seem trivial at first but is, in fact, a flaw that can sometimes prove serious. The trick of the trade when using FORM_TRIGGER_FAILURE is that it has to be RAISEd explicitly and then handled by means of an exception handler. Although an exception, it is not raised implicitly, like NO_DATA_FOUND, for example. A good example is to analyze the effect of code segments like the following:

```
BEGIN
  GO_ITEM(item_name);
EXCEPTION WHEN FORM_TRIGGER_FAILURE THEN
      <handle the error>
END;
```

Here, the exception is never raised, even when GO_ITEM fails. The correct way is to check for FORM_SUCCESS and then raise FORM_TRIGGER_FAILURE, as follows:

```
BEGIN
  GO_ITEM(item_name);
   IF NOT FORM_SUCCESS THEN
      RAISE FORM_TRIGGER_FAILURE;
   END IF;
EXCEPTION WHEN FORM_TRIGGER_FAILURE THEN
      <handle the error>
END;
```

This code illustrates using FORM_TRIGGER_FAILURE in a fool-proof way.

> **TIP**
>
> Don't expect Forms to do what you can do yourself! Explicitly RAISE
> FORM_TRIGGER_FAILURE.

FORM_SUCCESS refers only to the success of any code written in Forms triggers, built-ins checked, and Forms side program units. It also refers to form failure caused by an explicit RAISE FORM_TRIGGER_FAILURE. It *does not* refer to errors resulting from the failure caused by a Forms object property, in which case it may not evaluate to TRUE.

Errors Raised from Exceptions from Triggers and Program Unit Code

Errors raised out of exceptions from triggers and program unit code can be tracked in the exception handler using SQLCODE and SQLERRM. These are SQL and PL/SQL exceptions caused by the failure of SQL DML statements or PL/SQL statements. These are tracked by SQLCODE and SQLERRM in the WHEN OTHERS exception-handling section.

Always give an exception-handling section with the WHEN OTHERS clause, irrespective of whether the trigger or program unit body contains any DML statements. Exceptions do occur because of errors in the declaration section, such as PL/SQL value or numeric errors.

```
EXCEPTION WHEN OTHERS THEN
        MESSAGE(TO_CHAR(SQLCODE)||' '||SQLERRM);
```

Errors Raised on the Server Side and Propagated to Forms

Errors raised on the server side and propagated to Forms as a failure of integrity constraints, insufficient privileges on base tables, and so on, arise out of failure of DML statements or semantic checks on the server side. An example is

```
FRM-40508: ORACLE error: unable to INSERT record.
```

Also, a user-defined error message given in a stored program unit called from Forms, such as a message in RAISE_APPLICATION_ERROR, can result in the same message, if the same is caused during INSERT.

Although at first it appears that the error is an FRM error and is from Forms, the error is actually propagated from the Oracle server, indicating that an INSERT operation on a base table block failed in the form.

There are two ways to trap this error. You can press the <Display Error> hot key and determine what the resulting error from the database is. This approach makes sense from the programmer's point of view but not from the end user's.

You can also programmatically trap the error and replace it with a customized message that is user-friendly. This approach makes sense from either point of view.

You should use DBMS_ERROR_CODE and DBMS_ERROR_TEXT in an ON-ERROR trigger to trap errors propagated from Oracle server from Forms. For example, to trap a message in RAISE_APPLICATION_ERROR in a server-side stored program, which is being called from Forms, you can write an ON-ERROR trigger as follows:

```
ON-ERROR

DECLARE
    alert_button NUMBER;
    error_msg VARCHAR2(1000)
BEGIN
    error_msg := TO_CHAR(DBMS_ERROR_CODE)¦¦' '¦¦DBMS_ERROR_TEXT;
    SET_ALERT_PROPERTY('ALERT_ERROR',ALERT_MESSAGE_TEXT, error_msg);
    alert_button := SHOW_ALERT('ALERT_ERROR');
END;
```

This displays an Oracle message string followed by the user message string. You can shorten the message by eliminating the Oracle message string as follows:

```
error_msg :=  DBMS_ERROR_TEXT;
error_msg := SUBSTR(error_msg,1,INSTR(error_msg,'ORA-',1,2)-1));
```

Suppressing Errors Using :SYSTEM.MESSAGE_LEVEL

An alternative way of suppressing unnecessary messages, both informative and error, is by using the system variable :SYSTEM.MESSAGE_LEVEL. This is a read-write system variable, unlike most others provided by Oracle Forms. The following example illustrates this concept:

To suppress the message

```
FRM-40100: At first record.
```

or

```
FRM-40350: Query caused no records to be retrieved.
```

the following pieces of code describe the technique involved:

```
/* For suppressing FRM-40100 */
:SYSTEM.MESSAGE_LEVEL := '5';
FIRST_RECORD;
:SYSTEM.MESSAGE_LEVEL := '0';
/* For suppressing FRM-40350 */
:SYSTEM.MESSAGE_LEVEL := '5';
EXECUTE_QUERY;
:SYSTEM.MESSAGE_LEVEL := '0';
```

The first assignment of :SYSTEM.MESSAGE_LEVEL to 5 is required to suppress all error messages (informative and error) at level 5 and above.

The reassignment of :SYSTEM.MESSAGE_LEVEL to 0 is required to re-enable the default behavior, that is, display all messages when occurring.

> **TIP**
>
> The assigning of :SYSTEM.MESSAGE_LEVEL to a value suppresses all messages at that level or above. The only exception is the one specified earlier: Not all messages with severity levels less than or equal to 25 can be suppressed. Error messages can be suppressed only for errors causing damage that Forms can do away with.

> **TIP**
>
> When you want to suppress a message, use :SYSTEM.MESSAGE_LEVEL or the conventional method, with ON-ERROR. When you want to replace a message, use the conventional method with ON-ERROR. The conventional method is always superior because it eliminates the risk of suppressing unknown messages.

Deficiencies in Forms Error-Message Handling

Until now, you have seen that ON-ERROR trigger and FORM_SUCCESS are essential to trap and check for the occurrence of a Forms error. You have also seen how RAISE-ing FORM_TRIGGER_FAILURE helps freeze the operation in erroneous conditions till the error is rectified. The next few sections focus on the deficiencies and inability of Forms error-message handling with respect to errors that cannot be tracked by FORM_SUCCESS or FORM_FAILURE: the insufficiency of the ON-ERROR trigger in tracking Forms errors, the role played by FORM_SUCCESS or FORM_FAILURE in the case of nested triggers, the inadequacy of Forms in tracking overall form success, and the inability of Forms programmatically to track whether a particular trigger fired and which trigger fired.

Errors That Cannot Be Tracked by FORM_SUCCESS or FORM_FAILURE

There are many Forms errors that the built-ins FORM_SUCCESS and FORM_FAILURE cannot point out. One such error is

```
FRM-40600: Record has already been inserted.
```

This can be explained by the following scenario. Consider a base table master block having a detail block. The detail block has the Primary Key property set to TRUE. This facilitates the checking of duplicate records without making explicit SELECTs to the database for each record entered. Consider a Save button that contains the following code segment in the WHEN-BUTTON-PRESSED trigger:

```
COMMIT;
IF FORM_SUCCESS THEN
  <perform a sequence of actions>
END IF;
```

The sequence of actions can be, for example, to navigate to the detail block and perform an EXECUTE_QUERY.

As soon as the Save button is pressed, Forms raises the error FRM-40600 (just mentioned) whenever it encounters two records with the same values for the primary key combination. It is surprising to note that FORM_SUCCESS evaluates to TRUE and the code under the IF statement is still executed. What an alarming situation! The immediate idea is to use FORM_FAILURE and raise FORM_TRIGGER_FAILURE as follows:

```
IF FORM_FAILURE THEN
 RAISE FORM_TRIGGER_FAILURE;
END IF;
```

Unfortunately, this fails when there are multiple duplicate records involving the same primary key values. Now, what's the work-around? Obviously, to write an ON-ERROR trigger that captures this FRM error using ERROR_TYPE and ERROR_CODE, something similar to the following:

```
IF ERROR_TYPE = 'FRM' AND ERROR_CODE = 40600 THEN
  MESSAGE('Duplicate Record');
  RAISE FORM_TRIGGER_FAILURE;
ELSE
  MESSAGE(ERROR_TYPE¦¦'-'¦¦TO_CHAR(ERROR_CODE)¦¦': '¦¦ERROR_TEXT);
END IF;
```

Surprisingly, this also doesn't work, and the code under the IF condition is still executed. The only way to circumvent this situation is to assign a flag in the ON-ERROR trigger just described and to check explicitly for the flag in the code for the Save button before checking for FORM_SUCCESS. The modified versions of the ON-ERROR trigger and the WHEN-BUTTON-PRESSED triggers are

ON-ERROR

```
IF ERROR_TYPE = 'FRM' AND ERROR_CODE = 40600 THEN
   MESSAGE('Duplicate Record');
  : Error_flag := 1;
    RAISE FORM_TRIGGER_FAILURE;
ELSE
    MESSAGE(ERROR_TYPE¦¦'-'¦¦TO_CHAR(ERROR_CODE)¦¦': '¦¦ERROR_TEXT);
 END IF;
```

WHEN-BUTTON-PRESSED

```
COMMIT;
IF (:error_flag = 1) THEN
   :error_flag := 0;
   RAISE FORM_TRIGGER_FAILURE;
END IF;
IF FORM_SUCCESS THEN
   <perform a sequence of actions>
END IF;
```

(Here, :ERROR_FLAG is a form variable defined in the master block or some other control block.) This code makes the situation fool-proof.

TIP

Raising FORM_TRIGGER_FAILURE is a sure indication of FORM_SUCCESS evaluating to FALSE. Don't always rely on Forms implicit checking to conclude that FORM_FAILURE has occurred, and use error flags to make the situation fool-proof.

The Inability of the ON-ERROR Trigger to Track Forms Errors

This section deals with a different category of errors, ones that the ON-ERROR trigger is incapable of handling. In the alarming situation just described, the ON-ERROR trigger really helped. The following describes a scenario in which the ON-ERROR plays no part in tracking errors raised by Forms built-ins. A rule of thumb that most Forms programmers follow is that most of the built-ins in Forms do not call for an ON-ERROR trigger, which is reserved only for FRM-type errors.

Keeping this in mind, one good use of ON-ERROR trigger has been to keep track of the errors raised at the database side from the Forms side, such as errors raised by RAISE_APPLICATION_ERROR in a stored program from the Forms side. This can be done using DBMS_ERROR_CODE and DBMS_ERROR_TEXT in an ON-ERROR trigger. This highlights the insufficiency of the ON-ERROR trigger in the sense of using DBMS_ERROR_CODE and DBMS_ERROR_TEXT outside the ON-ERROR trigger. In other words, using DBMS_ERROR_CODE and DBMS_ERROR_TEXT in ON-ERROR is not enough to track all errors resulting from the database side. Using the FORMS_DDL built-in is one such scenario.

Consider the following piece of code:

```
FORMS_DDL('BEGIN UPDATE employee SET sal = '||TO_CHAR(:sal)||
          '  WHERE  empno IN '||:empno_list||' ; END;');
IF FORM_SUCCESS THEN
  COMMIT;
ELSE
  MESSAGE(TO_CHAR(DBMS_ERROR_CODE)||' '||DBMS_ERROR_TEXT);
  RAISE FORM_TRIGGER_FAILURE;
END IF;
```

If the UPDATE statement fails, the error cannot be detected by using either an exception handler or an ON-ERROR trigger, no matter if SQLCODE, ERROR_CODE, or DBMS_ERROR_CODE is used in either case. This illustrates the use of DBMS_ERROR_CODE and DBMS_ERROR_TEXT outside the ON-ERROR trigger and thus its inadequacy.

TIP

The ON-ERROR trigger is a good slave but a bad master. It cannot command Forms to always capture errors and sometimes falls prey to Forms built-ins like FORMS_DDL. FORM_SUCCESS might come to the rescue sometimes, but as seen in the preceding tip, raising FORM_TRIGGER_FAILURE always gives the optimum reward.

FORM_SUCCESS or FORM_FAILURE in Nested Triggers

This section begins by explaining the "smart-but-not-too-smart" role played by FORM_SUCCESS or FORM_FAILURE when it comes to *nested* triggers (triggers within triggers). There is the EXECUTE_TRIGGER built-in, by which one can force Forms to execute the code present in the trigger given as its parameter.

Consider the following code in the WHEN-BUTTON-PRESSED trigger of a button:

```
EXECUTE_TRIGGER('WHEN-NEW-RECORD-INSTANCE');
IF FORM_SUCCESS THEN
    <perform_a_sequence_of_events>
END IF;
```

or this code, in the WHEN-NEW-RECORD-INSTANCE of the corresponding block:

```
GO_BLOCK('<block_name'>;
EXECUTE_QUERY;
```

Even if there is no form event that implicitly triggers WHEN-NEW-RECORD-INSTANCE to fire, the code in it is still executed. In this case, the FORM_SUCCESS indicates the success of the code in the WHEN-NEW-RECORD-INSTANCE trigger, which indicates the success of the built-in. (I mean, if you have FORM_SUCCESS following a GO_BLOCK, it refers to the success of the GO_BLOCK, and similarly for most of the built-ins). Now, if the GO_BLOCK is a failure, the sequence of actions in the outermost trigger WHEN-BUTTON-PRESSED is still executed. What a negative FORM_SUCCESS!

To circumvent the problem, I modified code for WHEN-NEW-RECORD-INSTANCE as follows:

```
GO_BLOCK('<block_name'>
IF NOT FORM_SUCCESS THEN
    RAISE FORM_TRIGGER_FAILURE;
ELSE
    EXECUTE_QUERY;
END IF;
```

Now, if the GO_BLOCK is a failure, the sequence of actions in the outermost trigger WHEN-BUTTON-PRESSED is *not* executed. What a positive FORM_SUCCESS!

Two points should be analyzed here. First, if there is a

```
RAISE FORM_TRIGGER_FAILURE
```

in the WHEN-NEW-RECORD-INSTANCE, the FORM_SUCCESS immediately following the EXECUTE_TRIGGER returns FALSE.

Second, if there is a

```
GO_BLOCK('<block_name>');
```

which is a failure, and there is not a RAISE FORM_TRIGGER_FAILURE in the WHEN-NEW_RECORD-INSTANCE, the FORM_SUCCESS immediately following the EXECUTE_TRIGGER returns TRUE. Remember, the EXECUTE_TRIGGER is called from an "outer" trigger, so already there is one level of nesting triggers, and FORM_SUCCESS is smart enough to return FALSE in the first case and not in the second case.

Now, what if the WHEN-NEW_RECORD-INSTANCE has a second EXECUTE_TRIGGER in it? Also, what if the trigger this is invoking has a GO_BLOCK, which fails? This creates a second level of nesting. What does FORM_SUCCESS return for the failure of the innermost GO_BLOCK? The behavior is the same as in the case of one level of nesting.

It might be surprising, but this is how FORM_SUCCESS works. The rule is that FORM_SUCCESS gives the success of the immediately preceding Forms built-in and returns FALSE if this built-in is a failure or whenever FORM_TRIGGER_FAILURE is raised. Therefore, in the case of nested triggers, in the nested trigger follow any call to built-ins by an immediate check for FORM_SUCCESS, and then RAISE FORM_TRIGGER_FAILURE when the built-in fails. It is important to RAISE FORM_TRIGGER_FAILURE because this is the only way the effect of a form failure is carried over to the outer trigger.

The modified version of the WHEN-BUTTON-PRESSED and WHEN-NEW-RECORD triggers is

```
EXECUTE_TRIGGER('WHEN-NEW-RECORD-INSTANCE');
IF FORM_SUCCESS THEN
    <perform_a_sequence_of_events>
END IF;
GO_BLOCK('<block_name'>
IF NOT FORM_SUCCESS THEN
    RAISE FORM_TRIGGER_FAILURE;
ELSE
    EXECUTE_QUERY;
END IF;
```

This makes the situation fool-proof.

Forms' Inability to Track OVERALL FORM SUCCESS

Considering the overall form, there is no way in Forms to keep track of form success. Errors in Forms can occur for any of the following reasons:

- An explicit RAISE FORM_TRIGGER_FAILURE in any of the Forms triggers
- A failure of a built-in in any of the Forms triggers
- Implicit FRM errors that are a result of a validation due to Forms object properties

The first two types of errors can be tracked by FORM_SUCCESS, but the third type of error cannot. As an example, consider the error

```
FRM-40600: Record has already been inserted.
```

which occurs when the block property Primary key is set to TRUE for a base table block. There are many more examples like this. Of course, there is a workaround for this! (Refer to the bibliography in this book's front matter.) However, it becomes practically impossible to keep track of all such "behind-the-scenes" errors.

How nice and intelligent it would have been to have a built-in like ALL_FORM_SUCCESS that would take into account the three types of errors listed here. This would reduce a lot of code and effort by way of a simple call and also make the impossibility described here a possibility. For example, one could have a KEY-COMMIT trigger at the form level as follows:

```
KEY-COMMIT at form level

COMMIT_FORM;
IF NOT ALL_FORM_SUCCESS THEN
  RAISE FORM_TRIGGER_FAILURE;
END IF;
```

Forms' Inability to Track Whether a Particular Trigger Fired or Which Trigger Fired

In Forms, you have no way programmatically to keep track of whether a particular trigger fired and which trigger fired. (This inability should not be confused with Debug mode, which traces the order of execution of triggers in an interactive mode.)

Knowledge of this becomes important when developing an application that displays the execution steps or prepares the execution report of a form during runtime. This is something similar to the debugger, but the main difference is that the execution is tracked programmatically and recorded—a "programmatic debugger." In this section, I present an approach for implementing this.

The first part, tracking whether a particular trigger fired, can be achieved by means of a built-in, TRIGGER_FIRED, just like FORM_SUCCESS. Remember, no need exists for TRIGGER_SUCCESS because FORM_SUCCESS does the job. The second part, asking which trigger fired, can be regarded as the reverse of :SYSTEM.TRIGGER_ITEM, :SYSTEM.TRIGGER_RECORD, and :SYSTEM.TRIGGER_BLOCK. You could use something like SYSTEM.ITEM_TRIGGER, SYSTEM.RECORD_TRIGGER, SYSTEM.BLOCK_TRIGGER, and an additional trigger, SYSTEM.FORM_TRIGGER.

Now, using the TRIGGER_FIRED in conjunction with SYSTEM.<object>_TRIGGER—where <object> is one of ITEM, RECORD, BLOCK, FORM, and so on—you can circumvent this insufficiency. But where? You need a new trigger, WHEN-TRIGGER-FIRED, that can be defined at all levels, with the new <SYSTEM.<object>_TRIGGER returning only those triggers that make sense at that level. The need for a new trigger such as WHEN-TRIGGER-FIRED arises because not all triggers have cascading effects. Therefore, TRIGGER_FIRED cannot always be checked in one of the existing triggers .

There are two aspects to this:

- If <SYSTEM.<object>_TRIGGER returns the name of the trigger that fired most recently, what is the need for TRIGGER_FIRED? The answer is to check whether any particular trigger fired. Therefore, TRIGGER_FIRED should be a Boolean function that returns TRUE or FALSE. It can be called with :SYSTEM.<object>_TRIGGER as a parameter or with a particular trigger name as a parameter.

- What should TRIGGER_FIRED return if no trigger fired or the trigger supplied as a parameter is not defined? One set of valid answers can be TRUE for the first part of the question and FALSE for the second part. Because no such trigger is defined, it is also true that no such trigger also fired.

Summary

The purpose of this chapter was to highlight Forms error-message handling, including the types and causes of errors and ways to handle them. The inability of Forms to cope with making a situation fool-proof and the golden methods to circumvent these problems were discussed. The areas explored were

- Errors raised out of the failure of Forms built-ins

- Errors raised out of the failure of Forms object properties

- Errors raised out of exceptions from triggers and program unit code, that is, the failure of DML statements or PL/SQL errors, raised on the server side and propagated to Forms

- The various triggers and SYSTEM variables and their use

- When built-ins such as FORM_SUCCESS or FORM_FAILURE fail
- When the ON-ERROR trigger isn't enough and how the use of FORM_TRIGGER_FAILURE can prove to be wrong
- The smart-but-not-too-smart role played by FORM_SUCCESS or FORM_FAILURE in the case of nested triggers
- The inadequacy of Forms in programmatically checking ALL_FORM_SUCCESS and programmatically checking whether a particular trigger fired and which trigger fired

Object-oriented Methods in Forms

IN THIS CHAPTER

Oracle Forms supports object orientation (OO) in various ways by combining different database features, as well as Forms Designer features; these features include

- Inheritance
- Encapsulation
- Object and code reuse
- Polymorphism

This chapter does not go into the implementation details of the Forms objects tailored for OO. Instead, it focuses on the various tips and techniques—the rules of the game for achieving OO using these Forms objects, including the scope of OO provided by Forms.

Inheritance

Inheritance is the mechanism by which a newly created object shares the structure of one or more existing objects. Oracle Forms incorporates inheritance by means of property classes and subclassing.

Consider the standard toolbar application discussed in Chapter 1, "GUI Development." Here we used a property class, named PC_ICONICBUTTON, which was applied to each of the iconic buttons. An example of such a property class appears in Figure 6.1, and an example of applying this property class to individual buttons is shown in Figure 6.2.

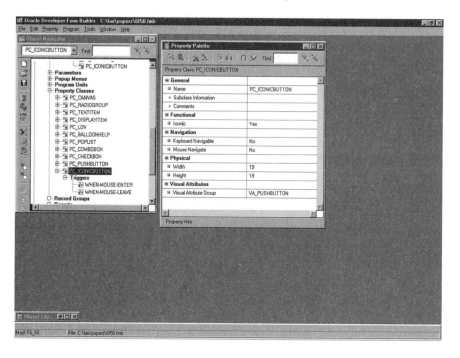

FIGURE 6.1

A property class for iconic buttons.

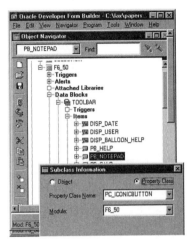

FIGURE 6.2
An example of applying a property class to an item.

This eliminates the need for specifying the common properties individually for each icon.

Inheritance by means of property classes is limited to

- Creating the property class and attaching it to a Forms object. The target object is automatically subclassed.
- Adding it to an object library. Then a Forms object can subclass it from the object library by a simple drag and drop or as a smart class.
- Directly subclassing or copying the property class across another Form module.

Here are some points to keep in mind about inheritance using property classes:

- An object based on a property class automatically inherits its properties.
- Properties that inherit their values from the property class are displayed with an = symbol in front of the property name.
- The inherited properties can be overridden if necessary.
- Triggers can be a part of a property class. For an object that has a trigger defined at its level and also in the property class that it inherits, the property class trigger is ignored.
- A property class can be attached to existing property classes. This enables inheritance from parents of parents of parents, thus providing additional reusability.
- Property classes can be copied between form modules.
- Properties to derived objects cannot be added through property classes.

Inheritance by means of subclassing is discussed in the "Object and Code Reusability" section.

Encapsulation

Encapsulation is the capability to combine and hide an object's implementation from its definition—in other words, to hide data from methods.

To put encapsulation to work, you use procedures, functions, and packages. (These can be stored in the database, form or a form library, an object group in a form, an object library, or a base template form.)

Object and Code Reusability

Reusability is the facility to use existing objects and code to create new applications.

For object reusability, use Copy/Paste properties; property classes; object groups; subclassing and copying for certain objects, property classes, object Groups, and object libraries across form modules; and template forms as a base for new forms.

For code reusability, use copying of triggers and program units across modules, and create form libraries or reference triggers across form modules. Also, the triggers attached to property classes, triggers and program units (from Forms 5.x onwards) in object groups, triggers and program units in object libraries, and the code reused from template forms contribute to code reusability.

Subclassing

Subclassing is the act of making an object inherit the properties of a base object, including code. You achieve it in five ways:

- Applying a property class to an object
- Dragging and dropping objects across form modules
- Dragging and dropping an object group across form modules
- Dragging and dropping an object from an object library
- Attaching a smart class to an object

In Figure 6.2, you noticed a red arrow on the left side of each button item. This is because, when a property class is applied to an object, it (the object) is subclassed.

Subclassing has the following characteristics:

- Subclassing can create new instances of the source object, such as when dragging from an object library into a form module.
- Subclassing allows you to redefine most of the inherited property values, including totally recoding subclassed triggers.
- Child objects of a source object, when subclassed from another object, reflect the new properties in the children of the parent subclassed object.

- When an object is subclassed from a property class, the properties in the property class are blindly inherited by the object. The point to be noted here is that Forms should be intelligent enough to ignore the inherited property and not mark it as inherited if it has the same value as the default value of that property in the subclassed object.

- Subclassing cannot add new properties to objects but can assign new properties to them. For example, a subclassed property class can be populated with an extra set of properties and their values, but it is not possible to extend the pool by adding altogether new properties.

- Do not work on the source form with a target subclassed form open.

- Subclassed objects can be specialized by modifying the inherited properties. Even subclassed trigger code can be changed. Referencing does not allow this kind of specialization.

Subclassing and Copying

You can copy or subclass across modules stored in a database or file system. When you subclass objects, the properties of the subclassed objects can be modified in the target module. This is an enhanced feature over referencing (available in Forms 4.5), in which only certain properties of the referenced objects can be modified in the target module—for example,

- For blocks, only the block name and comment can be changed.

- For items, the canvas view, comment, item name, and X,Y position can be changed.

- For triggers, only the comment can be changed.

- These changes are not reflected in the source form.

- When you copy a referenced object, the resulting object is also a referenced object.

Object Groups

Object groups enable you to reuse sets of functionally related objects by subclassing or copying the set as a whole. Again, consider the standard toolbar application. To construct such a toolbar, the following Forms objects can be used:

- A block named TOOLBAR with individual button items

- A canvas named CANVAS_TOOLBAR

- A property class named PC_ICONICBUTTON

These three Forms objects can be grouped together to form an object group, as shown in Figure 6.3.

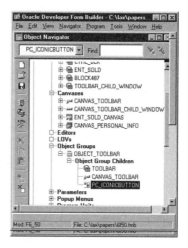

Figure 6.3

An example of an object group.

This object group can in turn be subclassed or copied across multiple forms where such a toolbar is required.

Here are some things to keep in mind:

- Base-level objects owned by blocks cannot be placed in an object group: Only items, item-level triggers, block-level triggers, relations, and so on, can be. Individual property classes, visual attributes, canvases, windows, alerts, record groups, LOVS, and so on, can be the children of an object group.
- Object groups can contain program units from Forms 5.x on.
- An object group cannot contain another object group.
- Deleting an object group does not delete the objects it contains.
- When an object is deleted, it is deleted from its object group automatically.
- Object groups store only pointers to objects, not copies of objects. Therefore, creating an object group does not increase module size significantly.

Object Libraries and Subclassing by Means of Smart Classes

In the section under subclassing, I discuss five ways of subclassing. Of these, the most intelligent way is smart-classing. Smart classes are part of object libraries.

An object library is similar to a Forms library in that it is sharable across forms. The only thing extra here is, an object library can contain both Forms objects and code. Creating an object library involves the following steps:

1. Create a module of type Object Library by double-clicking the Object Libraries node in the Object Navigator.

2. Add objects to it by dragging them from the Object Navigator and dropping them into the object library.

3. Mark them as smart classes. This is done by selecting the Object option in the menu and clicking on the Smart Classes suboption under it. The resulting smart class can be reused by a different object of the same type, in the same form or a different form. To do this, select the target object, right-click on it, and choose the corresponding smart class object under the Smart Classes node under it.

The object group OBJECT_TOOLBAR created in the preceding section can be added to an object library and marked as a smart class. Figure 6.4 shows how this is done.

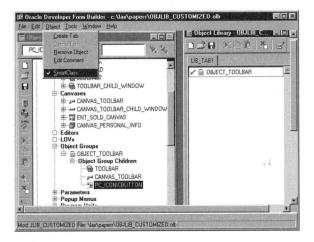

FIGURE 6.4

An example of an object library and smart classing objects in it.

Marking individual objects in an object library as smart classes is not mandatory, but doing so creates a higher level of subclassing.

There is some difference between subclassing by means of a smart class and the other sub-classing methods. The primary difference is that the first is the most intelligent way. The following tips suggest why smart classes are *smart*, and explain other related points:

- An object's smart classes pertain to only those classes that make sense for the object. In other words, a block smart class doesn't appear in the list of smart classes for a trigger object. The same holds true when a smart class is dragged from the object library and dropped in the Object Navigator.

- When a smart class is chosen for an object by clicking the right mouse button, the object under consideration will inherit the properties from the smart class object. The name of the target object will remain the same.

- Only those properties that make sense for the object are inherited.

- Smart-classed child objects cannot be deleted exclusively.

- Only those smart classes corresponding to the given object type are displayed in the Smart Classes list, when applying a smart class to an existing object. For example, when applying a smart class for a block object, a Property Class Smart Class is not shown in the list even though applying a property class to a block makes sense. This is an appreciable amount of smartness.

- Nested inheritance is supported. If a block is based on a block smart class that is based on a property class, the properties in the property class are inherited by the target block. This is true when you apply the smart class to the target block by choosing from the smart class list or by dragging and dropping a smart class from the object library.

- Smart class triggers enable the inheritance of their trigger text by a trigger, which doesn't make sense for the corresponding object, nor are the two triggers compatible. Consider a POST-QUERY trigger that exists as a smart class in an object library. Choosing it from the list of smart classes for an item that already has a WHEN-NEW-ITEM-INSTANCE trigger defined (by right-clicking on the WHEN-NEW-ITEM-INSTANCE trigger) simply replaces its trigger text with the trigger text of the POST-QUERY trigger. Thus, Forms has not recognized that a POST-QUERY trigger doesn't make sense at the item level and fails to understand that WHEN-NEW-ITEM-INSTANCE and POST-QUERY are two incompatible triggers.

- Smart classes do not support true multiple inheritance; that is, a given smart class cannot be based on two other independent smart classes. This is true even in the case of nested inheritance.

- An object cannot be smart-classed from two independent smart classes and in this way lacks multiple inheritance.

> **TIP**
>
> Only those smart classes corresponding to the given object type are displayed in the Smart Classes list when applying a smart class to an existing object, whereas any object that makes sense for the given object can be its subclass. For example, when applying a smart class for a block object, a Property Class Smart Class is not shown in the list, even though applying a property class to a block makes sense, whereas the same property class can be made subclass for the block without using the smart class. This overrides the extra smartness of smart classes.

Form Libraries

Form libraries enable sharing of common code. Here are some tips for using form libraries:

- Data variables can be shared at runtime using packages in form libraries. When a library is attached to two or more forms in a multiform application, the parameter data_mode of CALL_FORM, NEW_FORM, and OPEN_FORM specifies whether to share common library data at runtime. Valid values for this property are the Forms constants NO_SHARE_LIBRARY_DATA and SHARE_LIBRARY_DATA.

- If changes are made to the library, it need not be detached and reattached. Forms automatically checks and updates references to these changes.

- A library's program units are loaded dynamically into an application only when needed.

- Stick to indirect referencing of form variables (that is, data-bearing items, system variables, and global variables) inside form library program units. This can be achieved by using the built-in COPY for assignment and NAME_IN for reading a variable value.

Polymorphism

Polymorphism is the capability of using a method in more than one way. More clearly, different objects respond to the same method in different ways. You can use polymorphism in two ways:

- Overload procedures and functions
- Object class triggers, which can be executed at form, block, or item level

The second use is made possible by means of trigger execution style, which enables the execution of the same trigger when more than one instance of it are defined at multiple levels. This is discussed in Chapter 8, "Additional Interesting Techniques."

Summary

This chapter dealt with the object-oriented techniques in Forms 6.0. The basic principles of OO—such as inheritance, encapsulation, reusability, and polymorphism—and how Forms implements each of them were explained.

Intelligence in Forms

IN THIS CHAPTER

As IT made the transition from information systems to knowledge-based systems, information or processed data became knowledge or processed information. And knowledge gave birth to an altogether new component of IT called *intelligence*. A knowledge-based system in IT is now tailored towards incorporating the so-called intelligence—the capability of a system component to accept the right processed information sensible to it and ignore the insensible. In other words, it recognizes the appropriateness of the information being fed into it.

Oracle is second to none in incorporating an appreciable amount of this intelligence in its server and server-related tools that are Internet and object-oriented driven and are used to deliver knowledge as a part of handling applications ranging from workgroups, to the enterprise, to mission-critical ones. The Forms component of Oracle Developer is one of those tool sets with an appreciable amount of intelligence built into it. This chapter explores this aspect of Forms builder in detail and the benefits and inability of the same, with regard to smart classes, smart triggers, subclassing, normal triggers, form object properties, and form wizards.

Smart Classes and Smart Triggers— How Smart Are They?

This section explores the intelligence exhibited by smart classes and smart triggers. How well these work and to what extent these don't are highlighted briefly.

How Smart Classes Exhibit Intelligence

The following lists how smart classes are smart enough to recognize the appropriateness of the objects to which they are applied:

- An object's smart classes pertain to only those classes that make sense for the object. In other words, a block smart class doesn't appear in the list of smart classes for a trigger object. The same holds true when a smart class is dragged from the Object Library and dropped in the Object Navigator.

- When a smart class is chosen for an object, the object under consideration will inherit the properties from the smart class object. The name of the target object remains the same. Selecting an object in the Object Navigator or Layout Editor and clicking the right mouse button displays a pop-up menu. In this menu, choosing the Smart Classes menu option lists a set of smart classes applicable to this object, if any. The developer can choose one among the list, and the smart class automatically gets applied to the object.

- Only those properties that make sense for the object are inherited.

- Individual smart-classed child objects cannot be deleted without deleting the parent.

- Only those smart classes corresponding to the given object type are displayed in the Smart Classes list when applying a smart class to an existing object. For example, when applying a smart class for a block object, a Property Class Smart Class is not shown in the list even though applying a Property Class to a block makes sense. This is an appreciable amount of smartness.

- Nested inheritance is supported. For example, if a block is based on a block smart class that is based on a property class, the properties in the property class are inherited by the original block. This is true when you apply the smart class to the original block by choosing from the smart class list or by dragging and dropping a smart class from the object library.

How Smart Classes Lack Intelligence

The following list details how smart classes are not smart enough when applied to objects and how they exhibit improper behavior:

- Smart class triggers enable the inheritance of their trigger text by a trigger that doesn't make sense for the corresponding object or that isn't compatible with the smart class trigger. Consider a POST-QUERY trigger that exists as a smart class in an Object Library. Choosing it from the list of Smart Classes for an item that already has a WHEN-NEW-ITEM-INSTANCE trigger defined (by right-clicking on the WHEN-NEW-ITEM-INSTANCE trigger) simply replaces its trigger text with the trigger text of the POST-QUERY trigger. Thus, it has not recognized that a POST-QUERY trigger doesn't make sense at the item level, and it has failed to understand that WHEN-NEW-ITEM-INSTANCE and POST-QUERY are two incompatible triggers.

- Smart classes do not support true multiple inheritance; that is, a given smart class cannot be based on two other independent smart classes. Even nested inheritance is not supported.

How Smart Triggers Exhibit Intelligence

When choosing the trigger list of an object, Forms 5.0 is intelligent enough to provide smart triggers applicable to that object and at levels higher than the default level. Even the standard drag and drop is intelligent enough to recognize the appropriateness of a given trigger. The same holds true when a smart class trigger is dragged from the Object Library and dropped in the Object Navigator.

How Smart Triggers Lack Intelligence

By default, Forms doesn't include WHEN-LIST-ACTIVATED triggers in the list of smart triggers for a T-LIST item. This is intelligent for a pop-list and combo-box but not for a T-LIST. Although WHEN-LIST-ACTIVATED appears when the Others option is chosen from the smart triggers list, the point here is that it is a special trigger only meant for a T-LIST, and Forms should be smart enough to list this trigger under the predefined smart triggers list. Smart triggers aren't necessarily the most commonly used triggers.

A second point illustrating how smart triggers lack intelligence is that there are no smart triggers for a sound item.

Does Subclassing Exhibit Intelligence?

The intelligence exhibited during subclassing is almost similar to that shown by smart classes. When a smart class is applied to an object, it is automatically subclassed. The following points are worth noting:

- Child objects of a source object, when subclassed from another object, reflect the new properties in the children of the parent subclassed object.

- When an object is subclassed from a property class, the properties in the property class are blindly inherited by the object. The point to be noted here is that Forms should be intelligent enough to ignore the inherited property and not mark it as inherited if it has the same value as the default value of that property in the subclassed object.

- Only those smart classes corresponding to the given object type are displayed in the Smart Classes list when applying a smart class to an existing object, whereas any object that makes sense for the given object can be its subclass. For example, when applying a smart class for a block object, a Property Class Smart Class is not shown in the list even though applying a Property Class to a block makes sense. Whereas the same property class can be made a subclass for the block without using the smart class. This overrides the extra smartness of smart classes.

Normal Trigger Intelligence

Triggers behave diversely at different times depending on the level at which they are defined. This section presents some points favoring trigger intelligence. It also highlights some examples illustrating how trigger behavior is sometimes abnormal.

How Triggers Exhibit Intelligence

The following points show examples favoring trigger intelligence:

- While choosing from the trigger list of an object, Forms 5.0 is intelligent enough to provide triggers applicable to that object and at levels higher than the default level. Even the standard drag and drop operation is intelligent enough to recognize the appropriateness of a given trigger.

- Inapplicable triggers defined at a particular level are not fired at runtime. For example, a POST-QUERY trigger defined at item level is not fired.

- The behavior of a trigger is intelligent enough to decide whether that trigger should fire or not. If Fire-In-Enter-Query-Mode is set to Yes, a WHEN-VALIDATE-ITEM trigger still doesn't fire for a base-table as well as a non base-table item in Enter-Query Mode. This shows that Forms 5.0 recognizes that a WHEN-VALIDATE-ITEM is meant for validation purposes and has no purpose in firing in Enter-Query mode.

How Triggers Lack Intelligence

The following points demonstrate the abnormal behavior of triggers:

- While duplicating triggers with CTRL+D or overwriting the name, Forms still accepts a WHEN-VALIDATE-RECORD trigger at the item level. However, Forms does not show the same trigger when you create a trigger in the normal way by clicking the Create icon or dragging and dropping. This is how it allows you to define triggers at an inappropriate level.

- At the form level, Forms allows you to define a WHEN-TAB-PAGE-CHANGED trigger even if there are no tabbed canvases in the form. The point to be noted here is that it should not allow you to write the said trigger until there is at least one tabbed canvas in the form.

Intelligence with Regard to Form Object Properties

This section presents examples of how Forms uses object properties to exhibit smart rules. It also presents examples that show how Forms fails to be smart while using certain object properties.

How Forms Ignores Object Property Values and Thereby Enforces Smart Rules

Forms ignores object property values and thereby enforces smart rules. I will illustrate this with an example. The block property Single Record is ignored when set to Yes for a data block.

The block property Insert Allowed doesn't prevent the record(s) in the block from being de-marked for insertion. It only prevents you from entering a new record after it was turned off. Forms is intelligent enough to prevent the record(s) from being marked for an INSERT, UPDATE, or DELETE operation only from the point when the Insert Allowed, Update Allowed, or Delete Allowed properties are turned off, respectively. This means records already marked for DML before turning off the corresponding property maintain their status dynamically.

I will illustrate this with an example. Consider a data block with the Enforce Primary Key property set to TRUE. At design time, the Insert Allowed property for the block was True. In an appropriate trigger, before committing, based on runtime conditions, I dynamically set the Insert Allowed property for the same block as follows:

```
IF <condition> THEN
SET_BLOCK_PROPERTY('<data_block_name>', INSERT_ALLOWED, PROPERTY_FALSE);
END IF;
```

Note that I might have entered new records in the block before this code is executed. I also have a simple KEY-COMMIT trigger as follows:

```
KEY-COMMIT

IF FORM_SUCCESS THEN
  COMMIT_FORM;
END IF;
```

The uniqueness of the record is still checked and Forms raises the error:

```
FRM-40600: Record has already been inserted.
```

when it encounters a duplicate record. This shows that the record marked for insertion in the form before the resetting of the Insert Allowed property retains its INSERT status, and Enforce Primary key applies to those records that have INSERT status at the time of commit. Turning off the Insert Allowed property prevents subsequent entry of new records.

Finally, note that the item property Tooltip_Text, when dynamically set to null for an item, prevents the tool tip from being displayed when the mouse is on the item.

How Forms Fails to Be Smart While Using Some Object Property Values

Contrary to the ideas contained in the preceding section, Forms 5.0 isn't always smart enough to ignore object property values to enforce smart rules. The following subsections present examples that support this statement.

How Smart Is Forms in Implementing Query-Only Mode?

Calling Forms in query-only mode is as simple as specifying the constant QUERY_ONLY to CALL_FORM or NEW_FORM. Have you ever thought of how to check whether a form is running in query-only mode? There seems to be no direct way except to use a parameter or global variable. An intelligent Forms should give the capability of a form-level property, say QUERY_ONLY, for this purpose. But unfortunately, such a thing does not exist.

Now what about the properties Insert Allowed, Update Allowed, and Delete Allowed for each of the data blocks in the form? Does Forms turn them off automatically when running the form in query-only mode and reset them to their previously set values at other times?

The answer is an alarming "no." This shows that

- These object-level properties have nothing to do with the running functionality of the form, which is query-only. Though these properties are meant to toggle the operations of INSERT, UPDATE, and DELETE and though Forms prevents these operations in query-only mode, Forms doesn't keep their values in sync with the running condition. This might seem to be vague because there is no need to do so as long as it prevents DML, but my point here is: *The right properties should have the right values at the right times.*

- These object-level properties aren't really 100% dynamic (keeping in view the previous point), and SET_BLOCK_PROPERTY sets them dynamically only to a certain degree. At other times, they pertain only to the values set in the designer.

Another example to substantiate these two statements is the form level Validation property. Does it turn off the default validation when running in query-only mode? No. The value of the property is still TRUE.

Other Non-smart Object Properties

The block property Enforce Primary key, when set to TRUE for a data block, is taken into account when an ON-INSERT trigger is written for that block. My point of argument is that the purpose of an ON-INSERT trigger is to replace the default insertion into the base table. So most likely, its trigger text doesn't have an INSERT into the base table. If it does have an UPDATE of the base table, I still feel comfortable that Oracle doesn't allow an update of the primary key columns. Any other INSERT, UPDATE, or DELETE statements can be easily done with PRE- and POST- INSERT, UPDATE, and DELETE triggers.

Forms is not smart enough to check the text of the ON-INSERT trigger to check for this point so that it can ignore a check for the FRM-40600 error. This can be taken care of at compile time for the ON-INSERT trigger. What an intelligent compile time error this would be. Indeed it's not just intelligence, but complex or high intelligence to check for an insert statement in the trigger body, especially if such a statement is embedded in a program unit, either in Forms or in the database.

Let's refer again to the item property `Tooltip_Text`. Setting it to null dynamically prevents the tool tip from being displayed, but if you reset it to a non-null value, the tool tip still doesn't appear.

There are lots of Forms object properties that are smart enough in one way but not in other ways. The preceding two sections illustrated just some of them.

Intelligence with Regard to Form Wizards

This section presents the intelligence exhibited by the Forms Data Block wizard and LOV wizard and explains the features inherent and lacking in both these wizards.

How Smart Is the Forms Data Block Wizard?

While creating a data block using Data Block Wizard, checking the Enforce Integrity Constraints check box writes code for validation of a Foreign key against the corresponding Primary key during insertion, update, or deletion. This makes the wizard intelligent. However, the wizard doesn't automatically generate an LOV for the FK item. Doing so would be a very intelligent feature indeed. To get around this problem, an LOV has to be explicitly created for the FK item and assigned to it.

How Smart Is the Forms LOV Wizard?

Prior to Forms 6.0, to specify an LOV for an item requires two steps:

1. Create the LOV independently of the item.
2. Assign the LOV for the item explicitly using the item property palette.

Now imagine specifying LOVs for a large number of items. This calls for a lot of time and effort on the part of the developer.

In Forms 6.0, creating an LOV using the LOV wizard automatically applies the LOV to the item specified. This eliminates the previous second step thereby easing the development time and effort. In this way, the LOV wizard is smart enough.

However, it is lacking in one important feature: adding rows using the LOV at runtime. This becomes an often-requested requirement because, generally, an LOV is specified for look-up items like codes and so on, and the end user finds it handy to input nonexistent codes through the LOV at runtime and then use the new codes for the item in question. Otherwise, the look-up codes have to be created first using a separate maintenance screen and then can be used.

The LOV should first check if a particular code exists, and if not, insert the code and its description before using it. Providing a feature like this would make the LOV intelligent indeed.

Summary

The purpose of this chapter has been to highlight the level of intelligence exhibited by Forms builder. The topics under discussion pertained to smart triggers, smart classes, subclassing, the behavior of normal triggers, and the intelligence of Forms with regard to form object properties and Form Wizards.

Additional Interesting Techniques

8

IN THIS CHAPTER

This chapter presents some interesting techniques regarding cancellation of a query programmatically; the processes of navigation and validation; and defining triggers at multiple levels. The initial two sections explain techniques of programmatically canceling a query and the programmatic equivalent of Cancel Query when in Enter Query mode. The following sections explain the processes of validation and navigation with emphasis on two common triggers used for validation: WHEN-VALIDATE-ITEM and WHEN-VALIDATE-RECORD. With reference to this, two special techniques, one concerning an enhanced Exit Form functionality, and the second one on how to avoid the firing of WHEN-VALIDATE-ITEM trigger for control items—in query time—are discussed. The subsequent section outlines when to use the same trigger and how to make it fire, at multiple levels. The chapter concludes with a discussion of a block level commit.

Programmatically Canceling a Query

The capability to programmatically cancel a query was a much-felt need in Forms 4.5. This was needed for long-running queries in Forms data blocks with the option of canceling the query available to the end user. A get-around for this was to display an intermediate message like Query in progress... while the query was running. Although this served as a temporary patch to account for the boredom of waiting till the query was finished, it did not provide the user with the capability of aborting the query before it completed execution.

Forms 5.0 introduced non-blocking SQL that eases the problem. I will discuss the solution with regards to Forms 4.5 and Forms 5.0 and higher separately.

In Forms 5.0 and above, set the Form level Interaction Mode property to Non-Blocking, and Forms will automatically bring up a Cancel alert (similar to that in SQL*Plus) whenever an EXECUTE_QUERY is performed, either interactively or programmatically.

You set the Interaction Mode property to Non-Blocking to prompt for breaking a long-running query. This might terminate either the SELECT or the FETCH phases of query execution.

The Cancel alert is invoked only when the minimum amount of time has elapsed since the query has been submitted for execution. This might include both SELECT and FETCH phases.

In Forms 6.0 and above, the Interaction Mode property can be set dynamically using SET_FORM_PROPERTY:

```
SET_FORM_PROPERTY(:SYSTEM.CURRENT_FORM, INTERACTION_MODE, value);
```

The value is either of the character strings BLOCKING or NON_BLOCKING.

In Forms 4.5, it is easy to simulate non-blocking SQL for the fetch phase. To do the same thing for the SELECT phase requires complex programming using the ORA_FFI foreign function interface. Although a timer provides asynchronous operation to a certain extent, using a timer will not work because the expiration of the timer is deferred till the execution of the query.

As an example, consider a base table block based on the PERSON table with 10,000 records. We will analyze two cases, a simple EXECUTE_QUERY and an EXECUTE_QUERY(ALL_RECORDS) (or setting the block property Query All Records to Yes).

An EXECUTE_QUERY in the block, either interactively or programmatically, might not bring up the Cancel alert if the query is executed before the minimum amount of time required for the alert to display; that is, for non-blocking SQL to prompt for blocking or breaking the query. This will be the result even if there are 10,000 records to be fetched and displayed. For, by default, the number of records fetched is equal to the number of records displayed.

During an EXECUTE_QUERY(ALL_RECORDS) operation, there is maximum likelihood that non-blocking SQL will bring up Cancel during the fetch phase. This is because the SELECT phase is nothing more than

```
SELECT * FROM person;
```

and can be very efficient. As a result, the time taken might be less than the minimum required for non-blocking SQL to take action. But the fetch phase takes longer, as it has to do a repeated fetch and buffering in the Forms side.

The preceding fetch phase might be simulated in Forms 4.5 as follows. In the POST-QUERY trigger, check the :SYSTEM.MODE system variable for QUERY. Then, bring up an alert with a message This operation is continuing on the database side. and include a CANCEL button.

Now, do an ABORT_QUERY based on the response:

```
POST-QUERY

DECLARE
    Alert_id Alert;
    Alert_button NUMBER;
BEGIN
    IF :SYSTEM.MODE  = QUERY THEN
      Alert_button :=  SHOW_ALERT(alert_id);
      IF alert_button = ALERT_BUTTON1 THEN
         ABORT_QUERY;
      END IF;
    END IF;
END;
```

Here there are two special cases to be considered:

```
FRM-40350 Query caused no records to be entered.
FRM-40355 Query caused no records to be entered, Re-enter.
```

8

These messages are automatically taken care of as we try to block the fetch phase. Otherwise, there are two easy ways to track the number of records fetched:

- Execute COUNT_QUERY immediately followed by a GET_BLOCK_PROPERTY(<block_name>, QUERY_HITS). This technique is described in Chapter 2, "Advanced GUI Development: Developing Beyond GUI."

- Write a PRE-SELECT trigger, pre-execute the query using :SYSTEM.LAST_QUERY, and execute it using DBMS_SQL on the database side.

Programmatic Equivalent of Cancel Query

Here's a technique that is the equivalent of selecting the Cancel Query button when the form is in Enter Query mode. The technique used is simple but not conspicuous as we use the KEY-EXIT trigger. Write a KEY-EXIT trigger with the Fire In Enter-Query Mode property set to TRUE (in Forms 4.x) and to Yes in higher versions:

```
KEY-EXIT
  EXIT_FORM(NO_VALIDATE);
```

Note that programmatically simulating Cancel Query in Enter-Query mode is not the same as ABORT_QUERY. Simulating Cancel Query is aborting Enter Query mode.

Validation, Navigation, and Simulating Navigation

A Change event in Forms triggers a Validate event. In this situation, the WHEN-VALIDATE-ITEM and WHEN-VALIDATE-RECORD triggers come into the picture.

> **NOTE**
>
> A Change in Oracle forms is some change in an item value, either interactively through user input or programmatically. Overwriting the item with its original value is also a Change event.

A WHEN-VALIDATE-ITEM trigger fires when the item value has been changed and navigation is initiated out of the item either explicitly or programmatically. If no navigation needs to be initiated out of the item, there is a way to imitate navigation using the ENTER built-in.

COMMIT also imitates navigation and initiates validation.

Suppose there is a WHEN-VALIDATE-ITEM trigger for the last item of a record. The user enters a value into this item and does not press Enter. Instead, he clicks the Save button. As I just mentioned, COMMIT fires the WHEN-VALIDATE-ITEM trigger. But COMMIT is a form level event and in addition to this WHEN-VALIDATE-ITEM trigger, validation occurs throughout the form and multiple failures might cause multiple error messages to be displayed, which is confusing to the user as it messes up the process. Multiple failures might be because of failure of form object properties in addition to failure of the WHEN-VALIDATE-ITEM or cascading effects of these. Also there might be code that needs to be written before the call to the built-in COMMIT_FORM in the WHEN-BUTTON-PRESSED trigger of the Save button, such as assigning variables or simulating an UPDATE when the user enters non-base table items so that a PRE-UPDATE trigger fires and so on.

As an illustration, suppose that in our preceding example, there was code to assign a base table item to itself—to simulate an UPDATE operation—before the call to the COMMIT_FORM. The WHEN-VALIDATE-ITEM trigger fires after the assignment even if a RAISE FORM_TRIGGER_FAILURE is done in WHEN-VALIDATE-ITEM. So the record would be marked as an update before checking for the success or failure of the WHEN-VALIDATE-ITEM. To prevent this, in the WHEN-BUTTON-PRESSED trigger of the Save button, add the following code in the beginning:

WHEN-BUTTON-PRESSED

```
ENTER;
IF FORM_SUCCESS THEN
    <perform the assignment>
    COMMIT_FORM;
    IF FORM_SUCCESS THEN
       <Any further action>
    END IF;
END IF;
```

Note how ENTER simulates navigation and thus initiates validation. In this case, the WHEN-VALIDATE-ITEM fires. On its failure, the assignment is not done because FORM_SUCCESS evaluates to FALSE.

VALIDATION, VALIDATION_UNIT, and VALIDATE

The Validation and Validation Unit properties control the occurrence and scope of validation in a form.

The Validation property decides whether forms should initiate or not when the Validate event occurs. This property is ON by default and can be turned on and off programmatically by using SET_FORM_PROPERTY. The property is specified by the constant VALIDATION. For example

```
SET_FORM_PROPERTY(:SYSTEM.CURRENT_FORM, VALIDATION, PROPERTY_FALSE);
```

The Validation Unit property decides at what point validation should be initiated. In other words, until what point in time should Forms defer validating changes in the form? This property is valid only if the Validation property is set to YES. The valid values for this are `DEFAULT_SCOPE`, `ITEM_SCOPE`, `RECORD_SCOPE`, or `FORM_SCOPE`. For example

```
SET_FORM_PROPERTY(:SYSTEM.CURRENT_FORM, VALIDATION_UNIT, ITEM_SCOPE);
```

When set to `ITEM_SCOPE`, validation is initiated on navigation at the item level—that is, when control moves out of an item. The validation unit specifies at what level (item, record, or form) validation is initiated. This requires that the corresponding event initiating this validation should be an item-, record-, or form-level event, and this is what becomes the default scope of validation in the form from that point on. If the event initiating validation is an item-level event, the default scope is `ITEM_SCOPE`. Similarly, if the event initiating validation is a record-level event or form-level event, the default scope is `RECORD_SCOPE` or `FORM SCOPE` respectively.

The constant `DEFAULT_SCOPE` is environment specific and is `ITEM_SCOPE` on the GUI Windows platform. This should not be confused with the default scope previously discussed.

TIP

Turning off the Validation property automatically turns off Validation Unit property.

VALIDATE

Validation might be turned off for some particular reason; for example, during form startup. It can be later turned on—for example, just before committing. When turned on, the `VALIDATE` built-in has to be invoked to actually perform (execute) the validation.

Setting the Validation property to YES only indicates that validation should occur. Setting the Validation Unit property to the appropriate scope only indicates that validation should occur at the particular scope. Specifying a call to the `VALIDATE` built-in actually initiates the validation so that any `WHEN-VALIDATE-ITEM`, `WHEN-VALIDATE-RECORD`, and form object properties triggered by validation are fired.

The following example code illustrates this point:

```
WHEN-NEW-FORM-INSTANCE

SET_FORM_PROPERTY(:SYSTEM.CURRENT_FORM, VALIDATIION, PROPERTY_FALSE);

PRE-INSERT, PRE-UPDATE or PRE-DELETE

SET_FORM_PROPERTY(:SYSTEM.CURRENT_FORM, VALIDATION, PROPERTY_TRUE);
SET_FORM_PROPERTY(:SYSTEM.CURRENT_FORM, VALIDATION_UNIT, FORM_SCOPE);
VALIDATE(FORM_SCOPE);
```

In this code, setting the validation unit is not necessary because VALIDATE(FORM_SCOPE) automatically sets the VALIDATION_UNIT and then validates at form scope.

Note that after you set the Validation Unit constant for the whole form, even if you set it dynamically, it cannot be reset to hold for specific item(s), record(s), or block(s).

Initially, when a form is run, the validation is ON and the DEFAULT_SCOPE is the same as ITEM_SCOPE. If the validation is turned off and then turned on, even though the DEFAULT_SCOPE is ITEM_SCOPE, validation *might not* occur at the item level. As specified earlier, it depends on the event initiating the validation.

TIP

DEFAULT_SCOPE is not the same as ITEM_SCOPE when it comes to initiating the validation process.

Turning off Validation using

```
SET_FORM_PROPERTY(:SYSTEM.CURRENT_FORM, VALIDATION, PROPERTY_FALSE)
```

also turns off the validation occurring because of the Required property when set to TRUE/YES.

Turning off validation doesn't completely nullify the validation occurring in a form. Validation is nullified only for Validation initiating form object properties and validation triggers in forms.

An example of the former is the Required property. Other validations do occur. To exemplify this point, when the Enforce Primary Key property is set to YES and validation is turned off in the WHEN-NEW-FORM-INSTANCE trigger, the primary key enforcement is still checked in case of a duplicate record and Forms displays the following message on its failure:

```
FRM-40600: Record has already been inserted.
```

Oracle errors on the database side are also propagated to Forms.

When validation is turned off and then turned on at a later point of time, immediately call the VALIDATE built-in with the appropriate scope specified as its parameter. This is required to initiate the validation so that validation actually occurs.

When you turn off validation, if you are turning it on in a COMMIT event-initiated trigger, set it to Form scope. This is because COMMIT is a form-level event by default.

8

ADDITIONAL INTERESTING TECHNIQUES

For example, if the Validation has been turned off in the WHEN-NEW-FORM-INSTANCE trigger, and you are turning it on in, say, a PRE-INSERT trigger, specify the following:

```
SET_FORM_PROPERTY(:SYSTEM.CURRENT_FORM, VALIDATION, PROPERTY_TRUE);
VALIDATE(FORM_SCOPE);
```

Using DEFAULT_SCOPE will not work to validate form-level initiated events, such as pressing the Commit key.

Enhancing the Function of Exit Form

This section discusses a special re-definition of the default Exit Form functionality. This can be a requirement when the user tries to exit with pending data block changes, and the form should first prompt for saving these changes and then validate the changes if the response to the first prompt is a Yes. This goes in conformity with the dictum, "Validate only if you want to save changes, otherwise exit 'cool-ly'."

The default behavior of KEY-EXIT or EXIT_FORM is to first perform validation and, if successful, prompt for COMMIT, as shown in Figure 8.1. Specifying ASK_COMMIT, NO_COMMIT, DO_COMMIT, or NO_VALIDATE does not achieve our goal.

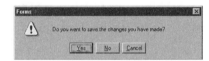

FIGURE 8.1
The Save dialog while exiting a form after successful validation.

If validation is a failure, KEY-EXIT or EXIT_FORM throws up another dialog to close the form, as shown in Figure 8.2.

FIGURE 8.2
The Close dialog while exiting a form after validation failure.

A better way is to prompt for COMMIT and when the user answers Yes to this dialog, validate. Why should it validate when the user doesn't want to commit? This way the functionality of KEY-EXIT or EXIT_FORM is enhanced over the default functionality.

To use this technique, you can re-define KEY-EXIT as follows:

```
DECLARE
    alert_button number;
BEGIN
/* Initially turn off the validation to avpid forms from validating by default
➡*/

  SET_FORM_PROPERTY(:SYSTEM.CURRENT_FORM, VALIDATION, PROPERTY_FALSE);
  ENTER;   --- This is required to mark form_success as changed. This will not
➡validate as VALIDATION is turned off.

/*  Prompt for save if form status is changed */

  if :system.form_status = 'CHANGED' then
   alert_button := show_alert('alert1');

/* If the user responds to above prompt as Yes, turn on validation and initiate
 it at form scope. */

   if alert_button = ALERT_BUTTON1 then
   SET_FORM_PROPERTY(:SYSTEM.CURRENT_FORM, VALIDATION, PROPERTY_TRUE);
VALIDATE(FORM_SCOPE);
     if form_success then
       exit_form(do_commit);
     END IF;

/* if the user response is a 'No', exit the form without validating */

  elsif alert_button = ALERT_BUTTON2 then
    exit_form(no_validate);
  ELSE
     null;
  END IF;

/* if form status is not changed, simply exit the form */
ELSE
  exit_form;
END IF;
END;
```

Preventing Validation of WHEN-VALIDATE-ITEM for Control Items During Query Time

This section presents a simple technique for preventing the WHEN-VALIDATE-ITEM trigger from firing while querying when such a trigger is defined for control items. This technique is useful when non-base items are part of a record and validation of these items is to be suppressed at the time of querying the records.

For a base table item, a WHEN-VALIDATE-ITEM will not fire during query mode. That's why you need a POST-QUERY trigger to populate any look-up items in the block that are based on the base table items.

For a control item, WHEN-VALIDATE-ITEM will fire when it is populated by means of a POST-QUERY. To prevent this, the following technique can be used:

WHEN-VALIDATE-ITEM

```
IF :SYSTEM.MODE != NORMAL THEN
    RETURN;
END IF;
<Actual Code For Validation>
```

Alternatively, you can force the item to be valid by setting the ITEM_IS_VALID property to TRUE in the POST_QUERY:

POST-QUERY

```
SET_ITEM_PROPERTY(item_id, ITEM_IS_VALID, PROPERTY_TRUE);
```

When to Use WHEN-VALIDATE-RECORD and When to Use WHEN-VALIDATE-ITEM

The need to use both WHEN-VALIDATE-RECORD and WHEN-VALIDATE-ITEM is quite often felt in coding applications where independent validations are to be done, at the record and item levels. As a special case of this, validation between interdependent items is best done using a WHEN-VALIDATE-RECORD trigger.

You should use a WHEN-VALIDATE-RECORD trigger to perform validation when control moves out of the whole record and not when it just moves out of an item in the record.

Use a WHEN-VALIDATE-ITEM trigger to perform validation when control moves out of an item. This also implies that the control might move out of the record in the process. But the subtle difference is WHEN-VALIDATE-RECORD fires only when the control exits the whole record. It does not fire while tabbing between items in the same record.

How Does the Validation Unit Property Influence This Behavior?

Setting the Validation Unit property to Record defers the validation process until the control navigates out of the record. This is similar to the behavior of a WHEN-VALIDATE-RECORD trigger except that it also postpones the firing of the WHEN-VALIDATE-ITEM trigger until this point. At this time, WHEN-VALIDATE-ITEM fires followed by WHEN-VALIDATE-RECORD.

Examples of situations requiring a WHEN-VALIDATE-RECORD are

- Range-based items in a record that involve a lower limit and an upper limit; for example, date items like start date and end date, number items like age lower and upper limits, and so on.

- Two or more items interdependent on one another like a type item, a subtype item, and a value item dependent on these two. Three WHEN-VALIDATE-ITEM triggers, one for each type, subtype, and value items would suffice. However they would involve complex coding to ensure correct values and to restore correct values when the user enters the first time and then goes back and changes the type and/or subtype items without changing the value item. The WHEN-VALIDATE-ITEM for the value item does not fire because its value hasn't been changed since it has been entered. So the code for the WHEN-VALIDATE-ITEM of value item has to be repeated in each of the WHEN-VALIDATE-ITEMS of type and subtype items.

Imagine the complexity when there are more than three items. A WHEN-VALIDATE-RECORD trigger, on the other hand, would require only one combined validation involving all three items.

Writing individual WHEN-VALIDATE-ITEM triggers for each of the interdependent items requires the code performing the combined validation to be repeated in each trigger. This increases the complexity of coding when a lot of these items are involved. Also the probability of error is greater in this case.

On the other hand, writing a WHEN-VALIDATE-RECORD trigger requires only doing the combined validation once, and this method is completely error-proof.

When to Use the Same Trigger and How to Make It Fire at Multiple Levels

This section discusses when to use the same trigger at multiple levels and how to override the default scope of a trigger by making it fire more than once. Examples are provided in the appropriate subsections as to when it is required to follow each method.

Using the Same Trigger at Multiple Levels

There are many situations in Forms when it is required to use the same trigger at multiple levels. The knack behind this is to use the same trigger at multiple levels if the trigger has to behave differently at any one level, for the same triggering event.

A quick example is the behavior of the KEY-NEXT-ITEM trigger for tabbing in a block. This is a requirement when groups of items are in a single-record control block and no two groups are similar functionally. A good example is an input parameter screen for a list of reports in which different parameters are grouped per report (and might be placed in different canvases). So there should not be any tabbing between two dissimilar groups. Also, think of the situation in which items in each group are in different canvases. One way to do this is to write KEY-NEXT-ITEM triggers: one at the block level, which nullifies the action, and one each for the first and last items in each group that enables tabbing.

Also, we do not write the KEY-NEXT-ITEM trigger for the remaining items in the block, assuming normal tabbing between them.

The KEY-NEXT-ITEM at block level fires while navigating between those items that do not have an item-level trigger attached to them. The KEY-NEXT-ITEM for the item level fires for the first and last items of each group. In the second case, the block-level trigger does not fire as the lower-level trigger always fires, by default.

Of course, using the properties Next Navigation Item and Previous Navigation Item would have done the same job, but keeping in mind a situation like the one previously described, it is best to handle the navigation using triggers rather than relying on default Forms functionality. The code for the two triggers previously described is as follows:

```
KEY-NEXT-ITEM at block level
NULL;
KEY-NEXT-ITEM at Item level
NEXT_ITEM;
```

The example of programmatically simulating a Cancel Query when in Enter-Query mode, as described in the previous section, suggests the behavior of the same trigger in two different ways in response to two different triggering events, exiting the form and coming out of Enter-Query mode. In this case, KEY-EXIT is fired when both these events are triggered.

Making the Same Trigger Fire at Multiple Levels More Than Once

The technique previously described involves the same trigger fire at two different levels by defining two instances of it. Now the question arises as to how to make it fire more than once at different levels. The default trigger that fires is the one at the lowest level.

To make the same trigger fire at multiple levels, set the trigger Execute Style property to Before or After to override the default trigger firing functionality. Then the same trigger can be made to fire more than once at different levels. (Note that the Execute Style property can be set only in the property palette of the corresponding trigger and cannot be set dynamically.)

A good example of this is pointed out in the preceding subsection, defining a KEY-NEXT-ITEM trigger, one at block level and one at item level. Here, the Execute Style property for the item level trigger is set to Before so that it fires first before the block level KEY-NEXT-ITEM trigger.

A Block Level Commit

This section attempts to remove the confusion of a block level commit in Forms. It explains what a true block-level commit is and continues to explain that what the developers presume to be a block-level commit is actually *not* a block level commit, and there is no such thing as a block level commit in Forms.

A block-level commit commits the changes in a particular block only, independent of the changes in other blocks not committed. Do not confuse it with being able to commit only when the control is in a particular block.

There is nothing like a true block-level commit in Forms. A commit achieved by the built-ins COMMIT or COMMIT_FORM, DO_KEY('COMMIT_FORM') or pressing of a hot key is always a form-level commit and does commit all valid and pending database changes in the form.

A block-level commit is *not*:

- The commit achieved by nullifying the KEY-COMMIT trigger for a block.
- The commit achieved by writing an ON-COMMIT, ON-INSERT, ON-UPDATE, or ON-DELETE trigger with a check for :SYSTEM.CURSOR_BLOCK in it. Of course, this prevents changes in other data blocks from being committed.

These two steps are often mistaken to be simulating a block-level commit, but in fact they are not.

Summary

This chapter deals with the often required techniques in Forms query processing and validation and navigation. The techniques for programmatically canceling a query and the programmatic equivalent of Cancel Query while in Enter Query mode were discussed. The subtle differences between WHEN-VALIDATE-ITEM and WHEN-VALIDATE-RECORD triggers and an enhanced Exit Form functionality were highlighted. Finally, the usage of the same trigger at multiple levels was discussed and the idea of a block-level commit was presented.

8

ADDITIONAL INTERESTING TECHNIQUES

Working with Trees

IN THIS CHAPTER

This chapter discusses the various techniques involving tree items in Forms 6.0. It begins by explaining what a tree item is and goes on to present the technique for creating a tree item. Next, the techniques for the various operations on a tree item are highlighted. Specifically, operations like dynamically populating a tree item, selection using single-click of a node, node activation using double-click of a node, expansion and collapsing of nodes including expanding and collapsing all nodes, searching for a particular node and dynamically adding and deleting nodes are discussed.

A tree item is used to represent hierarchical data and is query only. It is populated by means of a query and the query populating it uses `CONNECT BY` and `START WITH` clauses. A common example is the Object Navigator in the Forms Designer. Another example is the typical recursive relationship between Manager and Employee discussed in Chapter 1, "GUI Development," under the section "Simulating a Drill-Down and Drill-Up LOV Using T-Lists." The same LOV can be presented in a tree structure as shown in Figure 9.1.

FIGURE 9.1

A hierarchical list of employees.

The same list when represented as a native hierarchical tree structure appears in Figure 9.2.

The main operations of a tree are

- Creating and initializing with a data query
- Specifying an `ORDER BY`
- Populating the tree
- Altering tree properties

- Node operations: selection of a node (single-click), activation of a node (double-click), expanding and collapsing nodes, and searching for a particular node
- Growing trees: adding sub-trees dynamically, adding singular nodes dynamically, deleting sub-trees dynamically, and deleting singular nodes dynamically

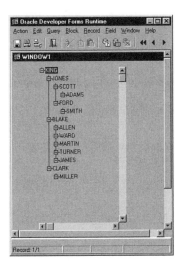

FIGURE 9.2

A native tree structure of employees.

Forms provides built-ins to implement the above operations. These are listed in Table 9.1.

TABLE 9.1   Built-ins to Implement Tree Operations

Operation	Built-in
Tree creation	At design time
Tree initialization	At design time by specifying a query for the Data Query property
Tree population	`FTREE.POPULATE_TREE(item, rg_id)` or `FTREE.POPULATE_TREE(item, query_string)`

continues

TABLE 9.1   Continued

Operation	Built-in
Altering tree properties	FTREE.GET_TREE_PROPERTY(item, property)
	property can be any of the following:
	1. DataSource: FTREE.DATASOURCE. Valid values are Record Group (FTREE.RECORD_GROUP) and query text (FTREE.QUERY_TEXT). Also we can obtain the actual Record Group (FTREE.RECORD_GROUP), which returns the record group ID or name (can be set dynamically). Query Text (FTREE.QUERY_TEXT) returns the query text as a character string by using the above constants (can be set dynamically).
	2. Allow_empty_branches: FTREE.ALLOW_EMPTY_BRANCHES. Valid values are TRUE and FALSE as character strings.
	3. Node Count: FTREE.NODE_COUNT.
	4. Selection Count: FTREE.SELECTION_COUNT.
	5. Allow Multi-Select: FTREE.ALLOW_MULTI-SELECT. Valid values are TRUE and FALSE as character strings. Can be set dynamically.
	FTREE.SET_TREE_NODE_PROPERTY(item, property, value)
	Only properties 1 and 5 can be set dynamically.
Node properties	FTREE.GET_TREE_NODE_PROPERTY(item, property)
	property can be any of the following:
	1. Node State: FTREE.NODE_STATE. Returns one of FTREE.EXPANDED_NODE, FTREE.COLLAPSED_NODE, or FTREE.LEAF_NODE.
	2. Node Depth: FTREE.NODE_DEPTH
	3. Node Label: FTREE.NODE_LABEL
	4. Node Icon: FTREE.NODE_ICON
	5. Node Value: FTREE.NODE_VALUE
	FTREE.SET_TREE_NODE_PROPERTY(item, property, value)
	All of these properties except Node Depth can be set dynamically.

Operation	Built-in
Node selection	FTREE.GET_TREE_SELECTION(item). Returns the selected node of data type FTREE.NODE starting from the top and numbered from 1 onwards. A node is considered selected if it is single-clicked.
	FTREE.SELECTION_COUNT: Returns the total number of selected nodes.
	The right trigger for performing an action based on node selection is WHEN-TREE-NODE-SELECTED. Use :SYSTEM.TRIGGER_NODE to get the node single-clicked.
Node Activation	WHEN-TREE-NODE-ACTIVATED trigger can be used to perform an action whenever the user double-clicks a node. Use :SYSTEM.TRIGGER_NODE to get the node double-clicked.
Searching a particular node	FTREE.FIND_TREE_NODE(item, search_string, search_type, search_by, search_root, start_point)
	search_type: FTREE.FIND_NEXT or FTREE.FIND_NEXT_CHILD
	search_by: FTREE.NODE_VALUE or FTREE.NODE_LABEL
	search_root: A valid node of data type FTREE.NODE or FTREE.ROOT_NODE.
	start_point: same as search_root.
Expanding and collapsing nodes	Use FTREE.GET_NODE_PROPERTY and FTREE.SET_TREE_NODE_PROPERTY to get the node state and set them accordingly depending on the current state of a node.
	To perform an action while expanding or collapsing, use WHEN-TREE-NODE-EXPANDED trigger.
Adding sub-trees	FTREE.ADD_TREE_DATA(item, node, offset_type, offset, data_source, data).
	offset_type: Either FTREE.PARENT_OFFSET or FTREE.SIBLING_OFFSET.
	offset: If offset_type is FTREE.PARENT_OFFSET, either (1-n) or FTREE.LAST_CHILD. If offset_type is FTREE.SIBLING_OFFSET, either FTREE.NEXT_NODE or FTREE.PREVIOUS_NODE.
	data source: FTREE.RECORD_GROUP or FTREE.QUERY_TEXT.
	data: Depending on the data source, a record group ID, name, or a query text string.

continues

TABLE 9.1 Continued

Operation	Built-in
Adding singular nodes	FTREE.ADD_TREE_NODE(item, node, offset_type, offset, state, label, icon, value). offset_type and offset are as described above. state is FTREE.EXPANDED_NODE, FTREE.COLLAPSED_NODE or FTREE.LEAF_NODE.
Populating a record group from an existing tree	FTREE.POPULATE_GROUP_FROM_TREE(recordgroup, item, node) starting from a given node. In this case, node is the start point of the tree from where data should be extracted.
Deleting sub-trees and singular nodes	FTREE.DELETE_TREE_NODE(item, node) Deleting a node that has children will automatically delete all of its children.
Finding the parent of a given node	FTREE.GET_TREE_NODE_PARENT(item, node).

Creating a Tree Item

We will use the following design to create a tree item based on a query and show how to get the EMP details by EMPNO for each tree node selection:

- A block named TREE_BLOCK with an item of type Tree named HTREE can be used. This item can belong to the primary canvas of the console window. Drag the tree item to cover a vertical rectangle visible enough to picture a hierarchical structure.

- The operations of expand and collapse are simulated as a toggle when a particular node is expanded or collapsed by clicking on it.

- The operations of Expand All and Collapse All are simulated as a toggle when a particular node is expanded or collapsed. These are relative to the depth of this starting node.

- A control block named CTRL_BLK with four iconic push buttons PB_EXPAND, PB_EXPAND_ALL, PB_COLLAPSE, and PB_COLLAPSE_ALL for the expand, expand all, collapse and collapse all operations on selected Tree nodes can be used. Expand and collapse are explained in the second point; Expand all and Collapse all are provided by clicking each node. These functions are also provided by means of buttons to give greater flexibility to the user.

- A data block EMP gets the details for the node selected EMPNO.

Begin by initializing the tree item with a data query based on a SELECT with CONNECT BY and START WITH clauses. This has to be specified in the Data Query property of the tree item:

```
SELECT -1, LEVEL, ename, NULL, TO_CHAR(empno)
FROM    emp
START WITH mgr IS NULL
CONNECT BY PRIOR empno = mgr;
```

This query lists all the organizations along with their reporting (parent) organizations at one level above them.

The data columns in the above query are selected as follows:

- The first column is to specify whether the tree is expandable or not. 1 is Expand to a Depth of All Levels Possible, 0 is Show Only One Level, and –1 is No Expand.
- The second column is self-explanatory—the LEVEL pseudo column for any hierarchical query.
- The third column is the text that will appear on a node when it is clicked.
- The fourth column is an icon name that will appear by the side of a node.
- The fifth column is the actual data value held by a node. The node value always returns a character value.

Next, populate the tree item on form startup. Write a WHEN-NEW-FORM-INSTANCE trigger using FTREE.POPULATE_TREE:

```
DECLARE
  item_id Item;
BEGIN
  item_id := FIND_ITEM(''TREE_BLOCK.HTREE'');
  IF NOT ID_NULL(item_id) THEN
    FTREE.POPULATE_TREE(item_id);
  END IF;
END;
```

Simply specifying a data query does not automatically populate the tree.

9

WORKING WITH TREES

TIP

Tree items should belong to single-row blocks, and the tree item should be the only item in the block.

Operations on a Tree Item

This section highlights the techniques for performing various operations on tree items. It begins by cautioning the developer with the effect of specifying an ORDER BY clause for a hierarchical tree query and then describing the technique for dynamically populating a tree item using a record group or a query. Node operations such as single click, double-click, expand, expand all, collapse, collapse all, and search on a particular node are described. Finally, techniques for adding and deleting sub-trees and singular nodes are presented.

Caution Regarding Ordering Tree Item Data

Be careful in specifying an ORDER BY clause for a tree item query. The ORDER BY takes precedence over the hierarchy. So the child nodes of a parent node might appear above the parent node if the ORDER BY order precedes the TREE HIERARCHY order.

Dynamically Populating a Tree

A tree can be dynamically populated by using record groups and using query text. Two ways to dynamically populate a tree are as follows:

- Specify an initial data query in the tree item properties. Use FTREE.POPULATE_TREE to populate the tree with data contained in the data query. This is illustrated in the previous section "Creating a Tree Item."

- Populate the tree item using a record group created programmatically. Use FTREE.SET_TREE_PROPERTY to do this. A call to this built-in replaces the existing tree data with the data contained in the record group and causes the tree to display the new data. The following code illustrates this concept:

```
DECLARE
  rg_id RECORDGROUP;
  ret_code NUMBER;
BEGIN
/* If the record group already exists, delete it. */

  g_id := FIND_GROUP(''RG_TREE'');
  IF NOT ID_NULL(rg_id) THEN
    DELETE_GROUP(rg_id);
  END IF;

/* Create the record group using a query */

  rg_id := CREATE_GROUP_FROM_QUERY(''RG_TREE'',
    ''SELECT -1, LEVEL, ename, NULL, TO_CHAR(empno)
    FROM emp
```

```
        START WITH ename = ''''JONES'''' CONNECT BY PRIOR empno = mgr'');

    /* Populate the record group using data from the query with which it was
    /created */

      ret_code := POPULATE_GROUP(rg_id);

    /* If the above populate is a success then set tree property as follows */

      IF (ret_code = 0) THEN
        FTREE.SET_TREE_PROPERTY(''htree.htree'',FTREE.RECORD_GROUP, rg_id);
      ;

    END;
```

The following points are to be noted here:

- The record group has to be created programmatically and has to be a query record group with a SELECT statement having a START WITH and CONNECT BY clause.

- The query for the record group has to conform to the five column query structure of the tree initial data query.

- There is no need to use FTREE.POPULATE_TREE. Using FTREE.SET_TREE_PROPERTY automatically populates the tree with the new data and displays it.

- The data source of a tree query can be of type record group or query text. It is specified by either the constant FTREE.RECORD_GROUP or FTREE.QUERY_TEXT.

> **TIP**
>
> The current data source of a tree can be obtained as follows:
> ```
> FTREE.GET_TREE_PROPERTY(item_id, DATASOURCE);
> ```

Selection of a Node

Selecting a node is the most important step in using a tree item. Selection of a node refers to single-clicking a particular node of the tree. Generally an action pertaining to the node value selected is initiated when a node is selected by means of a single-click.

In our example tree, when the user selects (single-clicks) an ENAME in the tree, the other related details pertaining to the employee name are displayed. To do this, write a WHEN-TREE-NODE-SELECTED trigger with calls to :SYSTEM.TRIGGER_NODE and GET_TREE_NODE_PROPERTY. The system variable :SYSTEM.TRIGGER_NODE points to the node the user single-clicks. A call to the built-in FTREE.GET_TREE_NODE_PROPERTY (as shown in the code below) gives the value contained in the node selected. The code is as follows:

```
DECLARE
  item_id ITEM;
  node_ret_val VARCHAR2(32767);
BEGIN
  item_id := FIND_ITEM(''TREE_BLOCK.HTREE'');
  IF NOT ID_NULL(item_id) THEN

/* Get the node value corresponding to the node selected. The specific node
➥selected is obtained by the system variable :SYSTEM.TRIGGER_NODE */

    node_ret_val := FTREE.GET_TREE_NODE_PROPERTY(item_id, :SYSTEM.TRIGGER_NODE,
➥FTREE.NODE_VALUE);

/* Get the employee details corresponding to the node value so obtained above.
➥This is done by setting the default where clause of the EMP block followed by
➥an EXECUTE_QUERY in the block */

    SET_BLOCK_PROPERTY(''EMP'', DEFAULT_WHERE,
                       ''WHERE empno = ''¦¦TO_NUMBER(node_ret_val));
    GO_BLOCK(''EMP'');
    EXECUTE_QUERY(ALL_RECORDS);
  END IF;
END;
```

Double-clicking a Node

Double-clicking a tree node activates a user-specified action. This is in conformity with the standard Windows functionality: single-click for selection and double-click for action. An example of this is Expand All or Collapse All for the currently selected node.

Write a WHEN-TREE-NODE-ACTIVATED trigger to perform the desired action. The use of this trigger is illustrated in the following sections "Expanding All Nodes" and "Collapsing All Nodes."

Expanding a Node

This is done to expand the current node to display depth one level below.

NOTE	

There is a difference between selection and expansion of a node. *Selection* is highlighting the node by clicking on the node name, whereas *expansion* is selection done by clicking on the icon next to the name. In other words, it's the difference between clicking on a <block_name> and the + icon to the left of it in the object navigator.

Collapsing a Node

This is done to collapse the current node to a height one level above. The functions EXPAND and COLLAPSE are controlled by default by the WHEN-TREE-NODE-EXPANDED trigger.

The following code toggles between expanding and collapsing depending on the current state of the node:

```
DECLARE
  item_id ITEM;
  node_ret_val VARCHAR2(32767);
  this_node FTREE.NODE;
BEGIN

/* Get the internal id of the tree item */

  item_id := FIND_ITEM(''TREE_BLOCK.HTREE'');
  IF NOT ID_NULL(item_id) THEN

    /*  Get the currently selected node */

    this_node := GET_TREE_SELECTION(item_id, 1);
    IF NOT FTREE.ID_NULL(this_node) THEN

/* If internal id is not null, switch this node''s state to the opposite of its
➡current state */

    IF (FTREE.GET_TREE_NODE_PROPERTY(item_id, this_node, FTREE.NODE_STATE) =
➡FTREE.EXPANDED_NODE THEN
      FTREE.SET_TREE_NODE_PROPERTY(item_id, this_node, FTREE.NODE_STATE,
➡ FTREE.COLLAPSED_NODE);
    ELSIF (FTREE.GET_TREE_NODE_PROPERTY(item_id, this_node, FTREE.NODE_STATE)
➡ = FTREE.COLLAPSED_NODE THEN
      FTREE.SET_TREE_NODE_PROPERTY(item_id, this_node, FTREE.NODE_STATE,
➡FTREE.EXPANDED_NODE);
    END IF;
  END IF;

  END IF;
END;
```

The user has to select by clicking on the node (thus highlighting it). The code gets the first such selected node and toggles between expanded and collapsed states. Note that a WHEN-BUTTON-PRESSED trigger can also be used to execute this code.

9

Expanding All Nodes

This is done to expand the current node to display all levels below to the atomic level.

We will use the following procedure to do the job:

```
PROCEDURE p_expand_or_collapse_all
  (htree VARCHAR2, exp_or_coll VARCHAR2, ret_cd OUT NUMBER)
IS
  item_id Item;
  current_node FTREE.Node;
  starting_node_level NUMBER;
  current_node_level NUMBER;
BEGIN
  item_id := FIND_ITEM(htree);
  IF NOT ID_NULL(item_id) THEN

/* Get the current node and its depth */

    current_node := :SYSTEM.TRIGGER_NODE;
    starting_node_level := FTREE.GET_TREE_NODE_PROPERTY(item_id, current_node,
➥FTREE.NODE_DEPTH);

/* Traverse down thr tree till the atomic node is reached. This atomic node is
/relative to the current node. While traversing expand each collapsed node in
/the path. We are sure that we have reached the atomic if there are no more
/nodes or we have reached a node whole depth is the same as the starting node
/ level */

    LOOP
      IF FTREE.ID_NULL(current_node) OR (current_node_level =
➥starting_node_level) THEN
          EXIT;
      ELSE

/* The literal ''X'' specifies that the operation is that od expansion. The
/literal ''C'' signifies collapsing */

        IF exp_or_coll = 'X' THEN
            IF FTREE.GET_TREE_NODE_PROPERTY(item_id, current_node,
➥FTREE.NODE_STATE) = FTREE.COLLAPSED_NODE THEN
                FTREE.SET_TREE_NODE_PROPERTY(item_id, current_node,
➥FTREE.NODE_STATE, FTREE.EXPANDED_NODE);
            END IF;
        ELSIF exp_or_coll = 'C' THEN
            IF FTREE.GET_TREE_NODE_PROPERTY(item_id, current_node,
➥FTREE.NODE_STATE) = FTREE.EXPANDED_NODE THEN
```

```
            FTREE.SET_TREE_NODE_PROPERTY(item_id, current_node,
➡FTREE.NODE_STATE, FTREE.COLLAPSED_NODE);
          END IF;
        END IF;

/* Reset the current node and the current node level. The immediately traversed
/ node becomes the current node and its depth becomes the current node level */

        current_node := FTREE.FIND_TREE_NODE
➡(htree, '', search_type=>FTREE.FIND_NEXT, search_point =>current_node);
        current_node_level := FTREE.GET_TREE_NODE_PROPERTY
➡(item_id, current_node, FTREE.NODE_DEPTH);
      END IF;
    END LOOP;
  END IF;
END;
```

Write a WHEN-TREE-NODE-ACTIVATED trigger to expand all nodes of the current node. This expansion to the current node as the root node is as follows:

```
WHEN-TREE-NODE-ACTIVATED

DECLARE
  retcd NUMBER;
BEGIN
  p_expand_or_collapse_all('TREE_BLOCK.HTREE','X', retcd);
  IF (retcd <> 0) THEN
      MESSAGE('ERR: Expand All/Collapse All failed');
      RAISE FORM_TRIGGER_FAILURE;
  END IF;
END;
```

Collapsing All Nodes

This is done to collapse the current node to a height of all levels above—that is, to the current node level.

The procedure described in the previous section can be used to collapse all nodes with the current node as the root node:

```
WHEN-TREE-NODE-ACTIVATED

DECLARE
  retcd NUMBER;
BEGIN
  p_expand_or_collapse_all('TREE_BLOCK.HTREE','C', retcd);
  IF (retcd <> 0) THEN
```

```
    MESSAGE('ERR: Expand All/Collapse All failed');
      RAISE FORM_TRIGGER_FAILURE;
  END IF;
END;
```

Note that the literal C is passed to indicate the operation of collapsing.

> **TIP**
>
> There is no automatic Expand All or Collapse All available at runtime for a tree item. The default toggle operation of expand/collapse can be used to toggle between these two node states.

Finding a Particular Node

Searching for a particular node is possible based on either the node value or the node label. This might be required when one is simulating drill-down LOVs using tree items. However, this search is not based on wildcard characters, unlike the one in a Forms-supplied LOV. You use FTREE.FIND_TREE_NODE with the search_string, search_type, search_by, search_root, and start_point specified:

```
FTREE.FIND_TREE_NODE(item_id, search_string, search_type, search_by,
➥ search_root, start_point);
```

The search_string is the value of the node or the label of the node depending on whether the search_by (the third parameter after the item_id) is node value or node label (FTREE.NODE_VALUE or FTREE.NODE_LABEL).

The search_type is the type of search: whether to find the next successive node (irrespective of child or sibling) or the next child node. Valid values are FTREE.FIND_NEXT for the former and FTREE.FIND_NEXT_CHILD for the latter.

Consider the tree shown in Figure 9.2.

Let the search_root be the node identified by ROOT NODE of the tree specified as FTREE.ROOT_NODE.

The following code

```
DECLARE
  item_id ITEM;
  current_node FTREE.NODE;
  starting_node_level NUMBER;
  searched_node_label VARCHAR2(15);
```

```
BEGIN
  item_id := FIND_ITEM('TREE_BLOCK.HTREE');
  IF ID_NULl(item_id) THEN
    MESSAGE('Invalid Tree Item');
    RAISE FORM_TRIGGER_FAILURE;
  END IF;
  current_node := FTREE.FIND_TREE_NODE(item_id,'', FTREE.FIND_NEXT,
➥ FTREE.NODE_VALUE,  FTREE.ROOT_NODE, FTREE.ROOT_NODE);
  searched_node_label := FTREE.GET_TREE_NODE_PROPERETY(item_id, current_node,
➥ FTREE.NODE_LABEL);
END;
```

yields KING as the next node of the tree ROOT NODE.

> ### TIP
>
> Specify a NULL search string to locate the successive or next successive child node without basing the search on a value.

Replacing FTREE.FIND_NEXT by FTREE.FIND_NEXT_CHILD also yields ADAMS. This is because, for the tree ROOT NODE, both the next node and the next child node are ADAMS, starting at the root.

Next we find the node identified by the label ALLEN. To do this, we replace the NULL value for the search string by the string ALLEN:

```
DECLARE
  item_id ITEM;
  current_node FTREE.NODE;
  starting_node_level NUMBER;
  searched_node_label VARCHAR2(15);
BEGIN
  item_id := FIND_ITEM('TREE_BLOCK.HTREE');
  IF ID_NULl(item_id) THEN
    MESSAGE('Invalid Tree Item');
    RAISE FORM_TRIGGER_FAILURE;
  END IF;
  current_node := FTREE.FIND_TREE_NODE(item_id, 'ALLEN',
➥ FTREE.FIND_NEXT, FTREE.NODE_VALUE, FTREE.ROOT_NODE, FTREE.ROOT_NODE);
  searched_node_label := FTREE.GET_TREE_NODE_PROPERTY(item_id, current_node,
➥ FTREE.NODE_LABEL);
  IF (searched_node_label IS NOT NULL) THEN
    MESSAGE(searched_node_label, ACKNOWLEDGE);
  END IF;
END;
```

The nodes label obtained is displayed to verify the fact. The `search_root` and the `search_point` are both `FTREE.ROOT NODE` in this case.

Next we perform the above search with ALLEN as the root node. As evident from the tree diagram in Figure 9.2, ALLEN has no child node. The above code is modified as follows:

```
DECLARE
  item_id ITEM;
  current_node FTREE.NODE;
  starting_node_level NUMBER;
  searched_node_label VARCHAR2(15);
BEGIN
  item_id := FIND_ITEM('TREE_BLOCK.HTREE');
  IF ID_NULl(item_id) THEN
    MESSAGE('Invalid Tree Item');
     RAISE FORM_TRIGGER_FAILURE;
  END IF;
  current_node := FTREE.FIND_TREE_NODE(item_id, 'ALLEN', FTREE.FIND_NEXT,
➥FTREE.NODE_LABEL,  FTREE.ROOT_NODE, FTREE.ROOT_NODE);
  current_node := FTREE.FIND_TREE_NODE(item_id,'', FTREE.FIND_NEXT,
➥ FTREE,NODE_LABEL, current_node, current_node);
  searched_node_label := FTREE.GET_TREE_NODE_PROPERTY(item_id, current_node,
➥FTREE.NODE_LABEL);
  IF (searched_node_label IS NOT NULL) THEN
    MESSAGE(searched_node_label, ACKNOWLEDGE);
  END IF;
END;
```

We get WARD as the resulting node label.

Next we replace `FTREE.FIND_NEXT` with `FTREE.FIND_NEXT_CHILD` in the call to `FTREE.FIND_TREE_NODE`. We get a null value.

TIP
The search type is always from the starting point and relative to the search root.

Planting and Growing Trees—Dynamically Adding Nodes Along with Data to an Existing Base Tree

Planting a tree (this is my terminology) is the process of creating a tree item in the Forms designer. There is no way to create a tree item dynamically. Initially it has to be created in the designer. A tree always has to be based on a query.

Growing a tree is the process of

- adding tree data sets under a given node (hierarchical sub-trees along with data under a given node).
- adding tree data elements (single nodes along with data).

Adding a data set amounts to dynamically adding child trees to an existing tree using a record group or query text. The base tree is and should be created at design time.

A child tree can be added either as a child of a specified node or below a specified node, both at a given offset. This is specified by the constants FTREE.PARENT_OFFSET or FTREE.SIBLING_OFFSET.

When added as a child of a specified node, the resulting node is at a level one below the specified node. The offset specifies in which node position, starting from the first child node, the new node can be added. It can be either (1-*n*), where *n* is the number of child nodes under the specified node's parent, or the constant FTREE.LAST_CHILD. FTREE.LAST_CHILD specifies that the new node be added after the last node at the current level.

When added below a specified node—that is, sibling—the resulting root node is at the same level as the specified node. In this case, the offset is either FTREE.NEXT_NODE or FTREE.PREVIOUS_NODE.

To grow a tree, follow these steps:

1. Use FTREE.ADD_DATA_TREE and pass either a record group or query as the value for the data parameter:

   ```
   FTREE.ADD_TREE_DATA(item_id, node, offset_type, offset, data_source,
   data);
   ```

2. Specify either FTREE.PARENT_OFFSET (adding a child to the given node) or FTREE.SIBLING_OFFSET (sibling to the given node).
3. Specify the offset and corresponding start (base) node.
4. The most important item is the data source—that is, RECORD_GROUP or QUERY_TEXT. This has to be a hierarchical query.

Again consider our example tree based on the EMP table in Figure 9.2.

We add the following two rows to the EMP table:

```
insert into emp values (1111, 'DAVID', 'MANAGER', null,
                        '25-FEB-84', 8000, null, 10);
insert into emp values (2222, 'ROSE', 'ANALYST', 1111,
                        '25-FEB-85', 5000, null, 10);
```

9

We add the sub-tree returned by the following query as the last child of the node the user selects by a single-click:

```
SELECT -1, LEVEL, ENAME, NULL, TO_CHAR(empno)
FROM    emp
START WITH ename = 'DAVID'
CONNECT BY PRIOR empno = mgr;
```

This is done when the user selects a node and then clicks a button labeled Add Sub-Tree. The following piece of code in the corresponding WHEN-BUTTON-PRESSED trigger does the job:

```
WHEN-BUTTON-PRESSED

DECLARE
  item_id ITEM;
  rg_id    RECORDGROUP;
  retcd    NUMBER;
  query_string VARCHAR2(1000);
BEGIN

  item_id := FIND_ITEM('TREE_BLOCK.HTREE');
   IF ID_NUL1(item_id) THEN
     MESSAGE('ERR: Invalid tree Item');
     RAISE FORM_TRIGGER_FAILURE;
   END IF;

  query_string :=
   'SELECT -1, LEVEL, ENAME, NULL, TO_CHAR(empno) FROM  emp START WITH ename =
➥ ''DAVID'' CONNECT BY PRIOR empno = mgr';
   rg_id := FIND_GROUP('RG_ADD_TREE');
   IF NOT ID_NUL1(rg_id) THEN
     DELETE_GROUP(rg_id);
   END IF;
   rg_id := CREATE_GROUP_FROM_QUERY('RG_ADD_TREE', query_string);
   retcd := POPULATE_GROUP(rg_id);
   IF (retcd <> 0) THEN
     MESSAGE('ERR: Tree Data Source Creation Failed');
     RAISE FORM_TRIGGER_FAILURE;
   END IF;

FTREE.ADD_TREE_DATA(item_id, :SYSTEM.TRIGGER_NODE, FTREE.PARENT_OFFSET,
➥ FTREE.LAST_CHILD, FTREE.RECORD_GROUP, rg_id);

END;
```

The before and after tree changes are shown in Figures 9.3 and 9.4, respectively.

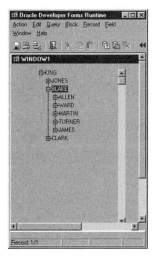

FIGURE 9.3
Tree structure before adding sub-tree. Mark the user-selected node labeled BLAKE.

FIGURE 9.4
Tree structure after adding sub-tree as the last child of the user-selected node labeled BLAKE.

> **TIP**
>
> No expanding or collapsing is done by FTREE.ADD_TREE_DATA.

Adding a Sub-tree to the Next Node of a Given Node and at the Same Level

So far, I have described how to add a sub-tree as a child node to a given node. Next I describe how to add a sibling of a given node. Adding a sibling adds a node next to a given node and at the same level. To demonstrate this, I will add a sibling to the very first node of the tree. To do this, the above trigger needs the following modification: Replace the constants FTREE.PARENT_OFFSET and FTREE.LAST_CHILD with FTREE.SIBLING_OFFSET and FTREE.NEXT_NODE as the values for offset_type and offset respectively.

The code with the given change is

```
FTREE.ADD_TREE_DATA(item_id, :SYSTEM.TRIGGER_NODE, FTREE.SIBLING_OFFSET,
➡ FTREE.NEXT_NODE, FTREE.RECORD_GROUP, rg_id);
```

The before and after tree changes are shown in Figures 9.5 and 9.6, respectively.

FIGURE 9.5

Tree structure before adding sub-tree. Mark the very first node labeled KING.

TIP

A sibling node cannot be added by specifying the start node as FTREE.ROOT_NODE. Note that FTREE.ROOT_NODE is not the same as the very first top level node of the tree.

FIGURE 9.6
Tree structure after adding sub-tree as a sibling of the very first node labeled KING.

Figure 9.6 shows the added sub-tree in a user-expanded fashion to illustrate the depth of query.

Adding a Sub-tree as the First Top-level Node of a Tree (Before the Node at Level 1)

This sub-section describes how to add a sub-tree to the very beginning of a tree. This means adding immediately after the root node. To do this, add a sibling to the very first node of the tree specifying FTREE.PREVIOUS_NODE as the offset. To do this, the above trigger line needs the following modification: Replace the offset value FTREE.NEXT_NODE with FTREE.PREVIOUS_NODE.

The code with the given change is

```
FTREE.ADD_TREE_DATA(item_id, :SYSTEM.TRIGGER_NODE, FTREE.SIBLING_OFFSET,
➥FTREE.PREVIOUS_NODE, FTREE.RECORD_GROUP, rg_id);
```

The before and after tree changes are shown in Figures 9.5 and 9.7, respectively.

9

WORKING WITH
TREES

FIGURE 9.7
Tree structure after adding a sub-tree as the first top level node.

Again, Figure 9.7 shows the added node in a user-expanded fashion to illustrate the depth of query.

Adding Tree Data Elements

Adding a data element means to dynamically add a single tree node to an existing tree using a value. The base tree is and should be created at design time.

A tree node can be added either as a child of a specified node or below a specified node, both at a given offset. This is specified by the constants FTREE.PARENT_OFFSET or FTREE.SIBLING_OFFSET.

When added as a child of a specified node, the resulting node is at a level one below the specified node. The offset specifies in which node position, starting from the first child node, the new node can be added. It can be either (1-*n*) where *n* is the number of child nodes under the specified nodes parent, or the constant FTREE.LAST_CHILD. FTREE.LAST_CHILD specifies that the new node be added after the last node at the current level.

When added as below, a specified node—that is, sibling—the resulting root node is at the same level as the specified node. In this case, the offset is either FTREE.NEXT_NODE or FTREE.PREVIOUS_NODE.

To add a single node, follow these steps:

1. Use FTREE.ADD_DATA_NODE and pass a value for the data parameter. Because the element to be added is a node, the state, label, icon, and value of the resulting node are also to be passed as parameters:

```
FTREE.ADD_TREE_NODE(item_id, node, offset_type, offset, state, label,
➥icon, value);
```

2. Specify either FTREE.PARENT_OFFSET (adding a child to the given node) or FTREE.SIBLING_OFFSET (sibling to the given node).

3. Specify the offset and corresponding start (base) node.

4. Most important is the quadruplet (state, label, icon, value). This has to be in conformity with normal tree values.

Consider our example tree based on EMP table. We will add a sub-node returned as the value of EMPNO of employee named SAMUEL, newly inserted as follows:

```
insert into emp values (4444, 'SAMUEL', 'ANALYST', null, '26-FEB-94', 4000,
➥ NULL, 10);
```

This is done when the user selects a node and then clicks a special button labeled Add Sub-Node. The following piece of code in the corresponding WHEN-BUTTON-PRESSED trigger does the job:

WHEN-BUTTON-PRESSED

```
DECLARE
  item_id ITEM;
  v_empno NUMBER;
  v_ename VARCHAR2(15);
  added_node FTREE.NODE;
BEGIN
  BEGIN
    SELECT empno, ename
    INTO   v_empno, v_ename
    FROM   emp
    WHERE  ename = SAMUEL;
  EXCEPTION WHEN NO_DATA_FOUND THEN
    RETURN;
  END;
  item_id := FIND_ITEM(TREE_BLOCK.HTREE);
   IF ID_NUL1(item_id) THEN
     MESSAGE(ERR: Invalid tree Item);
     RAISE FORM_TRIGGER_FAILURE;
   END IF;

  added_node :=  FTREE.ADD_TREE_NODE(item_id, :SYSTEM.TRIGGER_NODE,
➥FTREE.PARENT_OFFSET, FTREE.LAST_CHILD, FTREE.EXPANDED_NODE,
➥ v_ename,NULL,TO_CHAR(v_empno) );
END;
```

9

WORKING WITH
TREES

The before and after tree changes are shown in Figures 9.5 and 9.8, respectively.

FIGURE 9.8
Tree structure after adding a single node labeled SAMUEL as the last child of the user-selected node KING.

TIP

No expanding or collapsing is done by `FTREE.ADD_TREE_NODE`.

Adding a Single Node as the Next Successive Node of a Given Node and at the Same Level

So far, I have described how to add a single child node to a given node. Next I describe how to add a single sibling of a given node. Adding a sibling adds a node beside and at the same level of a given node. To demonstrate this, I show how to add a single sibling to the very first node of the tree. To do this, the previous trigger needs the following modification: Replace the constants `FTREE.PARENT_OFFSET` and `FTREE.LAST_CHILD` with `FTREE.SIBLING_OFFSET` and `FTREE.NEXT_NODE` as the values for `offset_type` and `offset`, respectively. The code with the given change is:

```
FTREE.ADD_TREE_NODE(item_id, :SYSTEM.TRIGGER_NODE, FTREE.SIBLING_OFFSET,
➡FTREE.NEXT_NODE, FTREE.EXPANDED_NODE, v_ename,NULL,TO_CHAR(v_empno) );
```

The before and after tree changes are shown in Figures 9.5 and 9.9, respectively.

FIGURE 9.9

Tree structure after adding a single node labeled SAMUEL as the sibling of the very first node labeled KING.

TIP

Similarly to adding data sets, a sibling node cannot be added by specifying the start node as FTREE.ROOT_NODE. Note that FTREE.ROOT_NODE is not the same as the very first top level node of the tree.

Adding a Single Node as the First Top-level Node of a Tree (Before the First Node at Level 1)

This sub-section describes how to add a single node to the very beginning of a tree. This means adding immediately after the root node. To do this, add a single sibling to the very first node of the tree specifying FTREE.PREVIOUS_NODE as the offset. To do this the above trigger line needs the following modification: Replace the offset value FTREE.NEXT_NODE with FTREE.PREVIOUS_NODE.

The code with the given change is

```
FTREE.ADD_TREE_NODE(item_id, :SYSTEM.TRIGGER_NODE, FTREE.SIBLING_OFFSET,
➡FTREE.PREVIOUS_NODE, FTREE.EXPANDED_NODE, v_ename,NULL,TO_CHAR(v_empno) );
```

The before and after tree changes are shown in Figures 9.5 and 9.10, respectively.

9

WORKING WITH TREES

FIGURE 9.10
Tree structure after adding a single node as the very first top level node.

Shrinking Trees

You can shrink trees in two ways:

- by collapsing nodes
- by deleting nodes

(Actually, shrinking by collapsing is not strictly shrinking because it only shrinks the view of the tree.) The actual shrinking of a tree takes place when particular tree nodes are deleted. To do this, you use FTREE.DELETE_TREE_NODE.

Continuing our earlier example, we will delete the node with label SAMUEL if the user clicks on it:

```
DECLARE
  item_id ITEM;
  this_node FTREE.NODE;
BEGIN
  item_id := FIND_ITEM(TREE_BLOCK.HTREE);
  IF ID_NULL(item_id) THEN
```

```
      MESSAGE(ERR: Invalid tree item.);
      RAISE FORM_TRIGGER_FAILURE;
    END IF;

/* Search for the node labeled SAMUEL relative to the root node and starting
/  from the root node */

    this_node := FTREE.FIND_TREE_NODE(item_id, SAMUEL, FTREE.FIND_NEXT,
➡FTREE.NODE_LABEL, FTREE.ROOT_NODE, FTREE.ROOT_NODE);
      IF (NOT FTREE.ID_NULL(this_node)) THEN

/* if such a node exists, delete it */

        FTREE.DELETE_TREE_NODE(item_id, this_node);

      END IF;
END;
```

Note that deleting a node does not delete the data from the corresponding table.

You can delete sub-trees from a tree using TREE.DELETE_TREE_NODE. To do so, just delete the root of the specified sub-tree.

Summary

This chapter discussed the various techniques involving tree items in Forms 6.0. Specifically it dealt with techniques for creating a tree item and the various operations on a tree item such as dynamically populating a tree item, selection using single-click of a node, node activation using double-click of a node, expansion and collapsing of nodes including expanding and collapsing all nodes, and searching for a particular node. Last, the procedures for dynamically adding and deleting nodes were discussed.

Oracle 8 and 8i Features in Forms Developer

IN THIS CHAPTER

Programming with objects involves using object tables (entire tables based on a single object type), VARRAYS, nested tables, REF columns, and stored procedures returning one of these object values. Oracle Developer 6.0 onwards has introduced the capability of performing CRUD (Create, Retrieve, Update, Delete) operations on block data sources based on some of these object categories. Also it has the capability of using some features of PL/SQL 8 from Forms and of incorporating JavaBeans components into Forms applications. This chapter explores these capabilities in greater depth. The remainder of this chapter is organized as follows:

- Techniques for querying and updating new data sources in Forms based on objects that includes CRUD on object table-based data sources in Forms and CRUD on object type-based items in Forms

- A new look at relations using REFs

- Record groups based on objects

- PL/SQL8 and 8i capabilities in Forms, including limitations

- Limitations of Forms in handling objects, including the inability to handle VARRAYS and nested tables involving objects stored in the database

Techniques for Querying and Updating New Data Sources in Forms Based on Objects

Oracle 8 introduced object tables (tables containing row objects) and tables having column objects. This section describes techniques for performing DML on blocks based on object tables and column objects.

CRUD on Object Table Based Blocks in Forms

Blocks in forms can be based on object tables that are based on user-defined types. A user-defined data type in Oracle 8 and 8i can be either an ADT (an abstract data type) or an object type. The latter can include member functions along with the type structure definition. Henceforth, I will refer to either of these as a UDT (user-defined type).

Oracle Forms explodes a UDT into its individual components. So INSERT, UPDATE, DELETE, SELECT, and LOCK boil down to these operations being performed on a normal base table item. Consider the following example:

```
CREATE OR REPLACE TYPE add_type AS OBJECT
                    (street VARCHAR2(20),
                     city  VARCHAR2(20),
```

```
               state VARCHAR2(2),
               zip   VARCHAR2(13));
```

```
CREATE TABLE address OF add_type;
```

Here `add_type` is a UDT consisting of four individual fields, namely, street, city, state, and zip. The database table address is based on this UDT. A block in forms based on the address table explodes the underlying object-type into four base-table items, each item corresponding to the respective individual field in the object type. An `INSERT` or `UPDATE` operation in this block generates an OID (object ID) for each row being inserted or deleted.

CRUD on Object-Type Based Items in Forms (Column Object)

Blocks in forms can be based on relational tables having user-defined type based columns. A user-defined data type in Oracle 8 and 8i can be either an ADT or an object type. The latter can include member functions along with the type structure definition. Henceforth, I will refer to either of these as a UDT.

Oracle Forms explodes a column UDT into its individual components. So `INSERT`, `UPDATE`, `DELETE`, `SELECT`, and `LOCK` boil down to these operations being performed on a normal base table item. (They are similar to the operations done on relational base table items.)

Item names based on UDTs are constructed as the UDT_name suffixed by an underscore and the exploded item name.

Consider the following example of the person table having two object columns `off_add` and `home_add`, based on the object type created earlier:

```
CREATE TABLE person
(id              number(10) PRIMARY KEY,
 lastname        varchar2(30) NOT NULL,
 firstname       varchar2(30) NOT NULL,
 middle_initial  varchar2(2) ,
 off_add         add_type,
 home_add        add_type);
```

The `PERSON` block containing two object-column based items `OFF_ADD` and `HOME_ADD` has its components exploded. For example, Forms creates four text items out of `OFF_ADD`: `OFF_ADD_STREET`, `OFF_ADD_CITY`, `OFF_ADD_STATE`, and `OFF_ADD_ZIP`.

No composite item—that is, one consisting of the entire object column—is created for an object-column.

The relevance of the exploded object-column items is no more than an ordinary base table item. Forms treats them just like ordinary items.

Direct and indirect referencing are valid for the individual component types. This means that direct selection and assignment of an exploded form item based on an object column and also using NAME_IN and COPY, are allowed.

Forms facilitates implicit instantiation, manipulation, and storage of underlying objects with the ease of a relational table.

DML statements based on objects in Forms are referenced as follows:

- Using REF operator
- Using the exploded item value
- Using the dot (.) notation

A New Look at Relations Using REFS

Relations in Forms are by far one of the best methods of creating and preserving data relationships between database tables, thereby maintaining data integrity. This concept of relations in forms has been extended to accommodate object tables and relational tables having object columns (henceforward referred to as object-relational tables).

A master-detail relation can be created to link:

- object tables
- object tables and object-relational tables
- object-relational tables; that is, to columns based on object types

A master-detail relation linking any of the preceding can be created by

- Using REF columns
- Using a join condition

Using Join Conditions for Forms Relations

This technique is similar to joining two relational tables having a primary-key (PK) and foreign-key (FK) relationship between them. Using join conditions for Forms relations is still reserved to preserve such PK-FK foreign key relationships.

The join condition for our ADDRESS_PERSON relation would look like

```
address.street = person.off_add_street AND
address.city = person.off_add_city AND
address.state = person.off_add_state AND
address.zip = person.off_add_zip
```

Using REF Items for Forms Relations

This subsection explains how to create a master-detail relation between blocks using REF items. First we tell what a REF item is and then explain how to create a relation using it.

The object table ADDRESS and the object-relational table PERSON—even though not "related" by means of a foreign key at the server end—are linked by a REF reference, and can be linked in forms using a master-detail relationship.

REF items provide a means of linking object and/or object-relational tables. This means the query and DML work behind the scenes as they do for a relation involving two relational tables.

You should always create a relation based on REFS while linking object and/or object relational tables.

A REF reference is required between two objects and/or object-relational tables for the following reasons:

- The scope of a nested object is limited to the context of the parent object.
- Thus, each row object (in case of an object table) and column object (in case of an object-relational table) cannot be referenced outside of the object table.
- Each row of an object table will hold its own PRIVATE instance of the row or column object and thus will have no accessibility to a second object table.

In the example form,

- The relation name is ADDRESS_PERSON.
- The master block is ADDRESS.
- The detail block is PERSON.

> **TIP**
>
> Select the REF column(s) while creating the detail block. All the REF columns have to be selected.

Figure 10.1 shows a sample screen while creating the PERSON table that has two REF columns OFF_ADD and HOME_ADD.

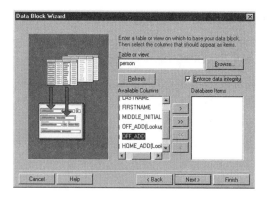

FIGURE 10.1

Creation of a Data Block with REF items.

The column OFF_ADD (highlighted in the figure) is the actual REF column from the PERSON table. This column holds a pointer to a row in the ADDRESS object table and Forms generates a unique Object Identifier for it that acts as an Object FK to the ADDRESS table.

You can see that the OFF_ADD is named OFF_ADD(Lookup). This is look up related and is generated automatically by Forms to populate an LOV for the OFF_ADD item.

The relation can be created in two ways. First, you can create the relation when you create the PERSON block. This is done by clicking the Create Relationships button and checking the Auto-join Data Blocks check box. Forms prompts for a choice of master blocks if there are multiple REF items in the PERSON block. This is shown in Figure 10.2.

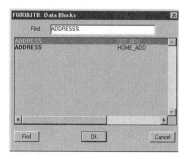

FIGURE 10.2

List of master blocks in case of multiple REF items.

The relation is created with the following special properties: Relation Type is set to Ref, and Detail Reference Item is set to the Ref item corresponding to the REF column in the base object table (in this case, OFF_ADD).

The following properties are set for the master and detail blocks:

- The Master block has the Include REF Item property set to Yes.
- Set the DML Returning Value property for the Master block. You have to set this explicitly after creating the relation.
- Both the Master and Detail blocks have the Alias properties set to the first letter of the respective block names.

Second, you can explicitly create a relation using the Relations node of the Object Navigator. The preceding properties for a relation have to be set in this case.

TIP

Always create one relation for each REF item included in the detail block.

The Master block should have the DML Returning Value property set to Yes. This has to be set to propagate the new OID generated each time a DML operation is performed on the same record—for example, an UPDATE operation. This OID is the referred to OID: referred to by the detail block.

If the master block is an object table, the property Include REF item should be set to Yes.

References to an object are made by using the REF operator with the table alias passed as an input parameter. The row of the child object table is located by comparing this OID, returned by REF, to the REF column in the child table. ROWID rather than a primary key value is used to locate the correct OID corresponding to the block record.

This is shown as follows:

```
........
........
CURSOR person_cur IS
    SELECT 1 FROM person p
    WHERE p.off_add = (SELECT REF(a)
                       FROM address a
                       WHERE rowid = :address.rowid);

........
........
```

Basing a Block on a Stored Procedure Involving Object Tables

The concept of basing a block on a stored procedure is introduced in Chapter 2, "Advanced GUI Development: Developing Beyond GUI." The same method is illustrated here with reference to object tables.

A block has to be based on a stored procedure when it is necessary to provide user-defined logic for replacing the default functionality of SELECT, LOCK, INSERT, UPDATE, and DELETE. This is required in the following circumstances:

- A block needs to be based on multiple tables involving complex application logic tying them. In this case, a view or a FROM clause query cannot be used because of the complexity of the underlying logic involved.

- There is DML to be performed on the server-side, using either dynamic DML or DML encapsulating application logic.

This method of basing a block on a stored procedure involves getting and returning result sets of data rather than processing one record at a time, thus reducing network traffic. This is helpful especially when the network involved is a WAN. Similar to the method of basing a block on a stored procedure involving non-object relational tables, this method also involves getting and returning result sets of data in the form of Index-by table of records.

The basic building blocks and the steps involved are as follows:

1. Create an object type DEPT_EMP with the following structure:
   ```
   CREATE OR REPLACE TYPE dept_emp AS OBJECT
   (empno      NUMBER(4),
       ename      VARCHAR2(10),
       job        VARCHAR2(9),
       hiredate   DATE,
       sal        NUMBER(11,2),
       deptno     NUMBER(2),
       dname      VARCHAR2(14));
   ```

2. Create an object table DEPTEMP_TAB of type DEPT_EMP:
   ```
   CREATE TABLE deptemp_tab OF dept_emp;
   ```

3. Create an object relational table dept_emp_addr with two REF columns deptemp of type dept_emp and addr of type add_type:
   ```
   CREATE TABLE dept_emp_addr
   (deptemp REF dept_emp,
    addr    REF add_type);
   ```

4. Define five separate procedures, included as part of a package called PKGDEPTEM-POBJ: one each for SELECT, INSERT, UPDATE, DELETE, and LOCK. All the procedures pass and return a table of RECORDS whose structure is the same as that of the object type dept_emp.

> **TIP**
>
> Data blocks can be based on a stored procedure returning a ref cursor, an index-by table, records, or a record type.

5. Create a block named STPROCOBJ that has these procedures specified as the values for Query Procedure, Insert procedure, Update Procedure, Delete Procedure and Lock Procedure Names in the Data Block Wizard for the block. The items in this block correspond to the columns in the object type dept_emp.

6. Make the following changes to the property palette. Set the Query Data Source procedure Name to PKGDEPTEMPOBJ.QUERY_PROCEDURE; set Query Data Source Columns to Result Set columns EMPNO, ENAME, JOB, HIREDATE, SAL, DEPTNO, DNAME; and set Query Data Source Arguments to RESULTSET and P_EMPNO.

    Similarly, under Advanced Database, set the corresponding properties for Insert, Update, Delete, and Lock accordingly.

    DML is performed internally on the object/object-relational tables DEPTEMP_TAB and DEPT_EMP_ADDR.

7. Forms generates four triggers called INSERT-PROCEDURE, UPDATE-PROCEDURE, DELETE-PROCEDURE, and LOCK-PROCEDURE at the block level. These can be thought of as replacements for ON-INSERT, ON-UPDATE, ON-DELETE, and ON-LOCK triggers for a base table block.

The code for the package PKGDEPTEMPOBJ can be found in Listing 10.1.

LISTING 10.1   Package with procedures for Query, Lock, Insert, Update and Delete operations involving Object Tables.

```
CREATE OR REPLACE PACKAGE PKGDEPTEMPOBJ AS

/* Variables which are of type of an index-by table of records, are used as
/IN OUT variables for the INSERT, UPDATE, DELETE and LOCK procedures. These
/parameters are IN OUT as they transfer data to and from the block and the
/database. */
```

continues

LISTING 10.1   Continued

```
TYPE dept_emp_rec IS RECORD
  (empno      NUMBER(4),
   ename       VARCHAR2(10),
   job        VARCHAR2(9),
   hiredate    DATE,
   sal        NUMBER(11,2),
   deptno      NUMBER(4),
   dname       VARCHAR2(14));

  TYPE dept_emp_tab IS TABLE OF dept_emp_rec INDEX BY BINARY_INTEGER;

  PROCEDURE query_procedure(resultset IN OUT dept_emp_tab, p_empno IN NUMBER);
  PROCEDURE lock_procedure(dmlset IN OUT dept_emp_tab);
  PROCEDURE insert_procedure (dmlset IN OUT dept_emp_tab);
  PROCEDURE update_procedure(dmlset IN OUT dept_emp_tab);
  PROCEDURE delete_procedure(dmlset IN OUT dept_emp_tab);

END PKGDEPTEMPOBJ;
/

CREATE OR REPLACE PACKAGE BODY PKGDEPTEMPOBJ AS
  PROCEDURE query_procedure(resultset IN OUT  dept_emp_tab,
      p_empno IN NUMBER)
IS
    CURSOR c_dept_emp IS
      SELECT DEREF(a.deptemp)
        FROM   dept_emp_addr a
        WHERE  a.deptemp.empno = NVL(p_empno, a.deptemp.empno);
    i BINARY_INTEGER := 1;
    v_deptemp dept_emp;
  BEGIN

/* The code below selects from the DEPT_EMP_ADDR tables into a cursor based
/ on dept_emp object type and outputs the result to the block. Note how the
/DEREF operator is used to get the actual record rather than the OID. The
/co-ordination and synchronization between the input resultset and the
/population of the block with these records is done by Forms automatically */

    OPEN c_dept_emp;
    LOOP
    FETCH c_dept_emp INTO v_deptemp;
    EXIT WHEN c_dept_emp%NOTFOUND;
        resultset(i).empno := v_deptemp.empno;
        resultset(i).ename := v_deptemp.ename;
```

```
          resultset(i).job := v_deptemp.job;
          resultset(i).hiredate := v_deptemp.hiredate;
          resultset(i).sal := v_deptemp.sal;
          resultset(i).deptno := v_deptemp.deptno;
          resultset(i).dname := v_deptemp.dname;
          i := i+1;
    END LOOP;
EXCEPTION WHEN OTHERS THENRAISE_APPLICATION_ERROR(-20101, SQLERRM);
  END query_procedure;


  PROCEDURE lock_procedure(dmlset IN OUT dept_emp_tab) IS
    v_deptemp dept_emp;
  BEGIN


/* The following locks each record in the input dmlset. The co-ordination and
/ synchronization between the input dmlset and the block's records that have
/been marked for LOCKING is done by the LOCK-PROCEDURE trigger written by
/Forms. Again note the use of the DEREF operator. */


      FOR i IN 1..dmlset.COUNT LOOP        SELECT DEREF(a.deptemp)
         INTO    v_deptemp
         FROM    dept_emp_addr a
         WHERE   a.deptemp.empno = dmlset(i).empno
         FOR UPDATE;
      END LOOP;
 EXCEPTION WHEN OTHERS THEN RAISE_APPLICATION_ERROR(-20102, SQLERRM);
  END lock_procedure;


  PROCEDURE insert_procedure (dmlset IN OUT dept_emp_tab) IS
    CURSOR c_dept_emp(i BINARY_INTEGER) IS
      SELECT DEREF(a.deptemp)
      FROM dept_emp_addr a
      WHERE a.deptemp.empno=dmlset(i).empno;
      v_deptemp dept_emp;
  BEGIN


/* The following inserts into the DEPTEMP_TAB table if already not found. It
/also inserts into the DEPT_EMP_ADDR table.  Note that the actual OID is
/inserted into the DEPT_EMP_ADDR table for the deptemp REF column. Each record
/ in the input dmlset is inserted.  The co-ordination and synchronization
/between the input dmlset and the block's records that have been marked for
/INSERT is done by the INSERT-PROCEDURE trigger written by Forms */


FOR i IN 1 .. dmlset.COUNT LOOP OPEN c_dept_emp(i);
 FETCH c_dept_emp INTO v_deptemp;
```

continues

10

ORACLE 8 AND 8i
FEATURES IN
FORMS DEVELOPER

LISTING 10.1   Continued

```
 IF c_dept_emp%NOTFOUND THEN
   INSERT INTO deptemp_tab
   VALUES (dmlset(i).empno,dmlset(i).ename, dmlset(i).job,
           dmlset(i).hiredate, dmlset(i).sal,
           dmlset(i).deptno,dmlset(i).dname);
   INSERT INTO dept_emp_addr(deptemp) SELECT REF(a) FROM deptemp_tab a
   WHERE a.empno = dmlset(i).empno;
 END IF;
     CLOSE c_dept_emp;
END LOOP;
 EXCEPTION WHEN OTHERS THEN RAISE_APPLICATION_ERROR(-20103, SQLERRM);
  END insert_procedure;

  PROCEDURE update_procedure(dmlset IN OUT dept_emp_tab) IS
    CURSOR c_dept_emp(i BINARY_INTEGER) IS
      SELECT DEREF(a.deptemp)
      FROM dept_emp_addr a
      WHERE a.deptemp.empno = dmlset(i).empno;
      v_deptemp dept_emp;
  BEGIN

/* The following inserts into the DEPTEMP_TAB table if already not found, else
/ it updates the same table. Each record in the input dmlset is updated.  The
/co-ordination and synchronization between the input dmlset and the block's
/records that have been marked for UPDATE is done by the UPDATE-PROCEDURE
/trigger written by Forms */

    FOR i IN 1..dmlset.COUNT LOOP
      OPEN c_dept_emp(i);
      FETCH c_dept_emp INTO v_deptemp;
      IF c_dept_emp%NOTFOUND THEN
         INSERT INTO deptemp_tab
         VALUES (dmlset(i).empno,dmlset(i).ename, dmlset(i).job,
                 dmlset(i).hiredate, dmlset(i).sal,
                 dmlset(i).deptno,dmlset(i).dname);
      ELSE
         UPDATE deptemp_tab a
            SET ename = dmlset(i).ename,
                job=dmlset(i).job,
                hiredate=dmlset(i).hiredate,
                sal      =dmlset(i).sal
          WHERE a.empno = dmlset(i).empno;
      END IF;
      CLOSE c_dept_emp;
```

```
END LOOP;
 EXCEPTION WHEN OTHERS THEN RAISE_APPLICATION_ERROR(-20104, SQLERRM);
  END update_procedure;

  PROCEDURE delete_procedure(dmlset IN OUT dept_emp_tab) IS
    v_deptemp dept_emp;
  BEGIN

/* The following deletes from the DEPT_EMP_ADDR  table. Note how the DEREF
/operator is used to find the matching record. Each record in the input dmlset
/ is deleted. The co-ordination and synchronization between the input dmlset
/and the block's records that have been marked for DELETE is done by the
/DELETE-PROCEDURE trigger written by Forms */

FOR i IN 1..dmlset.COUNT LOOP
   SELECT DEREF(a.deptemp)
   INTO   v_deptemp
   FROM   dept_emp_addr a
   WHERE  a.deptemp.empno = dmlset(i).empno;
   DELETE FROM dept_emp_addr a WHERE DEREF(a.deptemp) = v_deptemp;
END LOOP;
 EXCEPTION WHEN OTHERS THEN RAISE_APPLICATION_ERROR(-20105, SQLERRM);
  END delete_procedure;

END PKGDEPTEMPOBJ;
```

> **TIP**
>
> OIDS are generated automatically when the INSERT_PROCEDURE is invoked at the server side.

> **TIP**
>
> It is not necessary to set the DML Returning Value because the procedures use DEREF to get the actual row values, and hence are not based on the OID.

Record Groups and LOVs Based on Objects

This section presents the use of LOVs and Record Groups based on object tables and object columns. The procedure for dynamically creating such record groups is also highlighted.

Record groups and LOVs based on objects behave much in the same way as when based on tables.

Record groups can be on an object REF column, an object column, or an object type-based object table.

To create record groups based on Object Refs, select the columns from the corresponding object table or the object column corresponding to the object ref column from the table as the record group query.

The following query selects the individual columns from the object table ADDRESS. The OFF_ADD REF column in the PERSON table is based on the object type ADD_TYPE on which the object table ADDRESS is based:

```
SELECT REF(a), a.street, a.city, a.state, a.zip FROM address a
```

Do not select an object ref column by de-referencing it. For example, the following query is incorrect:

```
SELECT DEREF(a.off_add) FROM person a
```

TIP

Do not directly select the REF column because it displays the OID at runtime, which is like Greek or Latin to the user.

We will create an LOV based on the preceding SELECT and attach it to the OFF_ADD item (the REF item) in the PERSON block. This is to enable ad hoc querying in the PERSON block to enable the user to specify runtime query criteria in Enter-Query mode. This is shown in Figure 10.3.

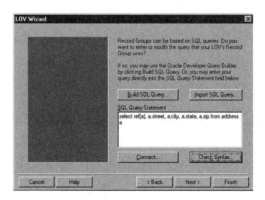

FIGURE 10.3
An LOV SELECT statement involving a REF column.

The Record Group column specifications appear as shown in Figure 10.4.

FIGURE 10.4

Record Group Column Specifications for a REF item.

Note that the data type of column OID is OBJECT REF and that of the other columns is similar to the columns selected from a purely relational table. The length of OID is 0 to hide it in the LOV.

The LOV Column mapping appears as shown in Figure 10.5.

FIGURE 10.5

LOV Column Specifications for a REF item.

At runtime, the LOV displays the following data, as shown in Figure 10.6.

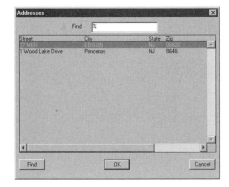

FIGURE 10.6
Addresses as they appear in the LOV.

The Effect of Directly Selecting the REF Column

Directly selecting the object REF column, as shown in Figure 10.7, will result in the Record Group Column Specification, LOV Column mapping, and a runtime LOV as shown in Figures 10.8, 10.9, and 10.10.

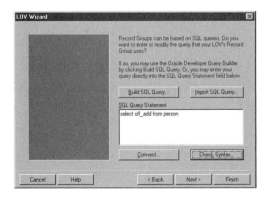

FIGURE 10.7
An LOV SELECT statement directly selecting only a REF column.

The Record Group Column specification appears as shown in Figure 10.8.

FIGURE 10.8

Record Group Specifications for an LOV based only on a single REF column.

Notice the data type of OBJECT REF.

The LOV column mapping properties appear as shown in Figure 10.9.

FIGURE 10.9

LOV Column Specifications for an LOV based only on a single REF column.

The preceding LOV—when attached to the OFF_ADD REF item in the PERSON block—displays the data shown in Figure 10.10 at runtime.

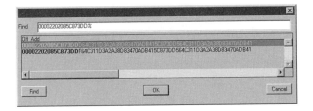

FIGURE 10.10
Figure showing an LOV displaying object REF OIDs.

Record Groups Based on Object Columns and/or Object-type Based Object Tables

The record group discussed earlier is also an example of a record group corresponding to an object-type based object table. Record groups based on object columns behave in the same manner as preceding and the corresponding query is similar. For example, consider the FOREIGN_ ADDRESS table. It has an object column FOR_ADD of object type ADD_TYPE that is specific to the country represented by the first column COUNTRY_CODE. The following query can be used to construct a record group that can then be used for an LOV for the FOR_ADD object column:

```
SELECT for_add.street, for_add.city, for_add.state, for_add.zip
FROM  foreign_address
```

Here FOR_ADD is deliberately not made as a REF column for illustration purposes.

Again, this LOV is useful for specifying query criteria. For example, the user can query for all foreign addresses belonging to a particular COUNTRY_CODE and city.

Dynamically Creating Object Record Groups

Dynamically creating object record groups amounts to dynamically generating a query for the record group based on object refs or object columns. Even non-query record groups can be created and populated dynamically with each column corresponding to the object type, which is pointed to by the OBJECT REF or object column.

TIP

Columns of OBJECT REF data type are not supported in Forms. The individual components of an object column or an object table pointed to by the REF column without the OID have to be selected.

Listing 10.2 illustrates a typical example.

LISTING 10.2　Procedure illustrating the use of Object REFs in Record Groups

```
PROCEDURE p_rg IS
  rg_id RECORDGROUP;
  gc_id1 GROUPCOLUMN;
  gc_id2 GROUPCOLUMN;
  gc_id3 GROUPCOLUMN;
  gc_id4 GROUPCOLUMN;
  gc_id5 GROUPCOLUMN;
  ret_id NUMBER;
BEGIN

/* Create the internal id of the record group */

  rg_id := CREATE_GROUP('RG_OBJ');

/* Add columns to the record group. Here the object id or OID column is added
/ as a LONG column */

  gc_id1 := ADD_GROUP_COLUMN(rg_id, 'OID',LONG_COLUMN, 128);
  gc_id2 := ADD_GROUP_COLUMN(rg_id, 'STREET', CHAR_COLUMN, 20);
  gc_id3 := ADD_GROUP_COLUMN(rg_id, 'CITY', CHAR_COLUMN, 20);
  gc_id4 := ADD_GROUP_COLUMN(rg_id, 'STATE', CHAR_COLUMN, 2);
  gc_id5 := ADD_GROUP_COLUMN(rg_id, 'ZIP', CHAR_COLUMN, 13);

/* Populate the record group with a SELECT statement. Note how the conversion
/functions, first REFTOHEX and then HEXTORAW are used to select the OID from
/the object table address */

  ret_id := POPULATE_GROUP_WITH_QUERY(rg_id,
  'SELECT HEXTORAW(REFTOHEX(REF(a))) oid, a.street street, a.city city,
➥ a.state state, a.zip zip FROM address a');
  IF ret_id <> 0 THEN
    MESSAGE(DBMS_ERROR_TEXT, ACKNOWLEDGE);
  RAISE FORM_TRIGGER_FAILURE;END IF;

/* Assign the record group so created to the LOV under consideration */

  SET_LOV_PROPERTY('LOV_TEST', GROUP_NAME, rg_id);
END;
```

Here LOV_TEST should have five columns already defined.

The OID column is defined as a LONG column in the record group and the object id REF(a) is first converted to HEX and then to RAW using REFTOHEX and HEXTORAW, respectively.

The Return Item for OID is specified as the REF item in the block. The data type of this REF item in the block remains as OBJECT REF. In this case, it is OFF_ADD.

The remaining four columns are defined with the same definitions as the STREET, CITY, STATE, and ZIP columns in the object table ADDRESS.

Following the previous technique and using the LOV to select the OIDS of address, the DML operations on the PERSON table work perfectly fine.

PL/SQL8 and 8i in Forms

This section briefly discusses which PL/SQL 8 and 8i features are supported by Forms 6.0 and which features are not.

PL/SQL8 and 8i in Forms 6.0

Client side PL/SQL does support PL/SQL 8, and some of the server-side PL/SQL 8 features can be used from the Forms side. Also large objects(LOBs) can be used. The following PL/SQL 8 features can be used as part of Forms-side PL/SQL:

- VARRAYS involving scalar data-types or record types.

  For example, consider the following VARRAY declaration:

```
DECLARE
  TYPE num_array IS VARRAY(10) OF NUMBER;
  v_arr num_array := num_array(101, 201, 301, 401);
BEGIN
    IF v_arr(2) IS NOT NULL THEN
      MESSAGE(' v_arr(2) is NOT NULL' );
      PAUSE;
    END IF;
END;
```

  This is valid in Forms 6.0

- Nested tables involving built-in types or an expression using %ROWTYPE.

  For example, consider the nested table declaration in Forms:

```
DECLARE
  TYPE num_table IS TABLE OF NUMBER;
  v_num num_table := num_table(101, 201, 301, 401);
BEGIN
  /* This below assignment will replace the value 101 previously
  assigned to the first element */
  v_num(1) := 99999;
END;
```

This is valid in Forms 6.0

- Direct DML on object tables and database tables having VARRAYS and nested table columns.

  Consider the following scenario:
  ```
  create or replace type addlist as varray(10) of add_type;
  create table source_locator(id number(6),
      src_loc addlist);
  ```

  The following PL/SQL block is valid inside any appropriate trigger in Forms 6.0:
  ```
  begin
      insert into source_locator values (1,
  addlist2(add_type('A','B','C','D','E'),
  add_type('A1','B1','C1','D1','E1')));
  end;
  ```

The following are not possible in Forms 6.0:

- Direct declaration of object variables

- Direct instantiation of an object using constructor methods

- Direct manipulation of an object using member methods

- Direct declaration and PL/SQL operations involving VARRAYS and nested tables involving object types stored in the database

For example, the following cannot be used:

```
DECLARE
    address1 add_type;
BEGIN
    ......
    ......
END;
```

Also, based on the above VARRAY based object type addlist, the following cannot be used:

```
DECLARE
    v_src_loc addlist;
BEGIN
    ....
END;
```

To indirectly perform DML on objects from Forms, wrap the PL/SQL8 code using stored procedures that return an Index-By table of records and call these outer procedures from inside triggers or directly against a DML source by basing form blocks on them.

Oracle 8 SQL operators and functions can be used to access objects from Forms. For example, the operators REF, DEREF, VALUE, MAP, and SELF can be used in Forms code.

Also you can use GLOBAL_SCOPE record groups instead of VARRAYS and nested tables to share data arrays among forms.

Pass Index-by table of records to account for object refs and parameters of object values, as explained in the section "Basing a Block on a Stored Procedure Involving Object Tables."

Also the PLSQL 8i features such as invoker rights, native dynamic SQL, and autonomous transactions are not supported by Forms 6.0. But invoking JavaBeans methods and incorporating PJCs (Pluggable Java Components) is supported from Forms 6.0.

PL/SQL Features Common to Oracle 8 and 8i

The analog of INSTEAD-OF triggers, in Forms, is built-in by means of ON-INSERT, ON-UPDATE, and ON-DELETE triggers.

The ON-INSERT, ON-UPDATE, and ON-DELETE triggers, also called transactional triggers, are for data blocks based on tables (object or non-object), blocks based on in-line SELECTs (FROM clause queries), and views and blocks based on multiple tables (directly specified in the DML data source separated by a comma and with a WHERE condition).

These are analogous to the FOR EACH ROW INSTEAD-OF triggers provided at the database level for performing DML (INSERT, UPDATE, DELETE ONLY) operations on views based on multiple tables.

Also, direct DML is possible in blocks based on views for which corresponding INSTEAD-OF triggers have been defined at the database level. In this case, there is no need for the ON- transactional triggers mentioned above.

Also note that from Forms 5.x on, there are five new triggers INSERT-PROCEDURE, UPDATE-PROCEDURE, DELETE-PROCEDURE, LOCK-PROCEDURE, and SELECT-PROCEDURE for implementing DML on a data block based on a stored procedure. These triggers are automatically generated when stored procedures are provided against the respective DML source names, and they cannot be modified.

Summary

This chapter discussed the techniques of handling objects from Forms. Specifically, it highlighted how to perform DML on blocks based on object tables and object columns, a new look at forms relations using object REFs, and the use of LOVs and record groups based on objects. Last, it gave a brief overview of the capabilities and limitations of using PL/SQL 8 and 8i features from Forms 6.0.

INDEX

SYMBOLS

A

Other Related Titles

The IT site
you asked for...

InformIT is a complete online library delivering information, technology, reference, training, news, and opinion to IT professionals, students, and corporate users.

Find IT Solutions Here!

www.informit.com